St Antony's Series

General Editor: **Jan Zielonka** (2004–), Fellow of St Antony's College, Oxford

Recent titles include:

Cathy Gormley-Heenan
POLITICAL LEADERSHIP AND THE NORTHERN IRELAND PEACE PROCESS
Role, Capacity and Effect

Lori Plotkin Boghardt
KUWAIT AMID WAR, PEACE AND REVOLUTION

Paul Chaisty
LEGISLATIVE POLITICS AND ECONOMIC POWER IN RUSSIA

Valpy FitzGerald, Frances Stewart and Rajesh Venugopal (*editors*)
GLOBALIZATION, VIOLENT CONFLICT AND SELF-DETERMINATION

Miwao Matsumoto
TECHNOLOGY GATEKEEPERS FOR WAR AND PEACE
The British Ship Revolution and Japanese Industrialization

Håkan Thörn
ANTI-APARTHEID AND THE EMERGENCE OF A GLOBAL CIVIL SOCIETY

Lotte Hughes
MOVING THE MAASAI
A Colonial Misadventure

Fiona Macaulay
GENDER POLITICS IN BRAZIL AND CHILE
The Role of Parties in National and Local Policymaking

Stephen Whitefield (*editor*)
POLITICAL CULTURE AND POST-COMMUNISM

José Esteban Castro
WATER, POWER AND CITIZENSHIP
Social Struggle in the Basin of Mexico

Valpy FitzGerald and Rosemary Thorp (*editors*)
ECONOMIC DOCTRINES IN LATIN AMERICA
Origins, Embedding and Evolution

Victoria D. Alexander and Marilyn Rueschemeyer
ART AND THE STATE
The Visual Arts in Comparative Perspective

Ailish Johnson
EUROPEAN WELFARE STATES AND SUPRANATIONAL GOVERNANCE OF
SOCIAL POLICY

Archie Brown (*editor*)
THE DEMISE OF MARXISM-LENINISM IN RUSSIA

St Antony's Series
Series Standing Order ISBN 0–333–71109–2
(*outside North America only*)

You can receive future titles in this series as they are published by placing a standing order. Please contact your bookseller or, in case of difficulty, write to us at the address below with your name and address, the title of the series and the ISBN quoted above.

Customer Services Department, Macmillan Distribution Ltd, Houndmills, Basingstoke, Hampshire RG21 6XS, England

Political Leadership and the Northern Ireland Peace Process

Role, Capacity and Effect

Cathy Gormley-Heenan

in association with
St Antony's College, Oxford

First published 2007 by
PALGRAVE MACMILLAN
Houndmills, Basingstoke, Hampshire RG21 6XS and
175 Fifth Avenue, New York, N.Y. 10010
Companies and representatives throughout the world

PALGRAVE MACMILLAN is the global academic imprint of the Palgrave
Macmillan division of St. Martin's Press, LLC and of Palgrave Macmillan Ltd.
Macmillan® is a registered trademark in the United States, United Kingdom
and other countries. Palgrave is a registered trademark in the European
Union and other countries.

ISBN-13: 978–0–230–50037–2 hardback
ISBN-10: 0–230–50037–4 hardback

This book is printed on paper suitable for recycling and made from fully
managed and sustained forest sources.

A catalogue record for this book is available from the British Library.

Library of Congress Cataloging-in-Publication Data
Gormley-Heenan, Cathy, 1973–
    Political leadership and the Northern Ireland peace process:role, capacity
    and effect/Cathy Gormley-Heenan.
        p.   cm. — (St. Antony's series)
    Includes bibliographical references and index.
    ISBN-13: 978–0–230–50037–2 (cloth)
    ISBN-10: 0–230–50037–4 (cloth)
    1. Political leadership—Northern Ireland.   2. Peace movements—
    Northern Ireland.   3. Northern Ireland—Politics and government—
    1994–   I. Title.
    JN1572.A91G67 2007
    941.60824—dc22   2006049483

10   9   8   7   6   5   4   3   2   1
16   15   14   13   12   11   10   09   08   07

Printed and bound in Great Britain by
Antony Rowe Ltd, Chippenham and Eastbourne

For Ronan and Hala

Contents

Acknowledgements

There are many people who have contributed to the production of this book. Many thanks to Professor Paul Arthur (University of Ulster) and Professor Mari Fitzduff (Brandeis University, USA) who supervised my PhD work, upon which the arguments of this book are based; to Professor Gillian Robinson at INCORE (International Conflict Research), who has always looked after me and has been a good friend and mentor during the prolonged gestation of this research; to Professor Lis Porter (University of South Australia), who is owed a huge debt of gratitude for her meticulous proof-reading and comments on various chapters; to Dr Roger MacGinty (University of York), for his initial advice on a daily writing plan for the various chapters, and for reading various drafts of this work; and to Grainne Kelly, for the discussions on almost every aspect of this research.

Some of the early ideas for this book were gathered during the course of a 12-month research project which looked at political leadership in societies in the post-agreement or settlement period whilst working as a Research Officer at INCORE (2000–01). This was funded by the Community Relations Unit, OFMDFM, and the support of this organization for the original research is gratefully acknowledged. Thanks also to the Center for the Advanced Study of Leadership (CASL) at the James MacGregor Burns Academy of Leadership, University of Maryland, for a research scholarship in April 2000 which allowed for a sharing of experience and knowledge with the staff there and with Leadership scholars like Jim Burns, Bernard Bass and Barbara Kellerman. Most importantly though, thanks must go to INCORE for my Tip O'Neill Fellowship in 2004. Without this fellowship, and the space which it afforded me to concentrate solely on this work, I doubt if it would have ever been finished.

Certainly, the final manuscript would not have been as forthcoming without the generous financial support of the Transitional Justice Institute, University of Ulster, of which I am currently an Associate Researcher. Also, the Social and Policy Research Institute, University of Ulster, has provided me with the much-needed financial and administrative assistance for the final stretch. Many thanks, in particular, to Hazel Henderson, for all her help with the preparation of this book.

To those political leaders who agreed to be interviewed for the research and who offered valuable insights both during interview and during subsequent informal conversations at conferences and events over the past few years, I am deeply grateful. Without you, this work would not have been possible. Thanks are also due to Melanie Blair at Palgrave Macmillan, Geetha Naren at Integra, and Jan Zielonka at St. Antony's College, Oxford, for their help and guidance.

On a personal note, special thanks are due to Ronan and Hala, to whom this book is dedicated; to Patricia, Duke, Lisa, Arlene and John – my family; and to Leza – my oldest friend.

* * *

Some of the arguments in this book have been presented in an abridged form in 'Chameleonic Leadership: Towards a New Understanding of Political Leadership During the Northern Ireland Peace Process', *Leadership*, 2, 1 (2006) pp. 53–75 (Sage). Chapter 4 is an amended version of the article 'Abdicated and Assumed Responsibilities: The Multiple Roles of Political Leadership during the Northern Ireland Peace Process', *Civil Wars*, 7, 3 (2005) pp. 195–218 (Routledge: Taylor and Francis Group).

List of Abbreviations

ANC	African National Congress
APNI	Alliance Party of Northern Ireland
CLMC	Combined Loyalist Military Command
DUP	Democratic Unionist Party
IDASA	Institute for Democracy in South Africa
INCORE	International Conflict Research
IRA	Irish Republican Army
LVF	Loyalist Volunteer Force
NDI	National Democratic Institute
NILP	Northern Ireland Labour Party
NIO	Northern Ireland Office
NIWC	Northern Ireland Women's Coalition
PUP	Progressive Unionist Party
SDLP	Social Democratic and Labour Party
UDA	Ulster Defence Association
UDP	Ulster Democratic Party
UFF	Ulster Freedom Fighters
UKUP	United Kingdom Unionist Party
UUC	Ulster Unionist Council
UUP	Ulster Unionist Party
UVF	Ulster Volunteer Force

1
Introduction

Background

On 10 April 1998 Northern Ireland joined a long list of countries which had produced peace agreements in the 1990s. The architects of the Agreement included eight local political parties and the British and Irish governments. Significant architectural influence of the US administration under President Clinton, and to a slightly lesser extent, of the experiences of other peace processes which had reached agreement before Northern Ireland, was noted. The Agreement was the culmination of a prolonged peace process, which had followed an equally prolonged and protracted conflict.[1] The origins of this peace process dated back to at least the mid-1980s with the secret dialogue between John Hume, leader of the Social Democratic and Labour Party (SDLP), and Gerry Adams, leader of Sinn Féin. The tentative discussions between Hume and Adams converged with the more formal 'talks process' in the early 1990s.[2] This 'talks process' gathered further momentum after both the republican and loyalist ceasefires in 1994 and the elections to the multiparty talks process in 1996 and eventually resulted in the signing of the Good Friday Agreement in April 1998.[3]

The story of the Northern Ireland peace process is not considered to be particularly unique since the 'decade of peace processes' of the 1990s bore witness to a multiplicity of ceasefires and political agreements spanning all continents.[4] As a consequence, academic studies of such political conflicts and peace processes have flourished considerably.[5] Many of the works have been comparative in nature. Some have made for more popular comparison than others. For example, most scholars of ethnic conflicts can recount various details of the peace processes in Northern Ireland, Israel/Palestine and South Africa and how a multiplicity of factors were married together to create 'settlements', however long their eventual life span.[6] Given the difficulties with many peace initiatives, the more recent attention has focused on those conflicts which have proved to be seemingly intractable, and which have had difficulty in reaching a settlement or in sustaining the peace.[7] This book seeks to further contextualize some of the current academic writing on peace processes by isolating and highlighting one of the key determining factors which can effect a societal transition from conflict to peace building. This factor is one of human agency. More specifically, it is political leadership.

It is argued, in normative terms, that many ethnic conflicts are triggered by 'bad leaders'.[8] They are defined as 'self-obsessed leaders who will do anything to get and keep power'.[9] By the same rationale then, those who help to trigger peace processes might be determined or presented as 'good leaders'. Not only could this be interpreted as an oversimplification in the extreme, but it is also arguable that the use of the terminology – 'bad' and 'good' leaders – lacks the academic precision that is needed to explain the role, capacity and effect of political leadership in conflicts and, more importantly, in peace processes. The basic rationale for this book takes the lack of academic precision, in respect of political leadership in peace processes, as one of its starting points.

Arguably, the role, capacity and effect of political leaders in peace processes risks being overlooked as both decidedly obvious and warranting little further explanation. We already know from real world experience that political leaders can act as the trigger to escalate violence, not only during conflicts but also during peace processes.[10] Similarly, we also know that peace agreements are usually not made by the masses but by political elites. Consequently, the majority of attention which does focus on political leadership in peace processes tends to come from a rather 'unacademic' background. The most obvious example of this is through the mass media and, in particular, their political commentators.[11] There are, of course, potential problems with such a narrow approach, not least that there can exist an unhealthy focus on political leaders as both the epitomization of the conflict and its possible solutions. In the context of Northern Ireland, O'Connor has acknowledged that 'the personalities of those who lead have mattered more, perhaps, than they ought'.[12] There is a significant emphasis on reporting their behaviour, on understanding what motivates the leaders and/or what makes them tick, and where such personalities are located within the wider political context.[13] All of this presents something of a conundrum. On one hand, there appears to exist a rather muted academic interest in understanding the role, capacity and effect of political leadership during peace processes. On the other hand, there appears to exist an overly enthusiastic interest in the behaviours and motivations of political elites during peace processes by those in the media charged with reporting the day to day events of those processes. It is puzzling that there is such interest in some quarters and yet not in others. In a sense then, this book serves to redress the imbalance and reintroduce an element of 'scholarly enquiry' into this subject.

The arguments of this book

This book aims to analyse more systematically the phenomenon of political leadership during the peace process in Northern Ireland from 1994 to 1998 specifically, and to move towards a new framework of analysis for political leadership in peace processes more generally. It argues that the interpretations of political leadership in peace processes offered by both the political leadership literature and the peace and conflict studies literature, to date, are often inappropriate in the context of Northern Ireland. It contends that an alternative interpretation of political leadership during the Northern Ireland peace process is critical to the development of any future analysis of the Northern Ireland peace process, and also to the development of the analysis of peace processes more generally. It suggests that political leadership during the Northern Ireland peace process was often necessarily contradictory in style and substance and argues that such contradictions and inconsistencies form the basis of the alternative interpretation that this book seeks ultimately to present. In the final analysis, this book asserts that political leadership during the Northern Ireland peace process can best be described as 'chameleonic leadership' – an inconstant leadership which shifted according to the opinion of others and the climate in which it existed, just as a chameleon can change its colour to blend with its background.

In developing this argument, Chapter 2 begins by introducing the phenomenon of political leadership through a critique of some of the more general interpretations of political leadership and the application of some of these interpretations to the context of Northern Ireland before moving to examine the Northern Ireland case study more specifically. It examines the case study in three distinct ways. First, Chapter 3 presents an analysis of some of the existing definitions and explanations of political leadership in Northern Ireland during the peace process. In doing so it asks whether the definitions of political leadership as given by interviewees, and/or the definitions of political leadership given by those analysing their behaviour during the Northern Ireland peace process from the sidelines, are useful in helping to define, explain and classify political leadership during that period. Such definitions, while useful, appear to offer only a very limited and often contradictory understanding. Thus, this book seeks to understand political leadership better by breaking it down into three distinct constituent parts for further examination – the role of political leadership, the capacity or influence of political leadership, and the effect of political leadership.

By deconstructing political leadership in this way, a number of research objectives associated with each chapter can be highlighted. Chapter 4 seeks to understand the role of political leadership during the Northern Ireland peace process. This chapter raises the question of whether their role was primarily to protect their own constituents during the peace process, or whether the role of political leadership was to make 'peace' at all costs. Ultimately, it considers whether there could ever be a single role for political leaders in the peace process and surmises that multiple roles may well have been incompatible with one another, thus leading to possible contradictions and inconsistencies within them. Chapter 5 seeks to explain the sources of influence available to the political leadership, as a way of opening up a discussion on their potential to influence the shape and direction of the peace process. Ultimately, it considers whether the most potent sources of influence were more structural or personal in nature and whether alternative sources of influence existed to undermine any possible influence that a political leader might have held. In this respect, any undermining of influence might have necessitated political leaders acting in different ways at different points in the peace process in a way that was directly relational to their perceived influence at that particular time. The potential of personal influence feeds into Chapter 6, which seeks to identify the effect that political leaders might have had on each other during the peace process. In doing so, any specific interactions between political leaders during this time which could be inductive of their effect on other leaders in particular and on the peace process in general are examined. The chapter questions whether the various attempts to bring political leaders together outside of the formal parameters of the 'talks process' in Northern Ireland significantly enhanced the leaders' ability to learn from and to understand their political adversaries and, consequently, whether this affected the nature and direction of the peace process.[14] It argues that leadership behaviour beyond the confines of Northern Ireland was often radically different to their behaviour within the 'talks process' and is demonstrable of further contradictory and inconsistent leadership behaviour during the peace process.

Through the course of this book, those factors which served to both help and hinder the role, capacity and effect of political leadership during the Northern Ireland peace process will be highlighted. These, however, are considered in detail in Chapter 7. This chapter argues that much of the experience of the peace process left Northern Ireland's political leaders with confused roles, undermined capacity and negated effect and identifies those issues which were the most significant contributors to this. It asserts that as a consequence of confused roles, undermined capacity and negated effects the new interpretation of political leadership during the Northern Ireland peace process can best be described as 'chameleonic leadership' – an inconstant leadership which shifted according to the opinion of others and the climate in which it existed. Chapter 8 concludes that using both the deconstructed understanding of political leadership, its limitations, and the interpretation of political leadership as 'chameleonic leadership', we can move towards the development of a broader understanding of political leadership in the context of the Northern Ireland peace process in particular, and of political leadership in peace processes more generally though this chapter also suggests how the framework of analysis could be developed further.

In terms of the approach taken for this work, it is acknowledged that there are different theoretical perspectives which can help explain the phenomenon of political leadership. To strengthen the subsequent arguments made within this book, it is useful to draw on two or three particularly relevant theoretical approaches.[15] Anything less than this could be perceived as little more than a 'reductionism approach'.[16] Indeed, such has often been the case of explanations offered in relation to the conflict in Northern Ireland. For example, many commentators hold Ian Paisley, leader of the Democratic Unionist Party (DUP), in some part responsible for the 'troubles' in Northern Ireland.[17] The essence of the reductionist argument presented is that without Paisley the conflict in Northern Ireland might well have developed in an entirely different manner. However, as Blondel argues, 'there is no full and complete "reductionism" which could entirely explain interpersonal reactions in terms of habits, religious fear or economic forces'.[18] Thus, while this book does have an agent-centred perspective, it also draws upon a combination of what Blondel determines as the three main branches of political thinking – the normative, behavioural and structural theories.[19] Clearly, no one approach is better than the other but, instead, they offer different yet complementary ways of viewing the political leadership phenomenon. In a sense, what each of these approaches seeks to uncover is how much importance should be attached to individual political leadership in the interpretation of political developments? In other words, does leadership make a difference and, if so, how much of a difference does it make? Edinger suggests that there are only two points of view in relation to the perceived significance of political leadership.[20] One is that political developments may only in the very last analysis be attributed to the leadership of a particular individual and the other assumes that individual leadership is a primary post-dictive or predictive causal factor in explaining political developments.[21]

In any study, it is necessary to state explicitly the initial core assumptions being made by the author. Given the area of this research, the obvious assumption is that political leadership matters, hence the agency oriented undertones.[22] The assumption that individuals matter is also made. This assumption is in contrast to much of that which is written on international relations theory where the primary actor is always the state and not the person.[23] Explaining the degree of how much it matters in terms of its role, capacity and effect during the peace process in Northern Ireland is, in the final analysis, the essence of this book. The assumption that leadership matters is just one reason for undertaking this work. There are, of course, other reasons. The more in-depth rationale for this research has been broken down into its component parts for further elaboration.

Why political leadership?

Other than 'because it matters', what are the fundamental reasons which would encourage a study of political leadership? One reason for studying the subject is that it is inevitably tied to a number of global realities. The most obvious of these is that neither institutions nor the average citizen within a democratic country actually govern that country on a day to day basis, but political leaders do. Renshon points to three characteristics of modern society that further illustrate the importance of political leadership in this respect – decision centrality, the extension of public sphere responsibilities and the structural amplification of effects.[24] The decision centrality argument suggests that you simply cannot have a public vote or a referendum on every political issue. More often than not, political leaders choose to take decisions in the absence of any direct input from the electorate. The extension of leadership responsibilities is directly relational to their decision-making role. The structural amplification of the effect of leaders' decisions is evidenced in the proliferation of government agencies and units charged with implementing the leaders' decisions, and means that the choices made by political leaders do not travel slowly throughout the bureaucracy and institutions of government.

Aside from these characteristics of contemporary society, another related reason for studying political leadership is, of course, that it represents the bare bones and/or the public face of contemporary politics. As Blondel says:

> If one reduces politics to its bare bones, to what is most visible to most citizens, it is the national political leaders, both at home and abroad, that remain once everything else has been erased; they are the most universal, the most recognised, the most talked about elements of political life.[25]

Indeed, reducing politics to its bare bones is a phenomenon which has become very common place in our contemporary political landscape. The war in Iraq, for example, has now been presented as a war against Saddam Hussein, as opposed to a war against weapons of mass destruction. As a result, such has been the focus on Saddam Hussein and his immediate family, that the general public would be less aware of the political structures that perpetuated Hussein's rule in Baghdad, or the ethnic cleavages between the Iraqi people. The Baath Party does not evoke the same degree of response or interest as the man himself. Equally, the public would be less well versed in the structures and ethos of Al-Qaeda than they would be in their knowledge of Osama Bin Laden, the leader of the Al-Qaeda movement. The media are not the only source culpable of dumbing down politics to equate with personalities. Indeed, it has been argued that politicians themselves have been keen to promote politics in overtly personal terms. This is a common argument articulated in respect of the position of Tony Blair, as leader of the Labour Party and current Prime Minister. Some suggest that Blair has attempted to reduce politics to its bare bones in the UK, by associating all of Labour's politics with Blair the leader.[26] For example, questions have been consistently raised as to whether the Blair style of leadership fits with a traditional British 'cabinet government' or is something more akin to the presidential style of the United States and, more importantly, whether this has been a conscious stylistic shift.[27]

A third reason for studying political leadership is directly related to the second and that is the public interest in political leaders. There is a public fascination with political leadership, personality politics and the personal elements of political affairs. Gaffney refers to this as 'the obsession with "personality politics" by everyone'.[28] Our obsession with personality politics and leadership is arguably one of great paradox given both our need for great statesmen and women and, equally, our preponderance towards either reading the dirt or dishing the dirt on politicians. Regardless, it is clear that there is greater public interest in the person than the policy and thus presents validity for further study.

A fourth reason is actually the reverse of the third. While there may be a public fascination with political leadership, the same cannot always be said within academic quarters. Indeed, in the UK particularly, leadership has often been seen as something rather 'superfluous' to understanding British governance.[29] Reintroducing the concept of political leadership to academic debates on governance is a worthwhile rationale for its study.

A final reason for studying political leadership is directly relational to its perceived problem-solving orientation. According to Tucker, political leadership means the diagnosis of a problem, the prescription of solutions and the mobilization of support for needed action.[30] Nowhere is the problem-solving orientation of leadership more important than in the context of violent conflicts and the search for peaceful solutions. It is to this context that I now turn.

Why peace processes?

A peace process is a prolonged peace initiative which invariably involves all of the main protagonists. Beyond this, the different variables involved in any one peace process make the general definition of a peace process more difficult to discern.[31] Adopting a rather critical approach in terms of the understanding of peace processes allows this book to connect with some normative issues. For example, a critical approach to the understanding of peace processes raises the question of whether or not a peace process is even necessarily a good thing. By extension then, it raises questions about the possible implications that this will have for analyses of leadership in peace processes. Arguably, many peace processes do not begin to address the root causes of the conflicts they seek to resolve.[32] Furthermore, peace processes can also serve to entrench the conflict and the actors within that conflict by reinforcing the roles that actors played during the conflict. For example, paramilitaries may be called to the negotiating table once a ceasefire has been declared irrespective of their capacity to adequately represent their community at that table.[33] With such reasoning, it is arguable that a peace process is not necessarily a good thing if it only deals with the manifestations of a conflict at the expense of the root causes of a conflict and also if it offers legitimacy to those holding weapons in the absence of any electoral mandate for them. Despite this, the benefits to be accrued from a potential peace process are often encouraging. A decline in conflict related deaths, an improved quality of life for those at the coal face of the conflict and an enhanced economic potential are the most obvious benefits to be accrued.[34] It is entirely plausible that political leaders involved in peace processes veer between perceiving the process to be a good thing on some occasions and to be a questionable practice on other occasions. By extension, this might explain any possible inconsistencies in their approach to the particular peace process with which they are involved. This is an obvious first reason for the study of political leadership in the context of peace processes.

The second reason is one of necessity, since the study of leadership has traditionally looked at leadership in conflict rather than the resolution of conflict. For example, Hamburg, Alexander and Ballentine note:

> large scale conflict between groups – like conflict between states – requires the deliberate mobilization efforts of determined political leaders. Without such leadership, members of ethnic, communal or religious groups who find themselves in adverse circumstances – for example, profound socio-economic inequality, political oppression and even deep intergroup animosity – do not spontaneously resort to warfare to retain redress. They tend instead to seek out non-violent means for improving their condition and resolving disputes, yet incendiary leaders can readily subvert such efforts and mobilize their followers for violence and hate.[35]

Much less has been said in relation to a leader's potential in terms of his or her contribution to the resolution of conflict. In fact, political leadership in peace processes is a subject that appears to have been ignored by general peace and conflict research. For those countries which have been subjected to extended periods of conflict stemming from the divisions within their societies, there exists a substantial body of literature. Much of the literature and research undertaken to date has focused on the nature of these divisions, a comparative analysis with other regions and the frameworks which exist to transform divided societies into 'liberal democracies'.[36] Issues such as policing, political violence/civil disobedience, and state control strategies have held the foreground in the recent past. The issue of political leadership and the transcendence of such leadership is not so often discussed.[37] At most, this notion of political leadership is referred to in scant detail, as just one of the many variables at play when deciphering why conflicts escalate, de-escalate and transform.[38] The dearth of literature relating to political leadership in the context of peace processes is another obvious rationale for the study.

Thirdly, in the areas where political leadership is examined more generally, there seems to be little within the general literature that is applicable to divided societies, despite the fact that the concept of political leadership itself is seen as universal. Many assumptions are made in the existing literature about the type of context in which political leadership operates. For example, Burns' seminal work on leadership in the 1970s argued that: 'conflict between and within parties is considered normal, predictable, and assuaged by time honored understandings about good winners and good losers, majority rule, "to the victor belongs the spoils" and so on'.[39] In functional liberal democracies this might well be considered to be the case. However, it could be argued that the 'time honored understanding' that Burns refers to is not so well understood nor accepted in ethnically and violently divided societies. In fact, part of the problem is often that there are few common understandings at all. Furthermore, the concept of good winners and good losers only emanates from societies where the competition/election procedures are considered fair, and where the administrative system is not contested. Majority rule has long been a major source of contention in many divided societies, with arguments made for 'mutual consensus' and the protection of minority groupings. Ultimately then, Burns' understanding of what is normal and acceptable about conflict and leadership within and among parties may be inappropriate to divided societies. The study of political leadership in the context of a peace process challenges some of the existing assumptions that are made in relation to political leadership and amounts to a third reason for a study which looks at political leadership in a rather specific context. In another example, the study of leadership in peace processes serves to contest the notion that political leadership is a wholly positive phenomenon. Kellerman has highlighted the implicit assumption assumed by many leadership scholars 'that to lead is to do right'.[40] It could be argued that the subject has not been broached because the implications of the relationship between leadership and conflict are difficult for some scholars to acknowledge. Yet it is clear that many divided societies are prone to leaders sometimes dubbed 'ethnic entrepreneurs', 'warlords' or 'power wielders', or, in other words, leaders whose motivations may not be so altruistic in both the conflict and in any subsequent peace process.

Fourthly, political leadership in the context of peace processes can raise some interesting anomalies which warrant further analysis. As an example of this, which relates to the previously articulated notion of leadership as a positive force, is that peace processes can highlight the interesting phenomenon of the political prisoner turned political leader.[41] This is not a normal convention in the majority of societies and appears to be something specific to divided societies. However, political prisoners have contributed to the emergence of new forms of leadership in societies where conflict is often related to the struggle for national independence, secession, self-determination or greater political accommodation. The transition of individual political prisoners to political leaders is an important one because it raises questions about what sort of dynamic, if any, exists between this band of leadership and the more conventional band of leadership during a peace process.

Finally, regardless of whether one is persuaded by the theoretical arguments of pluralism or elitism in general terms, it is abundantly clear that many peace processes are elite driven, with a relatively small number of people responsible for making decisions on the style and substance of peace negotiations. Collectively, the rationale presented here for the study of political leadership in the context of a peace process reinforces one of the arguments of this book that the political leadership literature and the peace and conflict studies literature often offer interpretations of political leadership that are lacking. Some do not engage at all with the concept of political leadership in peace processes preferring to remain focused on political leadership in war and conflict; others ignore the cultural specificities of divided societies and assume that the context in which political leaders operate is more universal; and those which have tentatively mentioned political leadership in the context of peace processes often ignore the very different leadership variables at play. That said, the study of political leadership in peace processes, in general, runs the risk of becoming immediately bogged down in the multiplicity of variables that exist within each individual context. Instead, it seems more appropriate to begin the study by focusing on a singular peace process in a particular region. The case study chosen for further examination is the Northern Ireland peace process from 1994 to 1998.

Why Northern Ireland?

Northern Ireland provides an interesting case study for the examination of political leadership in the specific context of a peace process.

Or does it? Some might ask why study Northern Ireland again? This is certainly a reasonable question by those who have argued that Northern Ireland is one of the most over-researched countries in the world.[42] However, despite the proliferation of academic works on the conflict in Northern Ireland, it has been argued that the research undertaken (at least until 1990) still fell short of a comprehensive understanding of the situation.[43] Moreover, academic disagreement continues to persist over the background, nature and long-term solutions to the 'conflict'. McGarry and O'Leary describe this as 'a "meta-conflict", a conflict about what the conflict is about'.[44] With the onset of the peace process in the 1990s, the nature of the research shifted slightly from the roots of the conflict towards the examination of possible settlements. But the reason for this study in particular is, firstly, that while political leadership might have been mentioned in the context of all other things, it did not appear to be singled out for individual attention during this period. Consequently, the comments made are less revealing than those which might have come from a more in-depth examination of political leadership. For example, Fred Halliday noted in his examination of the Northern Ireland peace process in the broader, comparative context of the 1990s decade of peace processes that:

> when it comes to internal conditions, the central issue remains the intentions of the main military and political players. Peace does not come, as many in the rush of 'civil society' expectations of the early 1990s may have hoped, through the replacement of the nasty people by nice people: would that it did. Protest, denunciation, scorn may play a role, but this is not enough to sway the 'hard' men and women, duros and duras. It comes through a decision by the nasty people that it is, at that particular moment, more advantageous to pursue peace than to pursue war.[45]

Arguably, discussing political players as 'nasty' or 'nice', while wholly understandable in one sense, sets up a dichotomy of political leadership which does not necessarily contribute to a more robust understanding of these actors during the peace process. Indeed, defining political leaders as either nasty or nice, and equating 'nasty people' with the pursuance of war fails to acknowledge the complex nature of political leadership during the Northern Ireland peace process, and their role, capacity and effect therein. Essentially then, the lack of attention towards an in-depth understanding of political leadership during the peace process provides the first and most obvious reason for concentrating on Northern Ireland.

The second reason for studying Northern Ireland is to reflect on the limited number of existing analyses which have looked at the issue of political elites in relation to the continuance, or otherwise, of conflict in Northern Ireland. For example, in 1995, McGarry and O'Leary looked at political leadership as one of the background conditions which were necessary for any likely settlement.[46] They argued, at that time, that there was an absence of the necessary elite motivations in Northern Ireland to move beyond conflict towards peace. For example, they claimed that the desire to avoid war had not been sufficiently intense and the desire to hold political office had also been insufficient; there was, moreover, the absence of sufficient elite predominance otherwise known as the ability to lead followers in directions which they might not necessarily wish to go; and finally there was the absence of intra-segmental stability which meant that the different political elites suffered intra-community fragmentation and consequently felt less secure about possible compromises, at that time.[47] Clearly, there was some sort of shift in elite motivations between 1995 and the eventual agreement in 1998, and ascertaining the possible reasoning behind such shifts is important.[48]

A further rationale for the study of political leadership in the context of the Northern Ireland peace process is that many of the key actors involved in the conflict were the same key actors involved in the peace process. While many of these actors engaged in a reassessment of their positions, policies and preferences in the late 1980s and early 1990s, this did not necessitate a change of leadership in Northern Ireland which makes for a rather interesting phenomenon. Contrary to some conflict resolution theory, which argues that leadership change is necessary for the transformation of a conflict, political leadership in Northern Ireland remained mostly consistent during this reassessment period. Of the four largest parties at the time of the negotiation process, the Ulster Unionist Party (UUP), the SDLP, the DUP and Sinn Féin, the leadership of the latter three had remained unchanged for almost two decades. The fact that many of the key players remained the same and yet the political situation dramatically changed is highly significant. Indeed, it raises the question of what allowed for the political changes to take place, if it had not been a significant change of leadership within the main parties. In other words, how exactly did a society with many of the same political leaders in place from the 1970s and 1980s come to make a peaceful agreement in the 1990s? How did these 'political protagonists' become the 'political pragmatists' of the 1990s? And how was this related to their role, capacity and effect during the peace process?

The answer may, in some ways, relate to the fourth reason for choosing Northern Ireland to study. While overt efforts were made in Northern Ireland at 'institution building' and at finding an acceptable mechanism of governance, more covert operations had gotten underway to afford the political leaders the space with which to explore possible transitional issues and 'were concerned with building up a culture of trust among politicians'.[49] Arthur argues that the point of a series of track two exercises with political leaders from Northern Ireland was that:

> the participants shared a concern that something needed to be done and that at the very least they should explore each others' options. Track two presented the best opportunities to do so. The absence of the media, the physical location, the neutral back-up support, all were as far removed as possible from the rawness of the Northern Ireland's political arena.[50]

The net gain of the series of peer learning initiatives that Arthur studied was, at best, that some politicians had learnt to trust one another and, at the very least, that some politicians had the measure of their adversaries in the bilateral and multilateral talks of the ensuing peace process. This engagement with leaders at a personal level outside of the confines of structured negotiations has not been examined in much detail and may have been a contributing factor to some of the positions taken at the negotiating table. It is critical, then, that this is re-examined in detail here.

A fifth reason for studying Northern Ireland in this particular context is, of course, that research on leadership during the Northern Ireland peace process has the potential to allow for 'borrowing' by other countries, should anything worth borrowing emerge. There is some evidence of this already with the borrowing of public figureheads from one peace process as an indication of what might be missing in another. Indeed, as Adrian Guelke noted: 'the most common metaphor that the South African transition inspired in Northern Ireland was the notion that what the province needed was a unionist de Klerk'.[51] The unionist de Klerk analogy was made by both republican and nationalist politicians, not least by Martin McGuinness and John Hume.[52] The 'unionist de Klerk' analogy was also referred to within the unionist tradition, although for entirely different reasons. During the peace process these unionists claimed that Trimble was selling unionism out, just as de Klerk sold out the White South Africans.[53]

Finally, and more practically, Northern Ireland also provides a relatively discreet time period for study (1994–98), a more accessible peace process than others and the potential to fill a niche in the literature, given that political leadership is a topic that has been largely unexplored in the Northern Ireland context. Overall, the reasoning behind the study of political leadership in peace processes, in the specific case study of Northern Ireland, is demonstrably complex. There are a multitude of valid reasons for undertaking such a study. The rationale presented here gives an overview of the potential added value of a research study of this kind and confirms that a new interpretation of political leadership during the Northern Ireland peace process will be a worthwhile contribution.

A note on methodology

The research for this book first began in 1999. At that time, the political context in Northern Ireland was in something of a state of flux. Although the Agreement had been signed in April 1998 and had been endorsed by the public in a referendum in May 1998, only very limited political progress had been made beyond that point. Elections to the newly created Northern Ireland Assembly had been held in June 1998 though the establishment of the Northern Ireland Executive was delayed by arguments over whether the IRA should decommission its weapons in advance of Sinn Féin being allowed to take their seats on the Executive. By the time the research began in 1999, the Assembly was still not fully functional and George Mitchell, the Chairperson of the multi-party talks process in Northern Ireland, had been recalled to Northern Ireland to conduct a review of the Agreement. Following this, power was eventually devolved to the Northern Ireland Assembly on 30 November 1999 on the understanding that decommissioning would begin to take place once the Assembly was fully functional. However by February 2000 the Independent International Decommissioning Commission, under John de Chastelain, reported that little progress had been made in terms of decommissioning. The consequence of this was the suspension of the Northern Ireland Assembly and its associated institutions by the then British Secretary of State for Northern Ireland, Peter Mandelson, in February 2000. This period of suspension between February and May 2000 coincided with the majority of the interviews that were conducted with political leaders as part of the research.

In designing the research, some of the key terms needed to be teased out further and explained. Principally, these were leadership, political leadership and peace processes.[54] The main interest of the research was *political* leadership though the author was fully cognisant of the role

that other leaders play in divided societies and in societies in transition, whether they were cultural, religious, community-based or business leaders, not least because such leaders can often have 'a moderating
effect on unwise political leaders'.[55] While it could be argued that many
of those other leaders mentioned above might act *politically* they are
often seen to be nonconstituted leaders.[56] Nonconstituted leaders, by
definition, lack the power that political science sees as intricately linked
to politics. In the context of the Northern Ireland peace process this
was evidenced in the fact that there was no formal space created at the
negotiating table for leaders other than party political leaders. For this
reason the nonconstituted leaders were omitted from the parameters of
this research. Instead, political leadership was taken to mean political
party leadership.

How far down a party organization one can go in terms of making a
distinction between the political leaders and the rank and file of a party
also requires further elucidation in order to more fully clarify the boundaries of the research. For the purposes of this research it was decided
that the concept of political leadership should be used to classify those
people engaged in a political capacity at the top level of their respective
political parties in Northern Ireland. The concept was not necessarily
taken to mean merely the individual political party leaders in isolation,
nor did it mean only those political actors who held electoral office.
Instead, the concept was more inclusive than exclusive in its classification and focused on those who had the capacity to effect influential
change both within their own parties and beyond their parties during
the peace process. It was felt that for the purposes of an exploratory
investigation any broader conceptualization of political leadership ran
the risk of becoming bogged down in a maze of variables, dimensions
and linkages that might 'obscure more than it reveals about the essence
of political leadership'.[57] Therefore, beyond this classification no definition of political leadership is offered here. Whilst aware that almost
everyone may have their own sense of who leaders are and what they do,
honing that into a set of 'off-the-shelf' features is a perplexing task. The
characteristics of leadership are often ambiguous, malleable, contingent
upon circumstance and potentially employable for multiple intents.
While it is true that political leadership is a universal phenomenon, it is
also a relative concept and what may be deemed to be overtly political
in one context may not be seen as political in another.

A qualitative methodology was employed for this research which
primarily involved in-depth interviews with some of Northern Ireland's
political elites. One of the primary reasons for using the concept of

political leadership more inclusively than exclusively was to afford added protection of anonymity for those interviewed for the research. If the political party leader (in the singular) were the only person interviewed for the purposes of the research then it would have been more difficult to maintain anonymity. Another consideration was that, it afforded the author greater likelihood of gaining access to elites if the net were cast beyond a handful of individuals. Devine argues that a qualitative approach is best when the 'aim of the research is to employ people's subjective experiences and the meanings they attach to those subjective experiences'.[58] In the case of this research, the aim of the interviews was to ascertain political leaders' perceptions of their role, capacity and effect during the peace process. In-depth interviewing allowed the political leaders to talk freely and offer their own personal interpretations of leadership.

Using a qualitative approach represented something of a marked departure from the usual methodologies employed in more general leadership studies, which tend to use qualitative research in the exploratory phases of researching a topic and then use quantitative analysis to refine and validate the hypotheses which might have been generated from qualitative research.[59] However, as Conger argues, the qualitative method offers a number of distinct advantages over quantitative methods, including a greater opportunity to explore the leadership phenomenon in significant depth and to do so longitudinally, the ability to detect unexpected phenomena during the research, the ability to investigate processes more effectively, a greater likelihood of sensitivity to contextual factors and a more robust approach for investigating the more symbolic dimensions of leadership.[60] The downside of a qualitative approach and, in particular, the potential problems with elite interviewing as a principal methodology were taken into consideration. For example, elite interviewees tend to provide a very subjective account of an event or an issue, thus the reliability of the interviewee can sometimes be questionable.[61] Furthermore, elites are, by definition, less accessible and thus interview samples tend to be a lot smaller and run the risk of being unrepresentative.[62] These issues notwithstanding, it still seemed clear that the qualitative approach offered more scope for research into a relatively untapped area in Northern Ireland's political analysis.

Whilst in-depth interviews were one of the primary sources of data collection, the actual interview format was somewhat informal, with topics raised for discussion rather than a number of specific questions asked. Keeping the interviews informal was a conscious decision taken to allow the interviewees the opportunity to talk about political leadership using their own terminology rather than being guided by the existing terminology in the leadership literature, which the author felt might prove to be more problematic than helpful. Additionally, the use of a semi-structured interview was useful as a sidestep to the potential problem of elites wanting to control the interview and refusing to answer specific questions. Whilst mindful of the degree of confidentiality offered to the interviewees, it is permissible to say that each of these players were either senior members of their various parties negotiating teams, and/or were actual party leaders, and/or were current or subsequent Ministers within the Northern Ireland Executive.

The interview material was supplemented by other political interviews, given by political leaders in Northern Ireland to the broadcast and print media. Transcripts of political interviews given on television programmes such as *On the Record* were utilized to this effect, though consideration was taken of the many problems of political interviews whereby 'journalists regard politicians as deliberately evasive or obfuscatory, while politicians see journalists as too eager to set someone up for a fall rather than act as a conduit for political discussion'.[63] In addition, life histories in the form of biographies and autobiographies of key players during the period of the peace process were examined as well.

In organizing and analysing all of the data collected, a grounded theory approach was used.[64] Critical to such an approach is that: 'one does not begin with a theory, and then prove it. Rather, one begins with an area of study and what is relevant to that area is allowed to emerge'.[65] Additionally, because of the risk that elite interviewees might, at worst, try to rewrite history in their own favour or, at best, present radically different interpretations of events and issues, a process of triangulation was used whereby the data collected from interviews was cross-referenced with other published first-hand accounts and documentary sources from the peace process and also with published secondary source materials.[66] A manual analysis of all data was then undertaken using the above materials and was supplemented by grey materials, such as conference papers, reports and proceedings and election manifestos from the 1994 to 1998 period. Some peer-debriefing took place which involved exposing the author's preliminary analysis and tentative conclusions to peers on a continuous basis which assisted in further analysis of the study. This took the form of conference papers presented at various conferences after the interview period in 2000. Papers were delivered at the International Leadership Academy/United Nations University Post-Conflict Peace-Building Conference in Amman,

Jordan in November 2000; the Ethnic Studies Network Conference at INCORE in July 2001; the Social Policy Association Annual Conference at Queens University, Belfast in August 2001; and at the Political Studies Association of Ireland Annual Conference at the University of Ulster in October 2002.

The overall result is an analysis of political leadership unconstrained by either a strict chronological approach or a unionist/nationalist tradition approach because through using the grounded methodological approach, it became clear that neither approach emerged from the research as necessarily important. In other words, no attempt has been made to ascertain types and styles of leadership that could be described as inherently unionist or nationalist. Nor has any attempt been made to chart shifts in behaviour on a month to month basis by various political leaders. Rather, the focus has been on political leadership in Northern Ireland in its generic form during the entire period of the peace process. This is critically important in terms of the progression of the overall argument which contends that an alternative interpretation of political leadership during the Northern Ireland peace process is critical to the development of any future analyses of the Northern Ireland peace process, and also to the development of the analyses of peace processes more generally. Focusing on a unionist/nationalist leadership dichotomy would be likely to result in a perpetuation of the academic argument that the conflict and its resolution was about two distinct ethnic groups. The research presented here seeks to offer an alternative analysis.

Conclusions: the potential contribution

It is argued that research projects should satisfy two main criteria in order to determine their likely value to the academic community. The first is that the research should pose a question that is deemed to be important in the real world. The second is that the research should have the potential to make a contribution to scholarly literature by increasing our ability to construct some scientific explanations of some aspect of the world.[67] This contribution can be made in many ways. It can take the form of challenging existing hypotheses, it can show that theories designed for some purpose in one literature can be applied in another literature, or it can also argue that an important topic has been overlooked in the literature and then proceed to contribute a systematic study to the area.[68] Marsh and Stoker add to this that: 'a characteristic of good political science, in our opinion, is that it should have the capacity to reach out to other disciplines'.[69]

Clearly, the subject of political leadership is one which is highly significant in the real world. Nowhere is this more true than in the context of violent and divided societies. The Carnegie Commission on Preventing Deadly Conflict argues that bold leadership is essential as part of the tools and strategies used in the prevention of conflict but laments that we know far more about the role of leaders in stimulating ethnic and communal conflict than we do about the role of leaders in diminishing it.[70] The question(s) posed by this book asks what was the role, capacity and effect of political leadership during the peace process in Northern Ireland and how (if at all) can we use what we know about the role, capacity and effect of political leadership in one specific, violent context, to help build a more general understanding of these issues in the context of other peace processes?

Given that the research must also contribute to the scholarly literature on the subject, the contribution seems best suited to the rationale which suggests that political leadership in peace processes is an important topic which has been overlooked in both the political leadership literature in general and in the peace and conflict studies literature in particular.

To sum up this introduction, consider the simple analogy of baking a cake. The ingredients are relatively simple – a combination of some flour, eggs, sugar, butter and milk. Deciding how much or how little of each ingredient to use is rather more difficult. Most people will use a cook book to assure themselves that they have all of their ingredients mixed in exactly the 'right' quantity and therefore will produce a perfect result. However, ingredients mixed in slightly different quantities do not necessarily mean that the 'mix' isn't quite right but it does mean that the outcome will be slightly different. More sugar will simply make the cake sweeter. Less eggs and the cake may not rise. In the absence of flour, there would be no cake at all. The point is that the same ingredients mixed in different quantities will affect the overall outcome. In the context of political leadership and peace processes, baking a cake can be equated with building and sustaining a peace process. Political leadership is just one ingredient within that process. The question is which ingredient does political leadership represent? Is it akin to flour – without which there would be no cake? Without political leadership would there be no process? Or is it similar to sugar – to sweeten what can often be a bitter process? We know that as an ingredient in a peace process political leadership is important. That is not enough. We need to have a clearer understanding of the role, capacity and effect of political leadership during the peace process in Northern Ireland in order to convincingly interpret the significance of the leadership ingredient. This book seeks to provide that clarity while remaining conscious that within such clarity may lie many contradictions and inconsistencies.

2
Conceptualizing Political Leadership in Peace Processes

Introduction

Reviewing the literature has the potential to be both complex and nuanced, not least because this topic straddles the confines of more than one academic discipline. On one hand sits the subject area of leadership studies, which itself is multidisciplinary in nature.[1] However, political leadership can be considered as a sub section of the more broadly based subject area and for the purposes of this book the emphasis here has been concerned with political leadership only.[2] The other body of literature falls within the broad, multidisciplinary subject area of peace and conflict studies and, in particular, that literature which focuses on conflict resolution and peace processes – both generally and in particular.[3]

A cursory glance reveals that within the general political leadership literature there appears a consistent failure to address the specificities of the concept in the context of divided societies. Equally, within the peace and conflict studies literature, there is a temptation to leave the leadership phenomenon as a factor so obvious as to overlook it. Moreover, in no known instances has the phenomenon of political leadership in the peace process in Northern Ireland been empirically examined using the theories, concepts and models from the political leadership literature, nor tested against some of the assumptions made by both political leadership and peace and conflict specialists.

Thus, the purpose of this chapter is to introduce the various interpretations of political leadership in peace processes, to the particular context of Northern Ireland, by marrying together the literatures of political leadership, peace and conflict studies and the more contextual material from the peace process in Northern Ireland with some theoretical positioning. In doing so, it is argued that this will highlight some of the problems and paradoxes with existing interpretations of political leadership in peace processes, when applied to the case study of Northern Ireland.

The chapter presents three separate literature synopses – an analysis of the political leadership literature and how that literature engages with the issues of political leadership in the context of peace processes; the peace and conflict literature and how that literature deals with role, capacity and effect of political leaders in conflicts and in peace processes; and the Northern Ireland peace process literature and how that literature deals with those political leaders involved in the process. It does so in order to extrapolate some of the interpretations of political leadership in peace processes generally which might be useful to our understanding of political leadership during the peace process in Northern Ireland.

Ultimately though, the chapter argues that the interpretations of political leadership in peace processes offered by both the political leadership literature and the peace and conflict studies literature are mostly inappropriate in the context of Northern Ireland. The chapter concludes with a series of interpretational problems and paradoxes which have been highlighted by the literature and explains how the remainder of the book will be conditioned by such issues.

Revisiting the political leadership literature

The literature on political leadership can be subdivided into four distinct bodies of work. First, there are the classical political theories which include the seminal works of Machiavelli, Plato and, more recently, Weber.[4] Secondly, there are the biographies and autobiographies of political individuals throughout history.[5] Thirdly, there are those works that have attempted to move away from the specific analysis of individuals towards the more general analysis of political leadership.[6] Finally, there is a body of knowledge which has examined the issue of political leadership in relation to other specific conceptual developments.[7]

Classical political theorists have been described as having only a limited concern for the detailed analysis of political leadership.[8] Much of their work focused on the creation and organization of a good society. In Blondel's analysis, this was because the classical theorists held a pessimistic view of leaders, having unsuccessfully tried to influence leaders at some point in their own lives.[9] However, while leadership does not appear to have been the main focus of the study in many classical works, a common thread runs through them all which further emphasizes their pessimistic outlook on leadership. This common thread is of issues related to conflict, violence and unethical behaviour. For the most part, violence and politics are seen as being both inextricably linked and necessary.[10] For example, Plato's philosopher rulers were recruited from the military guardian class. Machiavelli's Prince was advised that he did not have to be a good leader in order to be a successful leader.[11] Thus, in order to win and hold on to power a prince did not necessarily have to behave with a degree of moral conviction and could disregard any connection between ethics and politics.[12] As a result, Machiavelli claimed that the Prince could kill like a lion in order to get what he wanted if his other tactics had failed. More recently, Weber argued that the quite different tasks of politics could be solved by violence.[13] Like Machiavelli, Weber's account of political leadership headlined those with a strong instinct for power.[14]

These classic works have influenced much of the more contemporary writing on political leadership and what could be termed as 'the warrior approach' to leadership has continued. For example, Kaplan argued that leadership in the modern day demanded an approach similar to that taken by the 'ancient world', which was based on realism and on power politics.[15] Nice highlighted the various characteristics of a 'warrior model of leadership' and emphasized how leadership was inextricably linked to conflict and opposition; controlling the flows of information; seeing the end as justifying the means; an in-depth understanding of their followers and the enemies; selecting their battles wisely on the basis of this knowledge and also using other people as buffers during battle; and refusing to trust others.[16] Such is the perceived significance of the impact of war and conflict on leadership that the 'leadership secrets' of serving leaders during and after 9/11 in the US have even been revealed.[17]

Within the biographies and autobiographies of political individuals throughout history, the development of understandings of the concept of leadership has not necessarily been the priority for study. Partly, this is because political scientists, in particular, chose to leave it to the historians and the psychologists to write about the individual political leaders.[18] The consequence of this, as Blondel pointed out, was that: 'the historians who concentrated on leaders have not on the whole been concerned systematically with leadership as a phenomenon'.[19] As a result, the biographical literature often amounts to little more than a series of descriptives and narratives on a wide variety of leaders and politicians. Extrapolating from the specific to the more general using such biographical material has proved to be elusive, not least because much of the biographical literature is based on the uniqueness of the person and the uniqueness of the circumstances in which they were leaders. In other words, the lack of a conceptual framework for the selection, organization and presentation of data in most political biographies make generalizations almost impossible and serves as one reason why political scientists have, for the most part, steered clear of biographies as a means of conceptualizing political leadership.[20] Of those political biographies that do exist, a significant proportion focus on great leaders in wars, further endorsing the view that within political science the link between conflict and violence seems an accepted norm.[21]

Given the difficulties in understanding political leaders based solely on the classical theorists' views of leadership and the political biographies of 'great leaders', Blondel argued that there was need for more general classifications of political leadership.[22] In his mind, a general classification of political leadership must start from the effect that leaders have (or may have) on their society.[23] Classifying leaders in this way thus requires an examination of the personal characteristics of the leader, the instruments that they have at their disposal, and the situations that they face in order to see whether their impact is due to their personalities, their powers or the circumstances in which they are leaders. By way of illustration, Blondel presented a two-dimensional typology of potential leadership impact and classified the political leaders according to their goals since this was directly relational to the potential impact that they may or may not have.[24] Leaders were assessed on the basis of internal developments within a country and whether those developments were merely the maintenance of the status quo, some moderate changes or large changes. The second dimension for assessment was in terms of the actual scope for change and whether the scope was quite specialized (for example, only in one policy area), or a more moderate scope, or large scale-scope for change. In doing so, Blondel was able to categorize leaders from Mao, Lenin and Hitler, to Moses, Churchill and John F. Kennedy. The categories included leaders defined as saviours; paternalists/populists; ideologues; comforters; 'redefiners'; reformists; managers; adjusters/tinkerers; and innovators.[25] However, Blondel did caution that his two-dimensional categorization of goals was time bound. He considered this important since the position of a given leader can, and usually does, vary over time and that his categorization needed to be further developed on a longitudinal basis in order to improve his empirical understanding of the goals of political leaders.

As well as calls for political leadership in its generality to be considered, there were also calls that it should be considered comparatively. Edinger, in particular, applauded the move towards comparative analysis since he saw the study of political leadership as suffering from 'disciplinary and cultural parochialism'.[26] However, he did emphasize that any examination of political leadership in a comparative context would face three main problems.[27] First, it would suffer from definitional problems since the terminology of 'leadership' held different connotations in different countries. Secondly, it could suffer from the level of analysis problem in so far as some academics consider the significance of leadership to be of more importance than others do. More bluntly, explanations at the international and national levels of analysis tend to downgrade both the significance of leadership in general and the role of individual leaders in particular, while leadership studies scholarship has an air of ethnocentrism about it which evaluates the significance of leadership in all cultures and societies according to its own, predominantly US centric attitudes towards leadership. Finally, it might suffer from the problem of the 'counterfactual test' – in other words the test which works from the premise of exploring the impact of non-events by asking 'what difference would non-events have made in the course of political development?'[28] For example, what difference to the Northern Ireland peace process might there have been if David Trimble had been defeated in his 1995 leadership election? The primary problem with such testing is that it lacks scientific precision and requires some degree of imagination about what could or would have happened. Consequently, this approach sits uneasily with the plethora of work that takes a distinctly scientific and model based approach towards understandings of political leadership.[29]

Even within these tentative steps towards the formulation of a more general and comparative analysis of political leadership, the threads of conflict and violence can still be detected. For example, Rejai and Philips undertook a comparative analysis of loyalist and revolutionary political leaders, defining 'loyalists' as those who came to office through peaceful processes and 'revolutionaries' as those who seized power in violent ways.[30] This work presented the argument that among those considered as revolutionary political leaders could be found former loyalists. The reckoning was that loyalist turned revolutionaries participated in the political process of their society, found that process to be unresponsive to their needs and turned to revolutionary politics instead.[31] The converse was found to be equally true. Revolutionary-turned-loyalists operated outside of the political system until such times as they had more to gain from becoming part of that system. At this point in time, they opted into the system and became 'loyalists'. While Rejai and Philips did not study Northern Ireland in particular, their analysis has clear resonance for the Northern Ireland case study.

While some progress has been made in developing an understanding of political leadership in a more general way, further focus has also been given to the understanding of political leadership in relation to specific conceptual developments. The most obvious example of this is Kane's analysis of political leadership as moral capital.[32] Derived in part from Putnam's conceptual development of 'social capital', Kane argues that moral capital is derived by leaders from the positive moral judgments that people make about them. This moral capital is then used by political leaders to further their political objectives. A number of the leaders discussed have been leaders from countries which have been the seat of violent conflict. Hence, Kane is an author who ties up the concepts of political leadership, conflict and how moral capital can be used by leaders during conflict and peace process. Clearly though, the use of moral capital depends on the normative world view in operation in each society. In many respects, Kane's work is as close as the literature comes to dealing with political leadership in the context of peace processes. In another example, Putnam's 'social capital' theory is used to derive the concept of 'leadership capital'.[33] Renshon sees leadership capital as something beyond the moral. Rather, he argues that leadership capital consists of the competence, integrity and capacities for leadership.

However, despite these noted exceptions mentioned in the classic literature, the biographies, the more general analysis, and in relation to specific conceptual developments, the subject of political leadership, conflict and peace processes has not been approached directly by many. Perhaps, in part, this is due to a sense of denial about the relationship between leadership and conflict among some in the broader field of leadership studies, though clearly this is less true about political leadership scholars in particular. Kellerman made the point that those in the leadership industry 'assume[d] that to lead is to do right' which then allowed the leadership industry the necessary carte blanche to exorcise those political leaders throughout history who did not live up to the field's normative standards.[34] Indeed, it has been only by steering clear of the issues of what constitutes 'right' and 'wrong', that some authors have been able to make tentative steps into the research area of political leadership, conflict and peace processes.

For example, some attention has been given to political leaders in the context of conflict and territorial disputes by Chiozza and Choi, though their focus is only on two specific dimensions of leadership – how the length of a political leader's time in office would/could affect their overall capacity to make peace and how previous 'hawkish' behaviours might act to facilitate or impede making peace.[35] Their contribution has been one of the exceptions rather than the rule. Another relevant analysis has been Sechser's, who asks whether soldiers are less war-prone than statesmen, and uses a scientific modelling approach to investigate the question.[36] Sechser took the commonly held argument that civilian leaders are more prone to use force than military leaders because the military understands more fully the implications of war, having experienced war on the frontlines, and thus are more reluctant to engage in it. Using scientific modelling, he argues the reverse by offering the first cross national evidence in support of the argument that military officers are more likely than civilians to favour the use of force.

As the most recognizable embodiment of political groupings, it is intuitive to reason that political leaders are key actors in the creation, control and/or culmination of violent conflicts. However, despite their seemingly obvious centrality, and with the exception of the limited sources mentioned above, there exists a general dearth of writing that specifically addresses the role of political leaders in conflict situations. Such an omission is not only an academic oversight but is also one that has profound 'real world' consequences. Writing with reference to leadership during conflict, Brown observes that:

> Scholars have paid comparatively little attention to the roles played by domestic elites in instigating ethnic and internal conflicts. The result is a 'no fault' history that leaves out the pernicious effect of individuals... leaving elite decisions and actions out of the equation, as many social scientists do, is analytically misguided.... Under appreciating the importance of elite decisions and actions hinders conflict management efforts and fails to place blame where blame is due.[37]

In addition, the majority of the literature that does exist on leadership in peace processes remains unconvincing. The tendency to accord diametrically opposite labels of leadership does not convince as explanations for leadership behaviour. Setting up such dichotomies: 'good leaders' versus 'bad leaders';[38] 'leaders versus power-wielders';[39] 'warmongers versus peacemakers';[40] and 'weak versus strong leaders',[41] ignores a reality which is much more complex and nuanced and does not fit with the multi-dimensional nature of many protracted negotiations, which necessitates a much wider range of actors than a dichotomy might allude to.[42] For example, explaining South Africa's transition from apartheid to a multi-party democracy as a story of 'Mandela versus deKlerk' competition divorces other, equally important, political actors from this narrative.[43] In a similar vein, explaining the peace process in Northern Ireland as 'the David [Trimble] and Gerry [Adams] show' divorces other, equally important, actors from that particular narrative.[44] It is clear that this sets up too simplistic a dichotomy, tempting the reader to draw the cartoonish inference that some leaders are intrinsically 'good', while others are inherently 'bad'. Only some authors have recognized the futility of two-dimensional constructs. In the example of the dichotomy set up by Rejai and Philips using their categories of 'loyalist' and 'revolutionary', the dichotomy disproved itself. Eventually the authors concluded that such a dichotomy was not commensurate with reality and that there was, in fact, a great deal of heterogeneity between those that they had labelled as political opposites.[45] Therefore, in reality, leadership is neither one diametric nor the other. Rather, it is usually an activity conditioned and motivated by a diverse series of factors and influences within the leader's immediate environment.

There are a number of points to be distilled from the political leadership literature. The first and most important point is that it is clear that the contribution of the political leadership literature to our understanding of political leadership in the context of peace processes is limited, since it does not deal with the context quite directly. Indeed, the literature is at its strongest in terms of its interpretations of political leadership in conflict rather than in peacebuilding. Secondly, the classifications of political leadership which have been developed seem ill-suited to the context of Northern Ireland. The categories of leadership offered (for example as saviours, paternalists/populists, ideologues, comforters, redefiners, reformists, managers, adjusters/tinkers, and innovators) have limited resonance with the more traditional understanding of political leadership in Northern Ireland. Thirdly, the tendency of the literature to accord diametrically opposite labels of leadership to explain behaviours runs the risk of ignoring the more nuanced realities of political leadership, especially in the context of Northern Ireland, which has been equally fond of emphasizing its own limited dichotomies to explain the conflict; Catholic versus Protestant, nationalist versus unionist and loyalist versus republican. However, the following section articulates that the peace and conflict studies literature can be just as problematic, in terms of its applicability to the concept of political leadership in the context of the Northern Ireland peace process, as the literature discussed thus far.

Revisiting the peace and conflict literature

Peace and conflict studies is a multidisciplinary field which draws from the theory and research within political science, international relations, psychology, sociology, anthropology, philosophy, law and ethics.[46] There are two principal schools of thought associated with the field – the Nordic school, which is heavily influenced by a liberal philosophical approach and emphasizes consensus, and hence, is perceived as a 'peace research' approach; and the North American approach which is more focused on embracing and controlling diversity and is perceived as a 'conflict resolution' or 'conflict management' approach. Like much of the North American scholarship on leadership, peace and conflict studies has been broadly normative in its approach. In other words, it has often taken a value driven basis to the study of conflicts and their potential resolution. Given that the focus of this book is the context of peace processes only, the related literature can be subdivided into four separate bodies of work. Firstly, there is the work regarded as the contemporary classics of the field such as Burton, Galtung and Lederach.[47] Secondly, there is the more specific work that looks at issues of conflict management. Thirdly, there is the work that looks at conflict transformation and conflict resolution.[48] Finally, there is the literature that looks at some of the specificities of peace processes in isolation from the overall process.[49]

It has been more common to consider leadership in the context of conflict than in the context of peace. For example, Barash looked at the role of leadership in the course of war. He discussed the notion of 'strong leaders' and how they can make the case for war though acknowledges that weak leaders can also contribute to war in order to save face or to quell opposition at home.[50] In the context of peacebuilding, the contemporary classics do not engage with the leadership issue directly although they do signpost issues of particular significance to leadership. For example, Burton, as a human needs theorist, argued that one of the primary causes of protracted or intractable conflict was people's unyielding drive to meet their unmet needs at the individual, group and societal levels.[51] In applying needs theory to seemingly 'intractable' conflicts, Burton argued that these needs were often different to a party's 'interest' and could not be easily bargained away, thus necessitating a rather novel problem-solving approach to conflict resolution. Building relationships between the key political protagonists was considered to be part of that approach.

Indeed, there exists much synonymy between Burton's desire to 'problem solve' and using relationship building to do so and Lederach's more recent approach which suggested a need to move away from a primary concern with the resolution of issues towards a focus on the restoration of and rebuilding of relationships, given that the problem-solving approach insinuated the building of new relationships between participants.[52] Lederach's relationship building approach is multi-dimensional and specifically engages with relationship building at different levels of society. In particular, it focuses on the impact of leadership at the different levels.

In presenting his analysis of leadership, Lederach discusses the various levels of leadership as top, middle and grassroots leadership. Of particular significance to this work is his analysis of top-level leadership. Lederach defines these leaders as highly visible leaders locked into the positions taken with regard to the perspectives and issues in conflict, who are perceived as having significant if not exclusive power and influence.[53] Seeing political leaders as less able to effect change in terms of peacebuilding than some of the other leaders within a society, Lederach argues that the midlevel leadership approach – that is those people in academia, non-governmental organizations and religious groups who can access both those at the top-level and have influence over those at the grassroots level – are the most likely leaders to be able to influence the shape and direction of peacebuilding. Lederach is critical of top-level leadership and argues that too much emphasis has been placed on their significance in peacebuilding.[54] Pointing to the top-level assumption that achieving peace is primarily a matter of identifying the representative leaders and getting them to agree, Lederach argues that the reality is that identifying such 'representative' leaders is not always easy and that their agreement does not necessarily mean wider public agreement in so far as some leaders do not command the power and influence to guarantee their community's support for any agreements reached.[55] Overall, Lederach's view of a top-level leadership approach to peacebuilding is not an encouraging one in terms of political elites' potential influence.

The strength of Lederach's work, however, is that it is one of the few works which spells out clearly his interpretation of the role, capacity and effect of political leadership in peacebuilding, however limited that might be. The weakness is that this argument places little emphasis on the reality that many 'top leaders' are adept at finding ways around previously articulated goals when a process needs to move forward. The methods that leaders use in order to move from previously articulated positions have not really been examined. Some such methods, however, have been examined by Dixon in the case study of Northern Ireland. His interpretation of political events during the Northern Ireland peace process suggests that there was a large degree of choreography and stage management, or in other words, 'political lying', which catered for finding ways around previously articulated goals by Northern Ireland's political elite.[56] Equally, Aughey's analysis of the art and effect of political lying in Northern Ireland, as a method of explaining away the paradoxes in the Good Friday Agreement (GFA), indicates further the political leaders' capability of moving away from previously held positions.[57]

Although he is certainly one of the most obvious, Lederach was not alone in his focus on leadership. Nordlinger's work on conflict regulation in divided societies paid much attention to the 'critical role of conflict group leaders' in the context of managing conflicts as distinct from resolving them.[58] While Nordlinger observed six conflict regulating practices which could stabilize divided societies – a stable governing coalition between the political parties, a principle of proportionality, a mutual veto, purposive depoliticization, compromises, and concessions – he argued that in these conflict regulating practices noted, it was primarily the political leaders who took the initiative in working out the practices and implementing them.[59] He commented:

> it is obvious that they and they alone, were in a position to do so. Clearly the conflict group members (or non-elites) are too numerous, too scattered, too fragmented, too weak, and too unskilled to be able to work out and operate any of the six conflict-regulating practices.[60]

Nordlinger's book was primarily one of motive. He argued that political leaders would not take the initiative in working out the conflict management practice if it were not in their own interests to do so – in other words, he argued that leaders needed a motive to move. Nordlinger emphasized four conflict regulating motives which helped encourage the conflict regulating practices noted above – an external threat or danger that would submerge internal conflicts; the belief that intense conflict and its actual or possible consequences would detract from the economic wellbeing of leaders' segment or conflict group; the acquisition or retention of political power; and avoidance of bloodshed and suffering within their own communities as the rationale for leadership intervention.[61] Motivation, however, was not enough to secure elite conflict regulations. Nordlinger concluded that this had to be combined with conciliatory attitudes and the top leaders' own political security in order to explain adequately elite conflict regulating behaviour.[62] Overall then, the role, capacity and effect of political leadership in 'managing' conflict was determined by self-interested motivations, a sense of conciliation and safety of political positioning.

Miall, Ramsbotham and Woodhouse emphasized political leaders to the same degree as Nordlinger, but their analysis moved the debate away from a leader's role in conflict management towards that of their role in conflict transformation, whereby the status quo was not to be maintained but rather that the conflict would be deeply transformed within the parties, within their relationships and in the situation that created the conflict. These authors saw the true transformation of a conflict through a five point generic framework which included a context transformation; a structural transformation; an actor transformation; an issue transformation; and personal and group transformation. In particular, they saw an actor transformation coming about through a change of character, a change of leadership, a change in the constituency of the leader or adoption of its goals, values or beliefs.[63]

While their overall argument was that leadership change was just one of a series of changes that need to occur in order for conflicts to successfully transform from violence to non-violence, the authors of the framework readily recognized that, in particular, it was actor transformation, and the role of the actors (that is, the political leadership) which impinged directly onto the other various transformations. They argued that 'changes of position' are closely related to changes of interest and changes of goals, and hence are closely related to actor transformation, and also to the context and structure of the conflict.[64] Take, for example, a structural transformation which denotes possible change in the relationship between the dominant and weaker parties. The nature of this relationship obviously is affected by the leadership in power at the time. Indeed, the relationship changes only as a direct result of the behaviours and interactions of the party leaders. The same concept can be applied to issue transformations. When parties change their positions or when issues lose their salience, the transformation can only come into effect with the support, if not the direct input and guidance of the party leadership. The notion of actor transformation is one which holds particular salience for this research, since it is possibly the only example of the cross-pollination of terminology from the leadership literature with the peace and conflict studies literature. Burns' discussion of 'transformational' leadership and Miall, Woodhouse and Ramsbotham's attention to 'actor transformation' both indicate the necessity of change.[65] A leadership change is touched upon by others still. For example, Stedman argued that a leadership change can add fluidity to what can often be a log-jammed situation.[66] Kriesberg made a similar point when he noted that changes in leadership could often lead to various de-escalation initiatives.[67]

The literature, which focuses on the more specific aspects of peace processes and peace agreements, postulates a number of necessary conditions for a successful outcome that move beyond the 'change of leadership' arguments. Most of these focus on the need for a strong leader and a motivation towards peace. For example, Rothstein saw strong leadership as an absolute necessity.[68] He articulated the view that if both sides had strong leadership then agreements were more likely to survive, even if they took a while to get off the ground because the masses and extremists' views tended to lag behind leaders' views on the need to compromise in many cases anyway.[69] He warned that if both sides had weak leadership, and were unsure of their power base, then making agreements became less likely.[70] He argued that both sides, in such an instance, would be happy to maintain the conflict status quo, because they would lose nothing. Both might agree to the concepts of peace processes in theory because it shows some kind of movement on their part, but would not agree with peace agreements, per se, because it could require significant concessions down the road.

Rothstein observed that in the situation of one relatively weak and one relatively strong leader, there may be a requirement for mediation by an outsider influence since the weak leader would not want to negotiate a peace agreement from weakness, and the strong leader may not feel the need to make any concessions in such negotiations.[71] The strength of Rothstein's argument is that it deals with the issue of political leadership in a direct fashion. It makes an argument about the potential capacity of leadership in a peace process based on perceived strengths and weaknesses. However, while Rothstein's analysis is useful, it does not deal conceptually with issues such as what actually constitutes 'strong' leadership and 'weak' leadership. In fact, it is often the case that the strength of a leader even with significant self-motivation towards making peace is useless unless that leader is legitimized by the other side. If one considers the case of Northern Ireland, this can be illustrated. Sinn Féin, in general, and Gerry Adams, in particular, at least electorally, were in a fairly strong position during the peace process. Moreover, if their comments were to be taken at face value, their priority during that period was to 'reach a democratic peace settlement acceptable to all the people of this island'.[72] However, despite the strength of their support and their manifestations towards peace, the party leadership lacked legitimacy from almost all political leaders within unionism. As Lieberfeld argued, legitimacy and/or validity is not enough, if a leader's validity only comes from within its own national constituency. For example, he noted that the pre-negotiating concerns in South Africa and Israel/Palestine were not so much about each side's validity of its own leaders but rather about the other side's reluctance to acknowledge that no viable alternative partners existed.[73] Lustick makes a similar point.[74] Both are entirely relevant to the context of Northern Ireland.

Overall, the peace and conflict literature, in relation to its assessment of political leadership, is something of a mixed bag. Unlike the majority of the political leadership literature, which looks at leadership in conflict, the peace and conflict literature often assumes an onus on leadership to find a way out of conflict towards peacebuilding. In common with political leadership literature however, the peace and conflict scholars struggle to succinctly define the concept of political leadership in the particular context of peace processes.

Beyond this, there are a number of points which can be extracted from this review of the peace and conflict studies literature which help to illuminate the argument that interpretations of political leadership in peace processes offered by the peace and conflict studies literature are mostly inappropriate in the context of Northern Ireland. First, the idea of actor transformations and leadership changes as an explanation for progress in a peace process holds little appeal to the context of Northern Ireland whereby many of the same key political actors were involved in both the conflict and subsequent attempts to resolve that conflict through the peace process, and did not seem to digress far beyond their original stated goals. Secondly, some of the literature falls into the trap of creating dichotomous distinctions between leaders; Rothstein's elucidation of strong versus weak leaders in a peace process is a case in point. The point to be distilled is the same as before in that creating such dichotomies runs the risk of ignoring the more nuanced realities of political leadership in Northern Ireland. The importance of these points to the developing argument of this book is that they highlight the inevitable need for an alternative interpretation of political leadership during the Northern Ireland peace process which steers clear of dichotomous distinctions and the normative view that peace is made by political leaders who have in some way transformed. That said, it is important to review the existing Northern Ireland focused literature to ascertain the significance afforded to the political leadership phenomenon and the appropriateness of the explanations offered.

The Northern Irish peace process literature

While the analysis of the Northern Ireland conflict have proved exhaustive, the same cannot be said of that research which looks specifically at the peace process, though this can be explained in terms of the fact that the peace process is a very recent affair and thus further analysis can be expected in the future.[75] Of the analysis which does exist in relation to the peace process, it can be broken down into three distinct approaches. First, there has been the interpretation of the process from the perspective of journalists and political commentators who witnessed the process unfold, at relatively close quarters.[76] Secondly, there has been the interpretation offered by some of the key political players and their advisors who were intricately bound up in the process as it took shape.[77] Finally, there is the perspective and interpretation offered by academics, some of which were more removed than others from the day to day events as they unfolded.[78]

Interpretations of the peace process from the perspective of journalists and political commentators have focused rather heavily on the actors involved in the process. These analyses have personified the peace process to such an extent that the process is perceived to be about the people as much as it is perceived to be about the issues at stake.[79] Their interpretation of political leadership in this particular process is one which is basic – political leaders have the ability to make or break the process. Similarly, the interpretations offered by those involved in the peace process tend to emphasize the personal rather than the structural aspects of the process. For example, Thomas Hennessey, a member of the UUP negotiating team during the multi-party talks process, wrote an account afterwards which amounted to a study of a history of elite negotiations and a narrative of events.[80] Through the more academic analysis of the peace process we can see a limited attention and focus given to the concept of political leadership during the peace process. Only in rare instances has the subject been directly addressed and when it has, it has not been addressed in isolation but rather in terms of the structural context.

An interesting interpretation of the peace process and the role of leadership therein has been presented by David Trimble, both in his capacity as a political leader and also as an academic.[81] In a special issue of the

Fordham International Law Journal, various individuals were asked to reflect on their perceptions of the peace process. In analysing why the Good Friday Agreement was reached when previous attempts had failed, Trimble's answers were remarkably 'personal' rather than structural. Whilst clarifying his position somewhat by noting that he had not tried to find all of the reasons for the Agreement's success, the majority of those factors that he did mention, related in some significant way to the power of political leadership. His first 'factor' was the Blair factor. The substance of the argument given for Blair's role in making 1998 a success when other attempts at agreements had failed was more in keeping with New Labour party policy around devolution than Blair's role as an individual, but nonetheless the choice of heading as 'Blair' can only be interpreted as his acknowledgement of the personal effect of Blair. 'Ahern' is listed as Trimble's second factor of note and he argued that:

> the personal authority of the Taoiseach, Bertie Ahern, was considerably greater [than the previous coalition], and it was always going to be easier for de Valera's constitution to be changed by a Fianna Fail Government than against the opposition of that party.[82]

As a separate factor he again referred to the 'personal factors' – in particular, the commitment to the talks process by Blair, Ahern and Senator George Mitchell.[83] Finally, John Hume was singled out for particular mention in terms of his work in trying to redefine Irish nationalism to be a problem of peoples and not one of land.[84] In terms of this article, a quick overview of Trimble's reasoning for why an agreement was reached in April 1998 reveals that Trimble placed more emphasis on personal factors and on leadership than anything else.[85]

Others close to the peace process offer equally revealing narratives and their perceptions of leadership within that narrative. For example, George Mitchell talked of the necessity of 'true leadership' to eventually finding agreement in the peace process. He said:

> Prime Minister Blair and Ahern came to Belfast and showed true leadership. There would not have been an agreement without their personal involvement. Blair and Ahern did not just supervise the negotiations. They conducted them.[86]

More telling, he held up one leader for particular mention when he said that 'there is not a more impressive politician in Northern Ireland than David Ervine. . . . I think he is important to the Assembly and will be a leading figure for years to come.'[87] However, much of this analysis should be treated with a certain degree of caution. As Keith Alderman noted:

> Political biographies and memoirs take a variety of forms. Some are merely chronicles of a life and catalogues of achievements. In other, perhaps most, cases there are wider purposes, which may include a desire to set the record straight in some way, to continue old debates or to settle old scores.[88]

While it is clear that the interpretations of the centrality of political leadership in the peace process in Northern Ireland might have been somewhat clouded by those so closely involved in the process, it is interesting that academics have come to some similar conclusions, albeit stated less explicitly. For example, McGarry and O'Leary equate the ceasefires of 1994 and the subsequent peace process to four primary factors:

> political and military developments within both the republican and loyalist movements; the 'second-track' diplomatic activities of the leader of the SDLP John Hume and third parties, including an Irish American peace delegation; clandestine discussions or negotiations between the British government and the IRA; and the (eventual) co-operative diplomacy of the British and Irish governments following the Anglo-Irish Agreement.[89]

Hume's leadership can be extracted from the range of factors as something of significance, though it is interesting that the authors refer to his 'diplomatic activities' as distinct from any other activities which could be considered to have a diminishing effect. On the other hand, he is the only named leader in a list of probable factors which contributed to the development of the peace process.

It has only been in very rare instances that individual leaders have been the subject of entire academic works. Those examples that do exist have proved to be rather limited in their analysis. For example, Mastors looked at Gerry Adams in the peace process using a personality-at-a-distance method which analyses leadership in terms of what a leader says by drawing on television interviews and speeches.[90] Mastors began working from the assumption that 'personalities influence policymaking'. In relation to Adams, her findings suggested that:

Adams is a nationalist who is extremely distrustful of others and has a high need for power and affiliation. Other traits such as complexity, task, and self-confidence are average and are mediated by these other dominant characteristics.[91]

This could be considered a rather simplistic approach at unravelling the complexities of how a leader's personality may or may not affect their behaviour in negotiating a peace process. Clearly, there are very many basic assumptions made by the author that it is impossible to infer solely from the findings of an analysis of text based interviews, especially when the majority of those texts are leader's speeches, which the leader might not have even written. Her profile of Adams is of:

a man who will strive to get the most he can for himself and the party he represents. He will stand his ground at all costs, believing that his position is the correct one, and it is not likely that he could be swayed into changing his stated position. . . . [he] has a high need for affiliation, making him concerned with how others view him. This, in turn, will lead him to seek normalized relations with the opposition.[92]

Note the fundamental contradictions in the profile offered by Mastors of a man who will stand his grounds at all costs with one equally concerned enough to normalize relations with the opposition. Despite these obvious contradictions, Mastors argues that the findings are supported by some journalistic accounts and by interviews conducted with political leaders who were involved in the negotiation process. In the final analysis, it could be argued that what has been presented as 'fact' by Mastors is little more than perception. Trait theory, alone, cannot offer a fully robust explanation of why a leader has behaved in a certain way since it ignores much of the context that a leader operates within, which influences a person's behaviour as much as their inherent character traits.

Heskin, Cairns and McCourt, in an analysis which was undertaken at the very early stages of the peace process, were much more cautious in their approach to the study of individual leaders in Northern Ireland, choosing to focus on only the perceptions of political leaders using a factor-analytical study. Their findings indicated that:

neither group [Protestant nor Catholic] rated their local leader particularly high in any one dimension. In other words, there was no empirical evidence for the contention that John Hume and Ian Paisley were leaders who exert a powerful emotive, magnetic force on the hearts and minds of many in both communities.[93]

Indeed, a similar sentiment was echoed in Crozier's work on 'Good Leaders and "Decent" Men: an Ulster contradiction', when Crozier noted that:

> Observers of the political scene in Northern Ireland often wonder why, in a situation where there are two clearly opposed groups, no leaders of significant stature have emerged to guide their followers towards a solution.[94]

Crozier argued that any explanation of why Northern Ireland failed to produce strong leaders [at least by 1990 and by her understanding of what a 'strong leader' actually was] needed to consider a combination of historical, political and cultural imperatives. Crozier effectively lays the burden of responsibility for inhibiting the development of potential leaders, at local level, among followers 'by discouraging the individualism which might produce politicians with courage for bold initiatives, and constraining most "decent" men from being the good leaders the country so patently lacks'.[95]

In only one known instance in academia has the more recent Northern Ireland peace process been examined in a directly relational way to the concept of leadership – in O'Doherty's work on leadership and developing democracy where there is none. O'Doherty's interpretation of leadership in Northern Ireland is inclusive but vague; disappointingly, it does not appear to focus on the local political elites. He 'uses the notion of a "third party mediator" as a metaphor for anyone who would like to exert leadership to end ethnic conflict and advance democracy'.[96] Furthermore, he likens the complex process of achieving peace in Northern Ireland to 'an adaptive leadership challenge' and defines this as 'a challenge that requires someone to instigate a process for shifting the values in the cultures so that peace has a higher value than what it is that parties protect with their enmity'.[97] O'Doherty argues that in the case of Northern Ireland there has been a failure of leadership, on the part of third party mediators, evidenced in their abandonment of the various political parties in the immediate aftermath of the Good Friday Agreement. He sees this as irresponsible. Yet at no point does he discuss the actions or behaviour of the local political leaders as irresponsible. Instead, he argues that:

The peace process did not equip participants at the peace negotiation stage with the leadership capacities required to mobilize their
communities to do this work of forging this new relationship. Political and community leaders were not yet able to withstand the
enormous pressures on them to revert to the status quo of polariz-
ation and enmity... understood as adaptive work, the challenge of
third-party mediation is not simply to arrive at a peace agreement,
but to help the parties develop the leadership that can get them to
deal with the real problems in a democratic process.[98]

While O'Doherty clearly has a point here, the failure to highlight the
actions and behaviour of the local political leaders is a grave omission.
He treats local political leaders as passive entities in the process, thus
automatically negating any possible proactive role, capacity and effect
that they might have on the process. In other words, by equating leadership with the work of third party mediators, O'Doherty divorces equally
important other actors from the analysis. Similarly, by equating leadership with 'adaptive work', he implies that if the work is not positive in
nature then it is not really leadership.

Overall, there are a number of points which are important as part
of the developing argument of this book. First, with the exception
of the examples in the academic literature noted above, nowhere
has the subject of political leadership been explicitly addressed.
Rather, the implicit references made have seemed to suffice thus far.
Given the contention presented in this chapter that interpretations of
political leadership in peace processes offered by both the political leadership literature and the peace and conflict studies literature are mostly
inappropriate in the context of Northern Ireland, it is important to
emphasize that the interpretations of the role, capacity and potential
effect of political leadership in the Northern Ireland based literature
were given most attention by journalistic enterprise rather than scholarly enquiry and thus the appropriateness of such interpretations is
diminished.

Secondly, the mention of the role of certain individual political
leaders, as articulated by Trimble, Mitchell, McGarry and O'Leary, and
Mastors, runs the risk of creating false dichotomies between those
leaders perceived to have been 'good' by positively engaging with the
process and those perceived to be 'bad' by either disengaging from the
process entirely or actively seeking to undermine it. In its favour though,
the analysis presented here rarely referred overtly to the dichotomous
distinctions between good and bad leaders.

Noting the problems and paradoxes

Garnering an understanding of the role, capacity and effect of political leadership in the Northern Ireland peace process from the existing literature is difficult. The necessary task of weaving a coherent thread through quite disparate literatures reveals a subject area beset with problems and paradoxes. Some of these problems have already been illustrated, however they are drawn together here in a more succinct fashion. Essentially, there are three problems and/or issues to consider.

The first issue comes from a rather obvious paradox. Some leadership scholars sought to understand how the behaviours of certain leaders might have affected their 'effectiveness' or their ability to lead. Early peace and conflict studies scholars sought to explain why certain 'states' had a greater propensity towards war than others. Although one group tended to work at the macro-level (the state) and one group worked at the micro (the person/leader) they both sought to uncover key characteristics which could explain their subject area's propensity towards violence, and therefore by extension, the likelihood of its propensity towards peacebuilding. Despite this, neither group of scholars sought to cross-pollinate from the other. This has resulted in the development of distinct and separate fields of study which hold much merit individually but could have provided an added richness to the study of both had they been pulled together. One of the problems with looking at political leadership in Northern Ireland is the need to cross-pollinate between the two literatures without being able to rely upon any prior inroads in this regard.

The second issue relates to the theoretical underpinnings of some of the leadership literature and the peace and conflict literature. Both fields are essentially value driven and have a tendency to focus on how leadership ought to be, rather than on how leadership actually is. There are significant difficulties applying such values to leadership behaviours in conflict and peace processes, when the values are often in dispute among the warring factions. For example, if, as Bennis and Nanus suggest, leadership is about 'doing the right thing', the obvious question is, doing the right thing by whom?[99] Who determines what is the right thing to do in a peace process, if the options are as simple as surrendering your weapons or protecting your community? Who decides what is 'right'? Whose values take priority? And more importantly, why? In the case of Northern Ireland, values played a key role in the peace process. In fact, in order to gain admission to the multi-party talks process itself, the various political parties had to sign up to a doctrine of non-violence, known as the Mitchell principles, considered to be the British and Irish governments' norm, and in the case of Sinn Féin were a marked departure from their earlier approval of combining the ballot box and the armalite during the conflict. Again, one of the problems with looking at political leadership in Northern Ireland is the need to be cognizant of the focus on 'how leaders ought to be', particularly in terms of reviewing the literature and in the analysis of interviews with political leaders, since this often conditions what a person might say or write.

Thirdly, there is the problem of false dichotomies. The dichotomies of hero and villain; foxes and lions; transformational and transactional leaders; power wielders and power seekers are too simplistic in general and more so in the extreme of divided societies. Clearly, there is a discourse of analysis around political leadership that has not been sufficiently explained. The biggest concern of all is that the literature pays only lip service to the issue of violent conflict, and at best promotes a two-dimensional construct. Burns' work on leaders versus power wielders and Rejai and Philips' work on loyalist versus revolutionaries are cases in point. Blondel says that this notion of dichotomous distinctions is something which the field of social science has suffered from for a long time and suggests that:

> What has to be done therefore is to turn away from the very idea of a dichotomy and, by recognising that the reality is vastly more complex, slowly to elaborate models, and develop methodological techniques that will make it possible to grasp more realistically the contours of leadership.[100]

Presenting the vastly complex nature of political leadership in the context of the Northern Ireland peace process is the purpose of this book. In doing so, however, it will remain cognizant of the difficulties of marrying together two disparate academic fields of study, of the difficulties in marrying together the normative view of leadership 'to do the right thing' with the more complex and often nuanced realities in a conflict society engaged in a peace process, and of the difficulties in moving beyond the dichotomous distinctions so apparent in the leadership literature and in the historical context of Northern Ireland itself.

3
Explaining Political Leadership in Northern Ireland

Introduction

The phenomenon of political leadership in Northern Ireland during the peace process presents something of a problem in terms of academic research. It would be untrue to suggest that political leaders have been ignored, and have been reduced to mere footnotes in history. The plethora of authorized and unauthorized biographies and autobiographies serve as illustration of the point. However, it would be equally untrue to suggest that such material seeks or serves to define or explain the nature of that leadership during the peace process. Taking an overtly personalized approach to understanding these political leaders has often been the norm. Problematically, the personalized approach tends to present these political leaders as idiosyncratic, rife with anecdotal tales of personal transitions as part of the peace process, and with 'road to Damascus' conversions along the way. The phraseology is loose and often devoid of any real meaning. Indeed, many of the leaders are simply described as being 'charismatic', as a catch-all phrase, for their various qualities and attributes, and the reality, that charisma in one community has often meant loathing in another is ignored. As a result, we seem no closer to really understanding the nature of political leadership during the peace process. Therefore, this chapter introduces a number of different ways to define, explain and understand political leadership during the peace process. It does so by examining some of the various interpretations of leadership given by the political leaders themselves in interview with the author, and through secondary analysis of other interviews and autobiographical materials. Some of the limitations of existing definitions and descriptions are then examined. This is followed by the presentation of an argument on why it is necessary to develop an alternative understanding of political leadership during the Northern Ireland peace process and then how it might be possible to develop such a new understanding of political leadership.

Existing classifications of political leadership

There are already a number of existing classifications of political leadership, some more widely used than others. In exploring the different types of political leaders, some focus on the process of leadership, others on the outcome of that process, some on the style of leadership, and others on the different sources of power which they have at their disposal. Early political leadership classifications include Plato's timocratic leadership (ruling by pride and honour); plutocratic leadership (ruling by wealth); democratic leadership (ruling by popular consent); and tyrannical leadership (ruling by coercion).[1] Kellerman grouped the political leadership types into democratic, totalitarian, revolutionary, legal, traditional and charismatic, entrepreneurial, and non-constituted.[2] Some of the more recent definitions of leadership are less 'political' in terminology. For example, Hermann's crusaders, salesmen, agents and firefighters are more metaphoric than anything else, but her classification conveys the message that crusaders have a vision and seek to make that vision a reality; salesmen use persuasion to get their constituents to 'buy' an idea; agents act only as delegates for those whom they represent; and firefighters consistently respond to the emergencies which might affect their constituents.[3] Certainly, while there is much appeal in the metaphoric classifications, this could be considered as an illustrative example of loose phraseology.

However, within the field of leadership studies, there are a selection of leadership theories dating from the 1970s that might be of use in helping to explain political leadership in Northern Ireland. Referred to as the 'new leadership theories', they include theories of transformational (and therefore by association, transactional) and charismatic leadership.[4] Previously, such theories have been used to explain the leadership of successful social reforms and leadership of transitions from colonial rule and/or political tyranny to independence.[5] In other words, not only do these leadership theories attempt to present leadership behaviours that can account for and explain outstanding leadership, but the illustrative examples which they often use are not entirely dissimilar from the scenarios of deeply divided societies, and thus not entirely dissimilar from the case study of Northern Ireland.

The most well known and well researched of these is the theory of transformational leadership.[6] As a classically normative approach to leadership, transformational leadership is one which looks beyond the existing system, and offers ideas, hopes and aspirations to followers. Burns highlighted four types of transformational leaders – intellectual leaders, leaders of reform, revolutionary leaders, and heroes or ideologues.[7] The essence of transformational leadership is for the leader to transform people into better people. Thus, there is a highly moralistic premise to such leadership in so far as this type of leadership 'transforms people from the selves that they are into the selves that they should be. As a result of the transformation, people are poised to be true to their better selves'.[8] Because of the moral basis to transformational leadership, Burns refused to acknowledge some of the better known figures in history as leaders. For example, in Burn's analysis, Mussolini, Hitler and Stalin were regarded not as leaders but rather as 'power wielders'.[9] Burns was not alone in his refusal to afford a label of 'legitimacy' to those he deemed unworthy. As Kellerman pointed out in relation to the leadership literature:

> The powers that be – theoreticians and practitioners, researchers and educators, consultants and trainers – have entered into a tacit alliance: Omit from the collective conversation the notion of evil. The name Adolf Hitler does not cross our lips and so we pretend his ghost has been exorcised. In general, our work – indeed the way we use the English language – operates on the premise that the man who, arguably, had a greater impact on 20th century history than any other was in no way whatsoever, in no conceivable sense of the term, a leader. Needless to say this deep distortion has had a ripple effect. For example, the voluminous literature on leadership and management in the private sector implies that, by definition, leaders are meritorious and good rather than deficient and bad.[10]

This normative redefinition of the word 'leadership' has not gone uncontested in other fields, if not in the field of leadership. Kellerman argues that it is only those who work in the field of 'leadership studies' who make the distinction between leaders who do good and those who do not. Outside of the field, for example in political science, and equally importantly, among the general public no such distinctions are made. For example, Slobodan Milosevic was routinely referred to as the leader of the Serbs, and until recently Saddam Hussein was regarded the leader of the Iraqis. In Northern Ireland, Gerry Adams is regarded as the leader of republicanism. This raises the question – would the leadership studies scholars prefer not to consider as leaders those political figures in Northern Ireland with a democratically elected mandate who have links to paramilitaries, or are former paramilitaries themselves? It seems so. Using this sort of moral argument, it appears that there is no merit in examining political leadership in Northern Ireland, since a significant proportion of those leaders might actually be 'non-leaders' and can therefore be discounted from any analysis. However, an equally valid response is that those in leadership studies who refuse to acknowledge all genres of leadership have taken a departure that is 'ill-founded and ill conceived'.[11] To omit such leaders is to limit our understanding of who we are and of what we do.

Moreover, there has been a recent acknowledgement that the 'goodness' inherent in transformational leadership is not something which can be taken for granted, nor taken at face value.[12] Bass's analysis subdivides transformationalism into what he sees as two distinct types – 'true transformational' and 'pseudo transformational' leadership.[13] For Bass, truly transformational leaders either align public interest with their own interests or else sacrifice their own interests. They articulate followers' real unmet needs and can envisage an attainable future. Their leadership style is then to practice what they preach. They are conscious of only sounding alarm bells when real threats arise, thus their communication can be trusted. They uplift the moral values of their followers and by default are more mature ethically.[14] In contrast, pseudotransformational leadership simulates public interest but their own self-interest takes precedence. They create artificial demands in their followers and arouse the fantasies of followers. Their leadership styles are a case of 'do as I say: not as I do'. They have a tendency to manufacture crises when there are none and stretch the truth. They work on the premise that the end justifies the means and thus, are less mature ethically.[15]

As the converse to transformationalism, transactional leadership is based on a relationship between leader and follower whereby agreements and bargains are made with mutually beneficial results, and operates within the system as it stands. Transactional leadership is based on a system of trade-offs within the political system – for example jobs for votes, subsidies for campaign contributions, and patronage for loyalty. The most obvious transactional leaders are opinion leaders, bargainers or bureaucrats, party leaders, legislative leaders and executive leaders.[16] In other words, political leaders already embedded into the political system. However, much like transformational leadership, the transactional approach has been questioned in terms of its face value and has resulted in the concept's subdivision into definitions of truly transactional and pseudo-transactional behaviours. It is argued that truly transactional leaders will share rewards equitably between the group. They will give praise when it is deserved, keep any promises made, treat followers' failures as learning experiences and take corrective actions fitting followers' needs. The pseudo-transactional leaders will tend to hog the group benefits for themselves, use flattery as a leadership tool, make promises that they know they will be unable to keep, overreact to followers' failures and any corrective actions taken will seem arbitrary.[17] The overall thesis is that if the transformational or transactional leadership is 'pseudo' or inauthentic in nature then it is not leadership at all. This is entirely in keeping with Kellerman's earlier point which is critical of the field's compulsion to equate leadership with goodness. This is something of a questionable practice. Moreover, equating leadership with goodness sits uneasily with the realities of divided societies or societies engaged in peace processes where the behaviour of leaders is sometimes interpreted as less than 'good'.

Whilst transformationalism and transactionalism offer the most obvious dichotomist classification of political leadership, there have been other attempts to define and explain leadership behaviours. Many of these have synonymy or overlap with transformationalism/transactionalism. Consider, for example, the use of 'innovative leadership' as an explanation for leadership leading towards social reform. Sheffer argues that innovation in leadership is: 'as a result of a fresh scrutinizing of the real world; dissatisfaction with the reality that is observed; clear notions about desired changes in existing systems, goals and strategies for change; and dedication to implementing these changes'.[18] It differs from 'intellectual leadership' in so far as the latter might also have similar innovative ideas, but does not translate these ideas into actions. At the heart of innovative leadership are the soft qualities of inspiration, vision and creativity coupled with the ability to accurately grasp the nature, scope and complexity of political problems. Additional qualities include the capacity to overcome the different types of constraints that might be produced by domestic and/or external factors.[19] Innovative leadership appears to have elements of transformationalism in the leader's vision and innovative ideas, and transactionalism in terms of how the leadership might hope to overcome possible constraints, through the use of trade-offs.

While innovative leadership has its links with both transformational and transactional leadership, charismatic leadership often is described in a way that has synonymy with the concept of transformational leadership. However, charismatic leadership is not a concept upon which all are agreed. Introduced by Max Weber, he argued that charisma was a personal characteristic which amounted to superhuman or exceptional powers.[20] The theory of charismatic leadership was then developed further by House in 1976.[21] Key charismatic characteristics which were identified included being dominant, having a strong desire to influence others, being self-confident and having a strong sense of one's own moral values.[22] In using such definitions, the moral values of charismatic leadership sits easily with the moral values of transformational leadership. However, as with transformational leadership, the concept is contested. Lindblom saw charisma as a quality which can lead to socially undesirable and destructive leadership.[23] Using Lindblom's analysis, the link with transformationalism is severed. Clearly though, the concept of charisma can be divided into two specific types – that which is socially acceptable and that which is not. The first is a personalized charismatic leadership, which can be self aggrandizing, exploitative and authoritarian; the second, a more socialized form, which is altruistic, collectively oriented and egalitarian in nature. Again, the comparability with transformationalism is obvious – the latter overlaps with the concept that has been defined as 'truly transformational' and the former has synonymy with 'pseudo-transformational'.

There exists one model of leadership which is more difficult to locate on the transformational/transactional spectrum. This is sometimes referred to as the 'warrior model' of leadership.[24] Yet, while the classic 'warrior model' of leadership is much less well rehearsed – at least in a contemporary context – it is particularly useful for political leadership analysis in conflict prone societies. Despite being based on concepts of military leadership, many of the central principles are used by those in non-military positions of leadership, and can be applied to the leadership styles sometimes demonstrated in divided societies. The warrior model of leadership describes those operating both inside and outside of the political infrastructure. The principles of the warrior model are based on conflict and overcoming the opposition, information control, results being more important than the methods used to achieve them, knowing the people with whom the leader seeks to lead or to defeat, choosing battles carefully, and using intermediaries as buffers.[25] Obviously, the 'warrior leader' raises uncomfortable questions for the leadership studies field while it continues to perpetuate the argument that leadership equates only to goodness. For conflict resolution specialists however, it offers a more realistic interpretation of leadership behaviours in a divided society.

Collectively, the various definitions or labels of leadership reveal some possible ways with which to explain and define political leadership in Northern Ireland during the peace process. It has been important to highlight these interpretations for a number of reasons. Firstly, the majority of the classifications of political leadership presented here take the normative viewpoint that leadership, and thus by extension political leadership, is a positive phenomenon affecting change for the greater good. Those leaders more interested in affecting change for their own personal benefits are not regarded as 'true' leaders but rather denoted as 'pseudo' types. While this is a highly contestable viewpoint, it does raise questions about the applicability of the transformational model of leadership to the political context of Northern Ireland during the peace process. As an extension of the argument from the previous chapter which contends that the political leadership literature and the peace and conflict studies literature, to date, are often inappropriate in the context of Northern Ireland, it has been important to extrapolate any examples from the more general leadership studies literature which might have aided the development of a new understanding of political leadership during the Northern Ireland peace process.

The second reason for introducing the concepts of charismatic, innovative, and warrior leadership was in order to raise an awareness of some of the understandings of political leadership that currently exist and that might have some degree of resonance with the context of the Northern Ireland peace process. For example, as already noted, many of the political leaders in Northern Ireland have often been described as charismatic in nature.[26] Their innovation was, arguably, apparent in their ability to make an agreement which had sufficient space built into it to allow the different political leaders to argue its merits in their own way. So while Trimble could argue that the Agreement strengthened the Union, Adams could equally point to the provisions which weakened it. The 'warrior model' of leadership is an important concept in the context of Northern Ireland because it offers a more realist account of the peace process.

While such conceptual ideas are important, they are, however, somewhat disparate ideas. This leads to the third reason for introducing them into this chapter. The incompatibility of some of the conceptual ideas presented here supports the developing argument of this book that political leadership during the Northern Ireland peace process was often necessarily contradictory in both style and substance, and that such contradictions and inconsistencies form the basis of the alternative interpretation that this work ultimately seeks to present. As part of the development of this argument, it is important to understand how political leaders actually explain and define themselves and to illuminate any inconsistencies or contradictions therein.

What the leaders thought of themselves

Teasing out the terminology from political leaders in Northern Ireland, when attempting to ascertain how they themselves defined and classified their leadership during the peace process, has proved difficult. Most political leaders were either unable to or reluctant to classify their leadership, or the leadership of others in terms of particular styles and brands. Nor did they use the existing classifications of leadership to explain where they sat in the larger picture. This is unsurprising, especially given that the leadership scholarship has not been rehearsed as well as the conflict resolution scholarship among Northern Ireland's political elite. Nonetheless, upon further exploration most were able to identify certain aspects of their leadership behaviours which they felt defined them as political leaders. While this fell short of a classification of their leadership during the peace process, it did offer some insights.

Collective and individual leadership

Unlike the vast majority of the leadership literature which treats the concept of leadership in individual terms, the clearest message which came from more than one political grouping or community was in relation to the benefit of 'collective leadership'. The inference from their deliberations suggested that collective leaders tended to share the burden of responsibility, the decision-making process and the benefits accrued from any decisions made among a cohort of individuals within the top echelons of the party political structures. They were usually reluctant to present any leadership failings or successes in individual terms, preferring to see their style as more egalitarian. This can be illustrated as a leadership circle rather than a hierarchy. Given its progressive nature, many of the political leaders wanted to emphasize their collective leadership style and present it as something distinctive and separate from the other political leaders during the peace process. All appeared unaware that their style was not so unique. For example, a leading Sinn Féin politician argued that:

> There is an obvious difference between Sinn Féin and the other parties, first of all in negotiation and in everything else. We deal in 'collective leadership'. It's a republican way of doing things... because it makes sense that two heads are better than one

and so are ten. It is a tradition, if you like, and I actually think that it's a revolutionary way of approaching things.[27]

A leader from within the Northern Ireland Women's Coalition [hereafter referred to as the Women's Coalition] made a similar claim:

> Our style of leadership is very different. We work in a kind of team effort, and there is nothing that I wouldn't do, although I am constantly called on to speak publicly, that I wouldn't check out my messages and work all the time with a group of people, on a cross community basis, to make sure that what I am saying has some consensus attached to it.[28]

One of the front men for the Progressive Unionist Party (PUP) alluded to the same team effort as part of their peace process strategy arguing:

> I suppose in many ways what we did was that we tried to develop a partnership, rather than anything else.[29]

Only one leader, while acknowledging that collective leadership within the party existed, saw reason to question its contribution to the peace process. He said:

> I think that from a leadership point of view you have the experiences that we have in our party when we try as far as possible to encourage opinion, argument, debate, discussion, throughout the party, hoping that one can find a consensus that allows as many of us as possible to move forward . . . it is extremely difficult to do. I often wish at times that we had the capacity for executive leadership because democracy gets in the way.[30]

Despite this, the same leader made the case that the concept of collective leadership was needed beyond the confines of the individual political parties, and that there needed to be a collective leadership approach by all of the political leaders from the various parties during the peace process, which did not seem to happen. He argued:

> I believe in the epitome of inclusivity and collectivity if it is functioned properly, and therefore it's like the poles of a wigwam, take one leader away and they all fall, if one leader's in trouble we're all in trouble. I'm watching Adams, and then when Trimble is in trouble

Adams looks happy enough and when Adams is in trouble Trimble looks happy enough which flies in the face of the appreciation that only together will they actually get to where they want to go.[31]

While the Sinn Féin interviewee claimed that the rationale for collective leadership was that two heads were better than one in terms of strategic thinking and decision making, it is equally true that if the responsibility for decision making is spread beyond the individual party leader then the culpability for any 'wrong' decisions taken during the process is also spread beyond the individual party leader. More than anything, it seems that collective leadership is protective in nature, since it is difficult to pinpoint and isolate any particular individual for criticism. During the peace process, it was critically important that the various political parties displayed a united front. Unity was a sign of strength in negotiations. Collective leadership tended to emphasize such unity.[32]

Political prisoner and political leader

A second aspect of leadership could be described as 'political prisoner oriented leadership'. Some of the political leaders had spent time in prison during the course of the conflict in Northern Ireland. This was true both within the loyalist parties and within Sinn Féin. Hence, the role of political imprisonment in developing and enhancing political leadership was highlighted for particular mention by interviewees.[33] The reflection on this aspect of leadership was not necessarily restricted to those with personal experience of being imprisoned. Indeed, David Trimble's speech at the Vanguard Convention in 1976 mentioned Solzhenitsyn's *The Gulag Archipelago* and the proverb contained therein that 'we should look for our brave men in prisons and for the fools amongst politicians'.[34] More recently, a Women's Coalition leader, in considering some of the qualities that 'made' a leader in Northern Ireland, concluded:

> You know what makes a leader . . . prison. For some of the leaders here came the ability to take time out and reflect, and that's quite incredible to see that in loyalism. When that voice came to the table, in terms of having read widely and having studied the situation, having engaged with other people, they came to the table with a different analysis.[35]

A PUP leader concurred: 'I think for reflection, prison is the place to go. I don't advocate prison, but sure as hell if you want to reflect, it is the place to go'.[36] David Ervine, PUP party leader said: 'Prison was not where I wanted to be, but in hindsight I would not have missed it for the world', such was the effect of it on his political thinking.[37] Again, an interviewee from the PUP leadership pointed to the specific lessons that he felt prison has taught him and which were particularly useful in the context of the peace process:

> I think the things that I learned in prison in terms of leadership was that one, if you were a leader that it wasn't always sensible to make the popular decisions and two, if you have made unpopular decisions, if people really believed in you then they should understand why you did it, and three, if you want to be loved by people then you shouldn't be a leader, you know, because you will always make enemies and you have to actually balance that out.[38]

Moreover, for those leaders who had been imprisoned, it afforded them the opportunity to meet with their political adversaries in a different context. Arguably, this led to the formation of relationships between the two sides. Although borne of necessity, the cultivation of these relationships may have influenced the development of the relationships outside of prison, in the political arena. A PUP leader mentioned the work undertaken by himself together with a republican leader in prison and the political leadership skills which he derived from that:

> In 1988 myself and the leader of the Provos at that time, a guy called Pat Thompson from Crossmaglen, negotiated the release of 96 prisoners. They were all doing life sentences – every one of them – and they were all released within three years and there wasn't a word in the media about it and everyone of them was released. In the prison I was negotiating with the NIO (Northern Ireland Office) and Ministers, and we were always doing that. So prison does give you a good break in terms of if you are at the cutting edge of the prison then you can learn quite a lot.[39]

The most fundamental lesson to emanate from experiences inside prison was in terms of the prison compound leaders' interdependency on one another. Eventually, a similar concept of interdependency became central to the whole consociational arrangement within the Agreement in 1998. Again, one of the PUP leaders commented:

> I ran the UVF compound in the prison and we had a council where the Provos sat on it, and we met every 10 days and discussed what was

going on in the prison. We didn't always agree on what we were going to do but if I had been totally disagreeing with the prison authorities and said: 'Look I think that we should be protesting about this', then the Provos might have said: 'Well – look – hold on, we agree with your right to protest but we're not going to do it. We'll just withdraw, walk away and not interfere' but there was an interdependency where we knew that we would never go against the other. At worst, we would have said, 'OK – you'se just work away, we don't want involved in this'.[40]

From an analytical perspective, there is clear overlap between the definitions of collective leaders and formerly incarcerated leaders, specifically in terms of interdependency. McEvoy highlights this point in his discussion of paramilitary imprisonment in Northern Ireland. He notes:

The prison experience for non-conforming paramilitary prisoners in Northern Ireland has been largely a collective one. Paramilitary prisoner groupings have had their hierarchies, functional responsibilities, norms and values, support structures, and policing mechanisms . . . even prisoners who had left the collective wings of the Maze for integrated wings at Maghaberry acknowledged that the collective nature of the prison experience was a key strength.[41]

Reluctant leadership

The third classification of political leaders during the peace process, based on what some of the leaders said, can best be described as 'reluctant leadership'.[42] Frequently, the opinion was expressed that the political leaders did not seek out their office, nor particularly want their positions of office. This 'reluctance' spanned across many of the political parties:

I can honestly say it was never consciously my ambition to become leader because I'm regarded very much as a grass roots politician and unfortunately a lot of the work that I would normally have done has not been done as well as I would have liked because of all the other pressures, but as I say it was never a life long ambition to become leader.[43]

I didn't personally think of myself as automatically ambitious and wanting that because all the time at the back of my mind was how is this going to impact on my life, on my children, in particular, who were so young at the time. And so, it was the structural stuff that was kind of making me think that this was going to be difficult. But then I began to say if I don't do it, and I'm constantly encouraging others, then I can't speak with that voice if I'm not going to do it myself...[44]

I didn't really intend to be involved in it you know, not in public politics, maybe, I don't know, but certainly it was never my desire to be a public politician, but now that I am, I am.[45]

I was not anxious to put myself forward. It would have been a heavy burden – not just on myself but on my family. But I found as the week went on [before the election of the party leader] that there was an expectation by many people that I should put myself forward.[46]

Even some of those leading figures, who were not actually party leaders of their respective political parties but were, nonetheless, regarded as pivotal political figures during the peace, held the same sentiments.

I have no ambitions to be leader of the party, I have enough problems trying to run my own constituency without trying to run the party, so therefore it's not something that I aspire to.[47]

In a way, the point to be distilled is that some leaders were unhappy with the possibility that their leadership could be perceived as merely career-based. Articulating reluctance, in respect of a leadership position, simply reinforced the point that some leaders did not want to be seen to be engaged in the political process for personal gain or self-interest. As a Sinn Féin interviewee said, in an attempt to put clear water between their style of leadership and others:

They [others] are career politicians, you know, and I'm not saying it as if it is a dirty word or anything, but that's the way they operate, and I don't think that we've reached that stage. I think that our people are still in struggle mode, and rightly so. We are ideologically based... I'm not saying that there isn't ambition within Sinn Féin. Obviously it's an honour to do a Minister's job or whatever, ... [but] there is a difference. I think that it has to do with being in the struggle, and we have not settled down and I wouldn't really call myself a career politician. If there was another position for me in Sinn Féin which was not elected it wouldn't worry me. Maybe in the end, ... I mean we don't take a full wage, and maybe in the end, in a few years if you had a mortgage, . . . and I assume that that's what all these characters do. I didn't run out and get a mortgage when I got my wages.[48]

In terms of analysis, there are clear links between reluctant leadership and collective leadership. Reluctant leadership is also protective in nature. Apportioning blame for any problems during the peace process becomes difficult, when the leader claims that he/she is only in office because no one else wanted to be or because party colleagues and peers felt that they were the best person for the job. If the leader has not actively sought out the office, then their culpability for mistakes while in office is significantly diminished. This, however, is a very cynical interpretation of reluctant leadership. The case could be made that reluctant leadership was inextricably linked to a degree of humility among some of the key players. As one party leader noted of the negotiation process:

Maybe it speaks volumes for me that I actually like people who have a level of humility about them. You know that's a really good point and I hadn't thought about that before, [have the humility to] acknowledge the other person's existence and when I hear people saying that around a table I realise that they are going to be good leaders.[49]

In further conceptualizing the idea of reluctant political leadership in Northern Ireland, it is important to stress that politics was largely discredited as a career option in Northern Ireland, yet communities were under pressure to have political responses to external circumstances. Moreover, Sinn Féin and the PUP ideologies had consistently claimed that their respective communities had been sold out by the middle classes, church leaders and the more traditional political leaders. Therefore, reluctantly, they needed to have their own leaders.

Soft-skilled leadership

The final leadership behaviours which were highlighted could be termed as 'soft-skilled leadership'. Humility, social skills, and flexibility were just some of a number of soft skills which contributed to 'soft-skilled leadership' as indicative of the style and candour of some of the political players during the peace process. These are the skills not normally associated with political leadership. For example, one party leader said:

I think that humour is extremely important in this as well, I think that the sign of a good leader is to be able to laugh at himself, and to admit that they are wrong, which I think is quite a feminist thing to say, because a male may not say that. They would see mistakes as being a weakness. I actually think acknowledging your vulnerability and acknowledging your mistakes is a sign of strength, and the leaders that I endear myself to are the leaders who can do that.[50]

I also think that social skills are very important. That was one of the things I didn't mention. The ability to be able to say something to someone without being so dismissive, and some of the leaders are very egotistical, very 'power unto myself'.[51]

Acknowledging weakness is a well made point. Moreover, it is particularly important in the context of the peace and conflict studies literature, which has a tendency to focus on strong leadership. Just as 'strong leadership' is rarely defined in the literature, it is a concept used by leaders to describe their style of leadership during the peace process without definitional precision. One party leader said:

I mean traditionally politics here, for the last generation, somebody has been deemed to be a good politician just if they are seen to be a strong spokesperson for a particular party interest. You know if they can criticise this decision or that one, or just be as negative about anything they want just as long as they can hold their corner, then that's somebody that is then deemed to be good.[52]

Another argued:

As a strong leader you have to constantly explain to your constituency what you are doing, why you're doing it, and invite discussion, debate, argument, dissension, whatever it is, you have got to invite it, because you are seen then as arrogant, aloof, dismissive if you do not. Now, I think that you can be a strong leader provided that the avenues and opportunities exist for people to interact in dialogue and debate with you.[53]

A source of strength can come from flexibility, or from the leadership's 'elasticity' as one party leader noted of his party's style of leadership. The Sinn Féin interviewee said:

It can be described like an elastic band, where leadership has to stretch forward, and has to show leadership. We were, let me be clear, a substantial dynamic in all of this. And I think that we have stretched out constituents. But again, using the analogy, the problem is that the elastic can snap, and that can be very dangerous.[54]

In sum, it is clear that the self analysis revealed some important points. First, no one leader wanted to be held individually responsible for the successes and failings within the peace process, hence the drive towards emphasizing collective leadership. Secondly, very few leaders wanted to admit to having the drive and ambition to hold a position of leadership within their various parties in order to take the party in the direction which they wanted to go. Finally, pointing to imprisonment as a leadership building experience legitimized those political players who had been imprisoned and served to negate the assumption that leadership and goodness are inextricably linked. In totality, the self analysis by political leaders was, unsurprisingly, rather difficult and more than anything else indicated something of a lack of self-awareness on this issue among the political elite. Overall, it presented a rather subdued picture. What is most important about the articulation of collective leadership, political prisoner cum political leadership, and reluctant leadership is that they illuminate some of the contradictions apparent in terms of how political leaders in Northern Ireland behaved during the peace process.

What others thought of the leadership

While the political leaders might have struggled to articulate and define their brand of leadership during the peace process, political analysts have not done so. On the contrary, many of the analyses of the peace process are replete with comments about the personalities involved and examples of their leadership style. Many of the comments were quite benign. For example, at different points during the process, Adams was applauded as a statesman, or as a man of warmth and vision;[55] Hume was given the accolade of 'Saint John';[56] Trimble was regarded as a knowledge-based leader;[57] Paisley, Ervine, and McMichael were all described as charismatic.[58] Other comments were more pejorative. Adams was described as a terrorist;[59] Hume was still called 'Saint John' but the tone had become more wry; Trimble was denounced as 'a hardline sectarian bigot';[60] Paisley was still charismatic but the inference was towards the darker side of charisma; and Ervine was even described as practically 'nationalist' because of his political style.[61]

Some of the analysis offered was even more derogatory in tone. As an example, more than one leader has been compared either to Nazism or to Hitler himself: '[Sir John] Wheeler describes Adams as being akin to a Nazi, in charge of the bullet and the ballot box strategy, willing to use violence, to overrule the democratic will of others'.[62] Similar comparisons were made to Paisley [albeit in the period before the peace process in 1985] when it was said: '... Paisley's techniques are reminiscent of Adolf Hitler's method of beginning his speeches on a low key, then gradually increasing in force and loudness to a climatic attack on his enemy'.[63] Adding to this, Owen Dudley Edwards said: 'His distinctive talent, which he shares with Hitler, lies in capturing the mental framework of his audience, and specifically in arousing anti-Catholic sentiments from hitherto subconscious to the conscious mind'.[64] Given the propensity of leadership studies scholars to treat Hitler and those of his hue as 'non-leaders', the only conclusion that can be drawn is that comparisons between some of Northern Ireland's political leaders and Hitler were designed to de-legitimize their leadership positions and demonize them as people.

The analysis of leadership was not always directed towards the individuals. Concerns about the aptitude of the collective unionist leadership were apparent in the immediate period after the first IRA ceasefire in 1994. At this time McKittrick argued that unionist leaders: '... lack [ed] the political skills of their rivals. Politics had ... been a largely unregarded and faintly unpleasant activity for Unionists, so many of the best Protestant brains steer clear of it'.[65] This was a sentiment endorsed by the loyalist parties, who were equally critical of mainstream unionist leadership. For example, an Ulster Democratic Party (UDP) communication issued for the forum elections in 1996 stated: 'Our community has been plagued with political leaders who refuse to lead'.[66] Moreover, many of the loyalist party leaders claimed that they had been manipulated by mainstream unionist leaders into taking to the streets at their beckoning and being subsequently dumped by these same leaders when they were found guilty of paramilitary crimes and jailed.[67]

An overview of some individual leadership styles during the negotiations was detailed by McDonald and emphasized how Trimble's leadership style was questioned by some of those within the party. David Brewster, one of Trimble's negotiators said:

> The trouble with Trimble was he was trying to do everything himself. We, particularly Reg Empey and I, said, 'Look, you are the field marshal, so you should sit in your room in splendid isolation and the

guys who are fighting on the various strands can come to you and say, 'Here is our position. That will give you an overview'. Instead of which the stupid bugger was doing everything himself.[68]

This was in contrast to the earlier analysis of Trimble who began his tenure as party leader in a more cooperative fashion. Cochrane describes Trimble's leadership style as initially more inclusive (and therefore, by definition, more collective) in its approach than was apparent during Molyneaux's period in office.[69] He noted that after his election to office, Trimble appointed John Taylor as his deputy and said: 'It became standard practice for Taylor to accompany Trimble to meetings with the British or Irish governments, in contrast to Molyneaux's *mano a mano* chats and backstage whispers'.[70] Trimble himself, further endorsed the point (albeit after the Agreement was signed) when he was alleged to have referred to himself as more a chairman than a chief in a conversation with Adams. Adams recalled that:

A very senior unionist told me David Trimble was not a leader, he was a chairman. That very senior unionist was David Trimble himself.[71]

The analysis of the Sinn Féin approach to leadership was no more consistent in its emphasis on the collective over the individual in decision making and vice versa. On one hand, Mallie and McKittrick point to the variety of unnamed personnel who came along with Sinn Féin to meetings with the British Secretary of State, Mo Mowlam, during a critical period of the talks process.[72] It is implied by both the authors and also the Secretary of State at the time that these unnamed persons were part of the IRA's Army Council and were represented as part of the collective leadership approach undertaken by Sinn Féin.[73] On the other hand, and despite the collective aura, such egalitarianism was absent in McDonald's analysis, when he referred to the Sinn Féin leadership style, as 'run on Bolshevik lines with a politburo type leadership enforced with army style discipline' during the talks process.[74]

Contradictory interpretations

At best, all of this makes for interesting reading. However, it also presents something of an academic problem. Overall, there are numerous difficulties with the analysis of political leadership, as presented by both academics and political analysts, not least in terms of the contradictions between their interpretations and within their interpretations. First, the propensity towards mono-labelling leaders is not necessarily helpful as a tool of analysis and cannot be taken at face value. However, such mono-labelling does illustrate the depths of the contradictory interpret-ations of political leaders. During the peace process, each of the polit-ical leaders could be conceived of simultaneously, by different sources, as peace makers and peace breakers; as protagonists and pragmatists; as leading from the front and following from behind. Context and, more importantly, mutually exclusive perceptions of that context can lead to such dichotomous analyses being made, which do not take into account the possibility or probability of changes in leadership style and behaviour.[75] Indeed, political leaders in Northern Ireland during the peace process behaved in almost chameleon fashion, shedding old leadership skin for new leadership when necessity or circumstance dictated.[76] In reas-suring different constituencies that their interests were being protected, political leaders have had to present different faces, a different style of lead-ership, and a different message at different points in the peace process.[77] A leadership stance in public which might have been seen as distinctly hard-line or militant, was often replaced by a leadership stance in private which was more pragmatic in nature.[78] The hard-line reputation often acted as a 'smokescreen' and allowed for compromises to be made.[79]

Secondly, the tendency has been to discuss and review leadership behaviours in individual rather than collective terms, thus emphasizing a degree of contradiction between those leaders who preferred to talk of their leadership in collective terms, and those analysts who saw fit to emphasize the role of individual actors. Moreover, discussion usually focused on the leadership qualities which divided individuals rather than any points of commonality between them. This portrayal of a huge gulf between leaders in terms of both their abilities and their styles presented yet another political problem which would have to be overcome. In other words, in addition to the problem of actually finding accommodation between the various political positions, came the pseudo-problem of finding leaders with leadership styles which were compatible enough to allow them to work together under the terms of any agreement made. Much was made of the different leadership styles of David Trimble and John Hume, who would most likely have become First Minister and Deputy First Minister if an agreement were reached, and how incompatible they would have been with each other in their respective roles.[80] In reality, the incompatibility of leadership was something of a red herring, given that the structural problems within the Agreement were more problematic than personality problems.

Thirdly, there is a complete dislocation between how the various polit-ical leaders saw themselves and how they were perceived by others. The leadership characteristics derived from comments made by the leaders themselves – collective leadership, political prisoner cum political leader, reluctant leadership and soft-skilled leadership – were replaced by descriptions of political leaders which were either distinctly pejorative or presented a sanitized and sugar coated interpretation of political leadership and the personalities involved. These contrasting assessments of leadership raise obvious questions about the impartiality and objectivity of such assessments and have yielded little result in providing us with a definitive explanation of political leadership during the peace process. And yet, it is critically important to be able to identify those aspects of political leadership that might have made the difference between success and failure in the peace process. It is important to develop an understanding of political leadership which combines the alternative analyses above, and moves us beyond the rather simplistic argument which suggests that peace can be made by two strong leaders with a motivation to make peace.[81]

According to some conflict resolution specialists, the main attribute necessary for leaders in order that they can promote peacebuilding measures is simply one of strength. Moreover, the assumption is made that it is necessary to have two strong leaders and a willingness to make peace. This assumption ignores the reality of the peace process in Northern Ireland. The agreement was the result of *multi party* negotiations. Consequently, locating the two strong leaders who would 'deliver' was a futile exercise. Obviously, much attention was always paid to the 'big players' for much of the process. Nevertheless, there were ten political parties actively involved in the negotiations and their collective consent was a necessary requirement for the Agreement to hold. The fact that ten parties had a mandate invariably weakened some of the larger parties. This was most obvious within unionism. The PUP and the UDP, despite holding a small percentage of the vote held for entry to the multi-party negotiations, garnered their political strength from their links with the paramilitaries and used those links as part of their negotiating position. For example, the UUP would not have been able to hold any influence with loyalist paramilitary organizations over the issue of the decommissioning of weapons. The party leadership was particularly weak in this respect.

Additionally, the fact that the only other mainstream unionist political party had left the negotiations process weakened the UUP as much as it had strengthened it. On one hand, the UUP could garner political strength from being the only mainstream unionist party at the negotiating table. There was no other large party present to contradict their position from within unionism. On the other hand, the UUP were weakened by the departure of the DUP and the UKUP in September 1997 after Sinn Féin's admission to the talks process. The lack of unity within unionism weakened their position during the process. Even the UUP's attempted 'show of strength' by returning to the talks process later that month flanked by the leaders of the loyalist political parties damaged their position as much as it enhanced it. In short, it emphasized the fluidity of some of their previously held positions and arguments. The party's refusal to meet with Sinn Féin leaders or to talk to Sinn Féin as part of the negotiation process was on moral grounds. The party could not conceive of opening channels of discussion with political leaders who had links to paramilitary organizations, however tenuous the links. Yet, the possible paramilitary connections of those political leaders from PUP and UDP escorting the UUP leaders into the talks was ignored, at least in this particular instance.

The will and the motivation to make peace is even more difficult to locate consistently among the political players. John Hume's dogged determination to move the peace process forward by engaging in dialogue with Gerry Adams in the early 1990s was said to have been replaced by a rather distant and detached approach to the negotiations.[82] Arguably, some of his determination and motivation might have been lost as a consequence of the length and intensity of the talks process in a case of negotiation fatigue. Arguably, a lack of will and motivation was also detected in Sinn Féin's approach to the negotiations. The party leadership was unconcerned with entire strands and sections of the Agreement. It is argued that most of their attention focused on Strand Two – the strand which looked at North-South relations – and until the last moment they had only a rudimentary grasp of the mechanical underpinnings of Strand One, which dealt with the internal relations and practical arrangements for devolved government in Northern Ireland.

Key to the analysis presented here is the issue of consistency, or lack thereof. As subsequent chapters will show, circumstance sometimes dictated an inconsistent behaviour pattern. Equally key, is the issue of contradiction. This was most apparent in terms of the argument that two strong leaders are a necessity in order to make peace. The conclusion will build upon these issues further.

Conclusions – The need to develop a new understanding of political leadership

An argument can be made on moving towards a new understanding of leadership which explains political leadership in Northern Ireland during the period of the peace process because neither the understandings presented by political leaders, nor by political analysts have sufficed in terms of helping to adequately explain the phenomenon of political leadership in Northern Ireland during the peace process as being of a particular style or nature. It is clear that a definition which explains political leadership during the peace process must be about more than a list of words and phrases already given here. It must build on them and interpret them to present a more robust explanation of leadership at the time. Yet this has proved difficult to do.

Take, for example, some of the terms offered by leaders and their observers – collective and individual leadership. These terms are clearly dichotomous and, thus, seem difficult to explain as one word. Upon reflection however, 'presidential leadership' might sum up the interaction between the two. While collective leadership was focused on group decision making during the political process, and individual leadership focused on the role of the personality in the process, presidential leadership offers something of both. On the one hand, a presidential figure is clearly identifiable in individual terms. On the other hand, a presidential figure can be placed above party politics allowing a collective group beneath him/her to make the operational decisions. Equally, a presidential figure might want to be intricately involved in party politics but requires a strong team around him/her in order to do so.

Other definitions are less congruous. It proves almost impossible to find a way of demonstrating the linkage between those who see themselves as reluctant leaders and others who only see their naked ambition, or between those who see themselves as having been manipulated by other leaders in the past and those who were seemingly manipulating the peace process. Thus, political leadership in Northern Ireland during the peace process might best be described as contradictory or conflicted leadership, in both form and substance.

To be clear, the contradictions of such leadership are within the context of a single leader rather than between different leaders. Contradictory leadership allowed leaders to be both hard liner and moderniser; protagonist and pragmatist; transformational and transactional; reluctant and ambitious; innovative and pedantic; charismatic and 'robot-like'. The benefit of such a style of leadership was that it allowed the various political leaders to shift and adapt to changing political circumstances during the peace process without losing face. To its detriment, contradictory leadership left nuanced political observers, other political leaders and the general public unsure how best to describe and define their leaders. Moreover, and more importantly, contradictory leadership left the peace process without figures who could act as a benchmark of conduct.[83] It left the various political leaders, who were tasked with dealing with each other during the course of the process, feeling decidedly unsure of their political opponents. This, in turn, led to a lack of trust among political opponents, which was not conducive to a particularly positive peace process.

Bearing all of this in mind, how might it be possible to begin to develop a more robust explanation of the phenomenon of political leadership in Northern Ireland during the peace process? It is clear that the contradictions and inconsistencies of political leadership must form the basis of any new interpretation of political leadership. It cannot be ignored or explained away. Therefore, it is critical that the phenomenon of political leadership is broken down from the rather general analysis presented here into distinct parts for further examination. Such an approach necessitates an examination of the possible contradictions and inconsistencies within the role of political leadership during the peace process; the possible contradictions and inconsistencies within the capacity of political leadership to carry out their roles during the peace process; and the contradictions and inconsistencies in terms of the effect that political leaders actually had on other political leaders during the peace process.

An equally valid approach could be to use the attributes that are said to make up an adequate theory of political leadership and apply these to the context of Northern Ireland. The attributes necessary for an adequate theory of political leadership are: a definition of political behaviour; a specification of the conditions that enhance or impede the exercise of political behaviour; a specification of the sources of influence on which leaders can draw; a specification of the countervailing forces that exists in the context discussed; a specification of the motives and personality traits relevant to the exercise of power and political behaviour in organizations; a description of the kinds of behavioural tactics enacted in the pursuit of political objectives; a description of when such tactics will be used; a description of how politically motivated behaviour becomes legitimized; the moderating effects of organizational contexts on relationships between politically motivated behaviours and their effects and; the ultimate effects of politically motivated behaviour on organizational performance and survival.[84] A combination of both approaches will be used in this book, though the former will be dealt with explicitly in a chapter by chapter sequence, and the latter will be dealt with more implicitly throughout the following chapters. Turning first to the deconstruction of political leadership into its constituent parts, it is now time to consider its role, capacity and effect.

4
The Role of Political Leadership

Introduction

Some aspects of the Northern Ireland peace process have been likened to a theatrical metaphor. In using such an analogy, it is possible to view the political leaders as the 'cast' in the production. This 'cast' included the leading actors and actresses, support actors and actresses and a chorus line. The role of the 'cast' in a theatrical production is usually threefold: to narrate the story, to captivate the audience and convince the audience of the plausibility of the storyline, and to make it to finishing night without any major catastrophes on set. For example, should a 'cast' member momentarily forget their script then some degree of improvisation might be required in order that the production does not come to a grinding halt in full view of the audience. Translating the role of the 'cast' into the role of political leadership during the Northern Ireland peace process should then be relatively straightforward. Arguably, their role was to narrate the nature of the unfolding peace process to their party officials, constituents and followers, the media and wider society; to convince party officials, constituents and followers, the media and wider society of the plausibility of their 'analysis' of the peace process; and to avert the various crises which presented themselves during the peace process. The question is how, exactly, could they do that?

This chapter, therefore, seeks to present a more robust understanding of the perceived role of political leadership during the Northern Ireland peace process. It begins by charting some of the academic rather than metaphoric assessments of the role of leadership in general, and discusses how these might be applied to the particular context of Northern Ireland. It challenges some of the existing analyses on the role of political leadership during peace processes and argues that it is more important to emphasize the multiplicity of roles that a leader is likely to undertake during a peace process rather than focus on any primary role. It presents the multiplicity of roles, that political leaders undertake by categorizing them into three distinct areas: their interpersonal roles, their informational roles, and their decision-making roles and highlights some of the attitudes towards those roles by both the political leaders themselves and others.

In the analysis of this, the chapter then maintains that the multiplicity of roles led to a degree of role confusion and role conflict among the elite not least because many of their roles seemed often contradictory or incompatible with one another. The chapter concludes that such confusions, conflict and contradictions have the potential to further cloud our understandings of political leadership during the Northern Ireland peace process rather than crystallize the phenomenon but reminds the reader that it is these very contradictions and inconsistencies which will help form the basis of the alternative interpretation of political leadership, during the Northern Ireland peace process, that this book seeks to ultimately present.

Understanding the theory

Whilst seemingly reluctant to develop an actual classification of political leadership roles during peace processes, a number of peace and conflict texts do touch on probable roles and tasks that a leader may need to undertake. For example, Darby and MacGinty proposed that: '. . . during peace negotiations the primary function of leaders is to deliver their own people. Assisting their opponents in the process is secondary'.[1] They argued that the problem with assisting opponents is that it might alienate their own supporters and that '. . . the reality is that the loss of their followers is a greater threat to party leaders than the collapse of the process'.[2] Bloomfield, Ghai and Reilly took a more normative stance in their prescription of a leader's role and argued of political leaders that:

> They must often be ahead of the sentiment of a large proportion of their followers in counselling for peace, and they must have the authority to carry supporters with them through difficult times. This is especially difficult when the leaders at the negotiating table are often the very same ones who provoked or maintained the conflicts in the first place. It also requires leaders to put the long term interests of their nation in achieving a durable settlement before the short term gains that could be achieved by prolonging the conflict.[3]

They acknowledge, however, that their analysis is only theoretical and that, in reality, leaders will mostly make rational decisions about their own group's core interests in the peace negotiations first and foremost.[4] Nonetheless, they still conclude that successful transitions from conflict to peace-building depend upon '. . . far-sighted, courageous and creative political leadership'.[5] They define such leaders as those who are 'prepared to make sacrifices, to make deals with their political foes, to negotiate, to move forward when others are afraid or unwilling, as essential to building a sustainable democracy'.[6]

Any mapping of the more general leadership theory which might help explain the role of political leadership in the context of the Northern Ireland peace process highlights the contradictions between the more normative view of leaders and the more detached behavioural view.[7] This becomes important in the context of the Northern Ireland peace process because it illuminates the potential difficulties that political leaders in Northern Ireland faced in either interpreting their role as one in which they were supposed to do the 'right thing' during the peace process or as one in which they were obliged to protect both themselves and their followers at the expense of all other things. In addition, such literature highlights the possibility that political leaders can have a multiplicity of particular roles associated to their political positions. Some roles are given higher priority than others, by both academics and by the political leaders themselves, though this can seem a rather subjective hierarchy of roles, often conditioned by normative world views. Indeed, while there might be much merit in Darby and MacGinty's proposition that the primary function of leaders is to deliver their own people towards an agreement, this role only really becomes possible once the central tenets of that particular agreement have been established. Before that point in the peace process, there are other roles which must be undertaken by the political leaders in order to make the possibility of an agreement more likely, not least the interpersonal roles which involve interactions with others beyond the confines of one's own group of followers. The nature of these various roles have not been dealt with in any systematic way by either the political leadership literature or the peace and conflict studies literature. Consequently, Mintzberg's work on managerial leadership as opposed to political leadership has had to be utilized for the purposes of this chapter. He argued that leadership roles could be broken down into three main areas – interpersonal, informational and decision making – and it is these areas, in particular, which this chapter focuses on.

Interpersonal roles of political leadership

Earlier, it was argued that one of the roles of the cast in any theatrical production is to captivate the audience and to convince the audience of the plausibility of the story line. Translating this into one of the roles of political leaders during a peace process, their role is to convince party officials, constituents and followers, the media and wider society of the plausibility of their 'analysis' of the peace process. Essentially then, this role requires a great degree of interaction at the personal level. Thus, this section focuses on the interpersonal roles of political leadership.

One of the most outwardly apparent roles of political leadership during the peace process in Northern Ireland was interpersonal in nature, not least because this was the sort of role which attracted significant media attention. In their daily narratives of the unfolding peace process, the media concentrated on who met with whom, in what particular context, and with what potential affect. For example, much was made of the public handshake between Adams and Clinton during Clinton's first presidential visit to Belfast and the potential impact of that handshake in improving Sinn Féin's status within the peace process.[8] Equally, the first meeting between John Bruton, the then Taoiseach of Ireland, and Trimble, shortly after Trimble's election as leader of the Ulster Unionists, was hailed as a significant moment in the peace process by the media, since it was the first time that an Irish Prime Minister and an Ulster Unionist leader had held a formal meeting in over 30 years.[9] Clearly though, the interpersonal roles of leadership stretched far beyond the symbolism of handshakes and 'historic' moments. There was a much more substantive dimension to the role which can be examined in terms of their roles as figureheads, as points of liaison, and in terms of leader–follower relations.

Even in their more traditional role as figureheads, a role which was usually seen to be primarily ceremonial and symbolic, often perceived to be above party politics, and usually obliged to be involved in routine duties such as meeting and greeting guests and dignitaries, there are illustrative examples of how the political leadership in Northern Ireland were able to affect change within the peace process in their figurehead roles since the ceremonial and symbolic duties associated with their role as figureheads often afforded the political leaders in Northern Ireland numerous political opportunities. These opportunities were often critical during both periods of progress and periods of stagnation during the peace process.

First, the ceremonial element of being a figurehead allowed some of the political leaders additional avenues with which to gauge constituent reactions to progression in the peace process. Their attendance at various community functions and festivals allowed the leadership access to constituents in decidedly non-political contexts, in order that they could gauge levels of support or otherwise for the unfolding peace process. One obvious example of this was in Adams' role as a founding member of the West Belfast Community Festival. The festival was known throughout the period of the peace process as the place where frank discussions were often held about the nature and direction of the process. The exchange between Bernadette McAliskey, a former republican MP and critic of the Sinn Féin approach to the peace process, and Gerry Adams over the possibility of his peace strategy failing was just one example of this.[10] Question and answer sessions between Martin McGuinness, Albert Reynolds and Roy Garland before a packed audience was another.[11]

Secondly, the figurehead role afforded the leaders the opportunity to present their case to a variety of visiting dignitaries to Northern Ireland. The most obvious example of this was during Clinton's visit to Northern Ireland in 1995 when he held separate private talks with the leaders of the five largest political parties at that time. Trimble's meeting took place in the presidential limousine on a short trip from the nearby Queen's University to the Europa Hotel where Clinton was staying.[12] While it is clear that the invite to share the presidential limousine was designed to impress Trimble's community, in particular, and thus Trimble's standing within his community, it also afforded Trimble the opportunity to give the Americans a greater understanding of his position regarding the peace process.[13] Likewise, meetings with Adams and Paisley during the same visit afforded both players the opportunity to state firmly their positions on the peace process.

Thirdly, another important though less obvious aspect of the figurehead role was that, in addition to being able to present their own arguments and positions to potential supporters from outside, the Northern Irish political leaders were often simultaneously exposed to the thinking and rationale of other political leaders involved in other peace processes. Many key players received phone calls from Clinton in the final days of the multiparty negotiations and a number of key negotiators from the South African peace process made the journey to Northern Ireland to hold discussions with the various political parties. Arguably, such meetings resulted in the borrowing of ideas and strategies from other peace processes, as detailed by those political leaders involved in other peace processes.

A final opportunity afforded by the figurehead role of political leadership was that through these meetings with other international figureheads the different political leaders were able to garner additional legitimacy for their respective positions since the meetings were often used by the political leaders to shore up their own positions with followers. For example, the Sinn Féin manifesto for the Westminster election in 1997 claimed: 'Sinn Féin's committed and experienced leadership secured the active support for the peace process of world leaders such as Bill Clinton and Nelson Mandela'.[14]

While the political leaders' role as a point of liaison with other leaders had much in common with the role of a figurehead insofar as the figurehead position afforded the political leaders the opportunity to meet with other international leaders, the actual liaison role was much broader and the liaisons often stretched in multiple directions. Political leaders were a point of liaison for other political elites within Northern Ireland. They were a point of liaison for key personnel within both the British and Irish governments. They were a point of liaison for those international leaders who had taken a keen interest in the affairs of Northern Ireland, including both Clinton and Mandela. Yet even beyond these more obvious examples, their liaison role during the peace process cannot be underestimated.

By maintaining a self developed network of outside contacts and informers with 'leaders' from fields other than politics, who could provide favours and information, the different political leaders were able to discuss ideas and possible 'moves' within the peace process without those discussions being binding. One such example of the liaison role of leaders can be evidenced in Trimble's various liaisons with John Lloyd, Eoghan Harris, Ruth Dudley Edwards and Sean O'Callaghan during the peace process. The former three were all regarded as influential, leading journalists and the latter was a former republican and political prisoner who had turned his back on republicanism and subsequently became a key adviser to Trimble on all aspects of Irish republicanism.[15] All of these players came together at events such as the Friends of the Union pan-unionist conference, organized in late November 1997, allowing Trimble to coalesce his supporters in the London and Dublin media and to discuss possible political moves with them.[16] Another example of the usefulness of the self-developed networks of contacts was evident in the case of Hume's relationships with influential American congressmen, senators and aide workers. It is argued that the eventual US administration's involvement in the Northern Ireland peace process was secured through two decades of Hume's relationship building with various US administrations and certain individuals within them.[17]

The third and final interpersonal role was that of acting as political leaders which constituents could, and would, follow. In this role, the development of sound leader–follower relations was critical in order to maintain their confidence and support during the peace process. Some of the ways in which leaders traditionally interacted with followers and constituents to build and maintain their confidence and support were identical to tactics used in any other more 'normal' society. Generally, the tactics were to 'build networks and coalitions, define an agenda, inspire enthusiasm, shape and maintain an image, select and develop a staff, gather information and accomplish tasks'.[18] However, in their role as leading figures for the various political causes, the political leaders were both responsible to and responsible for constituent followers. The aforementioned tactics mostly used were in response to their role as being responsible to constituent followers.

More importantly however, in their role as being responsible for followers, the political leaders were required to ensure that the followers actually followed the strategic plan as set out by the leaders. In other words, one role of political leaders was to ensure that the unfolding peace process did not result in any splits or deviations from the process by their own immediate followers. In real terms, it was important that, through this role, the leaders faced down any accusations of a 'sell out'. Such accusations were always likely in the context of Northern Ireland, given the reality in any peace process that expectations will have to be disappointed, that political leaders will have to climb down from the heights of earlier rhetoric and that they will have to both satisfy a constituency but equally make a deal less favourable than at least part of that constituency will want to accept.[19] This was a point that had clear resonance for Sinn Féin, as a party from which splits were expected during the peace process, though did not manifest itself in the numbers expected. At one party conference during the peace process Adams noted that:

> In a struggle like ours there will always be fears of a sell out – of a leadership going soft. The greater the dependency there is upon a leadership and the more political underdevelopment there is among activists the more these fears will grow to be exploited by our opponents, to cause confusion and division. Fortunately, we have avoided this so far and to the degree that any confusion exists this can be easily dealt with in open and comradely discussions.[20]

In some instances, however, the key political players struggled to explain the nature of their interpersonal roles in the peace process. The interpersonal relationship between leaders and followers caused more concern than the interpersonal relationship with other party leaders and international leaders. A number saw their role as one of challenging constituents albeit recognizing that this was an ideal role rather than one rooted in the realities of the peace process. One party leader said that 'you would never, very rarely do something that your entire constituency is against but you would do stuff that you have to explain, argue, and debate about'.[21] Concurring with this, another highlighted the interaction between leaders and followers in their definition of the role of leaders in a peace process:

> It's challenging your own people all the time, speaking to the best hopes of what you would like them to do, rather than reinforcing their fears, recognising your dependency on the other person in a negotiation process, that you are as dependent on that leader as he is on you, or she is on you, and also making a collaborative team effort, and all the time disseminating any decisions that you make, and finally obviously there's the element of being radical and risk taking, but that being made in the context of all the other things.[22]

Overall though, a number of points in relation to the interpersonal role of political leadership during the Northern Ireland peace process are worth noting. First, the significance of the interpersonal role of leadership was, at times, underestimated by some political players who preferred to deal with structural issues at the expense of interpersonal issues. This issue will be dealt with in greater detail in Chapter 6 which looks at the degree of relationship building between political leaders during the peace process. For now, it is sufficient to say that many of the relationships between political leaders in Northern Ireland during the early part of the peace process were either not good or non-existent indicating that the leaders were either unwilling or unsuccessful in some aspects of their interpersonal roles.

Secondly, while non-existent relationships proved troublesome for the peace process, the over-emphasis on interpersonal relationships was to prove equally problematic for some political leaders during the peace process. Arguably, it was the 'special relationship' between the UDP and the Ulster Freedom Fighters (UFF) that led to the UDP's exclusion from the talks process in early 1998, when it became clear to the British government that the UFF had broken the terms of its ceasefire.[23] By the same measure, it was the perceived interpersonal relationship between Sinn Féin and the IRA which led to their exclusion from the talks process in early 1998 also, when it became clear to the British government that the IRA had broken the terms of its ceasefire also.

Both of these points help to clarify the argument that there was something inherently contradictory about the interpersonal roles of political leadership during the peace process in Northern Ireland. At times the interpersonal role was under-emphasized, at other times it was over-emphasized. The most obvious contradictions inherent within the role were that while one of the purposes of the interpersonal role was to assuage fears and allay concerns, the possible consequence of engaging with those who held reservations about the nature and direction of the peace process was alienation from the process for being guilty by association. As a result, some political leaders preferred to emphasize roles other than those which were interpersonal in nature.

Informational roles of political leadership

Returning again to the earlier theatrical metaphor, one of the roles of the 'cast' is to simply narrate the story. In the context of the Northern Ireland peace process, one of the most important roles for political leaders was the narration of the unfolding peace process to their party officials, constituents and followers, the media and wider society. Central to this narration were three distinct informational roles. These informational roles of leadership during the Northern Ireland peace process involved the monitoring of information relevant to the process, the dissemination of either some or all of that information to constituent followers and the articulation of the political parties' proposed forms of action and reaction to the various events which took place during the period of the peace process. These various informational roles are examined here individually, in order to ascertain if any inconsistencies or contradictions become apparent here also.

First, as monitors of information the leadership of the various parties were required to pay particular heed to key documents circulated by both the British and Irish governments and to the responses by other political parties. Most of this information was circulated within a fairly public domain. However, additional significant statements were often to be found in political speeches or in newspaper articles.[24] Beyond this, however, there was always other information that was circulated in a more restricted fashion. For those outside of the formal parameters of the process, and without immediate access to government information, information monitoring was often facilitated for them by back channels and 'off the record' briefings. For example, the revelation in

1993 that a back channel of contact had been taking place between republicans and the British government highlighted the fact that republicans had been receiving advanced copies of various Secretary of State speeches, the details of Ministerial meetings on Northern Ireland, and even confidential briefing papers on the progress of the Brooke talks taking place in Northern Ireland in the early 1990s.[25] Ultimately, in their role as monitors of information, the political leaders were able to scan all such information pertaining to the process and then issue their respective responses to that information. The purpose of such a role was to understand the strength of their political adversaries' commitment to their current positions, insofar as there would have been little point in conceding on an issue during the talks process if it were detected that the other side was about to concede on the same issue. By the same measure however, it often made more sense to concede on an issue if it became clear that the other side was unlikely to move on it at all.[26]

Secondly, in their role as disseminators of information, the political leaders were tasked with passing certain information on to constituent followers. How they chose to do that varied between parties and what they chose to divulge equally varied between parties. For example, the Sinn Féin leadership was well renowned for consistently going back to the party members for discussion and debate, and for holding a series of extraordinary meetings with their rank and file during the course of the peace process. Much like Sinn Féin, the loyalist parties said that talking to the paramilitaries and hard liners within their constituency base, and also conveying any received information to them, was critical to the continued stability of the peace process. In this respect, one party leader said:

> I tended to do the work with the military people in terms of trying to keep them on board, selling them the idea, and using conflict resolution, whereas _____ went towards, and I don't want to be disrespectful, the do gooders in the community, and, basically, the political parties. That's the way we have always played it. I have tried to do the hard work in the background going to talk to people and say 'here's what's happening' and try to get people to hold their nerve, and it has worked.[27]

Conveying such information to hard liners was not always easy; however, the potential impact of any misinformation given remained a cautionary tale. This was experienced by Ervine after a series of meetings with Dublin officials in 1996. Ervine recalled that misinformation relayed to the loyalist paramilitaries from some Dublin officials meant that some of the loyalist paramilitaries had begun to question Ervine's representation of them within the peace process, and accused him of playing a dirty trick campaign against them along with the Dublin officials he had been meeting.[28] Ervine said of the incident that he was in a lot of trouble over it: 'At a meeting to thrash the matter out, I was going to be taken away and my head blown off. There were those who certainly wanted to do it'.[29]

The necessity of properly briefing paramilitaries with information received stretched beyond those with immediate associations to such groups. Even Trimble took an unprecedented step for any leader of the UUP by going into the Maze prison in 1996 to talk to the loyalist prisoners held there, and to encourage their continuing support for the progression of the peace process.[30] That this contradicted his subsequent argument for refusing to directly negotiate with Sinn Féin during the talks process on the grounds of their links to paramilitarism, is discussed further in Chapter 7. At this stage, it is sufficient to simply note the contradiction.

In terms of their role as disseminators of information, the most pertinent question was how much the political leaders were either obliged or willing to 'tell' as part of the political process that was unfolding, bearing in mind the previously articulated interpersonal role which was to work with constituents and to keep supporters onside. Attitudes towards the dissemination of information varied among some of the political leaders. One party leader argued that 'leadership didn't always require you to be totally explicit and honest, with your own constituency'.[31] However, another disagreed and suggested that:

> In being what people might describe as a strong leader, you have to constantly explain to your constituency what you are doing, why you're doing it, and invite discussion, debate, argument, dissension. Whatever it is you have got to invite it, because [otherwise] you are then seen as arrogant, aloof and dismissive if you do not. Now I think that you can be a strong leader provided that the avenues and opportunities exist for people to interact in dialogue and debate with you.[32]

This highlights a contradiction in the attitudes of political leaders about what how much or how little information was appropriate to disseminate to followers. For some, disseminating widely was of paramount significance. For others, it was the potential death knell of the process.

The third and final information based role of the political leaders was as a spokesperson during the peace process. This spokesperson role took a number of forms in Northern Ireland. First there was the necessitated megaphone diplomacy which took place during the early period of the peace process conveying messages to those outside of the party and beyond the ranks of followers. In their role as spokespersons engaged in megaphone diplomacy, they were able (at least in theory) to explain to those outside of their own support base their intentions during the process, aided by the constant media exposure.[33]

Secondly, there was the spokesperson who tried to convey to their own support base the intentions of the leadership during the peace process though it is clear that this role had significant overlap with the previously mentioned dissemination role. Of this role, one leader commented that what was needed was to be 'as honest and explicit as you may dare with your own constituency, but also to be as honest and explicit with those you may have to work with politically'.[34] This role was often difficult and required much communication and education of constituents and followers. Another leader noted that 'it is again very difficult, because it's all about communication and the more convoluted your argument the more explanation is required'.[35] One of the greatest difficulties in being as honest and explicit as one dared to be with political adversaries was the absence of any long standing relationships that had developed between them, and by extension, the likelihood that such honesty and explicitness would be taken at face value was remote.

There are a number of key points to distill from the various informational roles of political leadership during the Northern Ireland peace process. Firstly, too little information sharing led to suspicions from hard-line constituents about the nature of the activity that the leaders were engaged in. This was particularly true for the loyalist parties involved in the peace process, as the example of Ervine's liaisons with the Dublin officials illustrated.

Secondly, too much information sharing ran the risk of adversely affecting the negotiating positions of the political leaders since their political opponents could become privy to information that was designed for certain constituencies only. In an interview towards the end of 1997, Mo Mowlam, then the British Secretary of State in Northern Ireland, said that civil servants leaking information to the press and to political parties were undermining the peace process.[36]

Thirdly, it was clear that different types of information were often necessary for different audiences. The information conveyed to paramilitaries was likely to have been tailored differently to that information which was conveyed to the public. Moreover, rather than having one leader disseminate information to multiple audiences, the inclination in some parties was to have certain leaders for certain audiences. For example, Adams and McGuinness were the main points of contact for the IRA and party members, while McLaughlin was the main contact for wider community, and particularly with opposition.[37] Within the PUP, Hutchinson was the main point of contact with paramilitary figures with which the party had association, while Ervine tended to do more of the front publicity work.[38]

Fourthly, and perhaps most critical to the overall argument of this book, the priority of the information roles seemed to shift for the political leaders at different junctures of the process. In other words, there was an inconsistent approach to role priorities. Certainly, as the process gathered momentum and moved into its very final stages of negotiations, monitoring and disseminating information was only important insofar as it afforded political leaders the opportunities to subsequently take decisions about the nature and scope of the peace process.

Decision-making roles of political leadership

As articulated in the introduction, one of the roles of political leaders during the Northern Ireland peace process was to avert the various crises which presented themselves during the peace process. In doing so, some of the political leaders undertook a number of related roles which helped deal with such potential crises.

The first such role was as an entrepreneurial leader. In general terms, the role of the entrepreneurial leader emphasized the need for leaders to find ways of adapting to changing conditions and environments.[39] In the context of Northern Ireland, this role necessitated that leaders strategically moved from previously held positions while managing to retain the majority of support within their respective political parties and constituency bases. The tactic most often used in this respect was to articulate such changes as being on the grounds of confrontation rather than mere concession.[40] Indeed, it was this tactic of alleged confrontation which allowed Trimble to sit down alongside Sinn Féin during the talks process, after publicly stating that he would not do so.[41] It allowed the Sinn Féin leadership to turn from its slogan of 'no return to Stormont', to one of endorsing the Agreement complete with a 108 seat legislative Assembly at Stormont.[42] It also allowed Sinn Féin to take offices in Westminster after years of vowing to end the British connection by presenting such a move as a victory.[43] Holding on to previously held positions in the face of changes in the 'political environment' was seen by some as a foolish strategy. One party leader noted:

> My view of leadership has to be measured in your determination to succeed in the strategy that you have adopted but also not to be a fool because the circumstances and issues change and situations develop and you have got to be logical and potentially flexible.[44]

Nonetheless, not all agreed with the idea of being flexible during the peace process. When the conditions and the environment surrounding the peace process shifted, particularly in 1997, when Sinn Féin were formally admitted to the multi-party talks process, both the leadership of the DUP and of the UKUP felt unable to adapt to the change in circumstance which resulted in their withdrawal from the talks process for the subsequent duration. On the other hand, once the Agreement became a reality, both the DUP and UKUP accepted that new reality insofar as they both fought for seats within the new legislative assembly and the DUP took their allocated Ministerial seats as part of the assembly executive. This change in stance from being un-entrepreneurial in one instance towards behaving more entrepreneurially in another is one of the most obvious examples of contradiction within the DUP and the UKUP stances.

In their role as disturbance handlers, the political leaders were charged with having to handle any particular point of pressure which arose from time to time during the process. The most obvious pressures were those instances through which the entire peace process threatened to miscarry or abort. The issues included the annual parades saga at Drumcree, the temporary exclusion of Sinn Féin and of the UDP from the process and the withdrawal of the DUP and the UKUP from the process.[45] Given that the peace process did not abort before the Agreement was eventually signed, this suggests some measure of success in the leaders' disturbance handling role. However, there were other pressures within the process that the leaders tended to have much less control over. Elections, in particular, were seen to have the potential to disrupt the entire process.

Between the time of the first IRA ceasefire in 1994 and the signing of the Agreement in April 1998 there were three major elections of note – the May 1996 Northern Ireland Forum election, the May 1997 Westminster General Election, and the May 1997 local government election. Additionally, there was also the election of the leader of the UUP in September 1995. The possibility of forthcoming elections has always had the effect of hardening political attitudes within many of the various political parties and the elections which took place during the period of the peace process were certainly no different. Primarily, this was because the elections tended to create a degree of uncertainty for political leaders. By behaving more conservatively during an election period, political leaders could not be accused of risking some of the short term interests of their constituents in favour of some longer term interests at wider society levels. In the absence of such accusations then, political leaders could feel relatively confident about the outcome of the elections. By the same token however, observers could feel relatively dismayed at the potential impact of this on the progress of the peace process.

Handling the pressures of elections, whilst a role of leadership in and of itself, also required political leaders to consistently emphasize some of their other roles within the peace process. This was usually evident in the various election manifestos produced by the party leaders. One Sinn Féin manifesto showed photographs of Adams shaking hands with Mandela and Clinton.[46] Sinn Féin were clearly emphasizing their leadership role as both interpersonal and informational. Adams was demonstrating his role as a figurehead of the party by illustrating his meetings with other figurehead leaders, as well as his role as spokesperson of the party by conveying his message beyond the confines of the party and constituent followers, to a much broader, international and influential audience. Like Sinn Féin, the DUP chose to demonstrate their views on leadership roles in pictures also. One DUP manifesto showed pictures of some of the different political elites from Northern Ireland shaking hands with Dick Spring whom they called 'the most detested politicians in Ulster'.[47] Those pictured were David Trimble, John Taylor and David Ervine. Another picture showed Gary McMichael sharing the same stage with Sinn Féin's Mitchell McLaughlin.[48] The subliminal message of this manifesto was that the DUP leadership saw its role as one of monitor and disseminator of information to subordinates, informing followers and potential followers of the developing interpersonal relationships between other political leaders during the peace process and emphasizing the potential negative consequences of this interaction.

The third decision-making role of political leadership during the Northern Ireland peace process was to act as a resource allocater. In other words, their role was to help determine who got what and when, as a consequence of the peace process. Much of the resource allocation role was undertaken during the course of the multi-party negotiations and sat neatly with the fourth and final decision-making role of political leaders in Northern Ireland which was seen as the most critical role during the peace process. This role was as a negotiator whereby the leaders had to make commitments to other parties engaged within the talks process whilst simultaneously trying to extract concessions from others within that same process. While the governments acted as gatekeepers, time-keepers and organizers, the political leaders were, in fact, the primary negotiators, albeit using both governments as conduits for negotiating with their political adversaries when circumstances dictated so.

Certain aspects of the political leaders' negotiator role need further elucidation here. Negotiations usually require a degree of compromise by all sides. It was clear that all of the leaders had to compromise at some point during the process in Northern Ireland. Had any revelations of such concessions become public knowledge before the deal between leaders had been completed in its entirety, then some leaders ran the risk of being undermined by more extreme opponents from within their respective communities.[49] This was particularly true for the UUP leadership, given that the DUP and the UKUP had already departed from the talks process but were following the process closely.

In one example of how this played out, the DUP claimed to have been given a leaked memo which was originally sent from Downing Street offices to the NIO in February 1998 which said that '. . . any settlement would have to include meaningful North-South structures . . . in these circumstances national boundaries obviously become less relevant over time'.[50] In relation to the UUP stance at the talks, the leaked memo continued to say that 'the Unionists had signed up to North-South structures'.[51] Although the authenticity of the leaked memo was strenuously challenged by the UUP at the time given that the DUP refused to show the original document and only a photocopy of the selected comments, the story itself was enough to cause a degree of concern about possible UUP concessions within the negotiations at a critical stage of the process.

Overall, there are a number of points to be made in relation to the decision-making roles of political leaders during the Northern Ireland peace process. First, the decision-making roles must be considered in the context of the earlier comments made by key political leaders in relation to the concept of 'collective leadership' and, equally, the comments made which indicated a measure of 'reluctant leadership' among their numbers. It has already been argued that the concepts of both collective leadership and reluctant leadership had a protective nature to them insofar as it afforded the leadership a possible rebuttal to any blame game played out during the course of the peace process or afterwards. In light of this, it is plausible that the decision-making roles were not necessarily the responsibility of a number of individual party leaders representing their various political parties. Instead, decision making during the peace process was most likely undertaken as a collective rather than an individual activity. The importance of this point is that it contradicts the notions that peace can be made by two strong leaders with the motivation to make peace. Indeed, this point stresses that the decision-making roles of political leaders in Northern Ireland were often inclusive rather than exclusive affairs and thus involved more than one individual key player on each side of the political divide and demonstrates the inappropriateness of this concept from the peace and conflict studies literature to the context of the peace process in Northern Ireland.

The second important point in relation to the political leaders' various decision-making roles is that some of the roles actually accommodated the changes of approach by certain political leaders rather than hampered them. For example, the entrepreneurial role encouraged leaders to find ways of adapting to changing conditions and environments; the disturbance handling role, at least in the context of potential upset from elections, allowed some of the leaders to behave more conservatively than at other points in the process; and the negotiator role often necessitated compromise which amounted to a changing position.

Overall, the various roles of political leadership, as identified here, highlighted two key themes. The first theme was one of multiplicity and the second was one of inconsistency. These themes can be used to make some points which are important to the development of the overall argument of the book. First, they highlight the fact that the political leaders engaged in the Northern Ireland peace process had no single role to play. Rather, they had multiple roles which were prioritized according to the political demands of the day. On some occasions, the most important role seemed to be liaising with constituents to keep them on board during the process. On other occasions, the most important role seemed to be the very selective dissemination of information to constituents lest any more information might jeopardize the unfolding process. Secondly, they highlight the fact that compartmentalizing the various roles of political leaders during the Northern Ireland peace process was, indeed, a difficult task. Many of the roles overlapped. For example, often a political leader would develop personal relations in order to ensure that they had access to all relevant information and opinion. Trimble's noted relationship with Sean O'Callaghan could be construed in this regard. The emergence of the themes of multiplicity and inconsistency from within this chapter are most important to the developing argument presented here because they illustrate that the multiplicity of roles coupled with the inconsistency of approach within these roles negate the most extreme normative argument that the role of political leadership in a peace process is to make 'peace' at all costs and also the more realist argument that their role cannot stretch beyond delivering one's own constituents towards an agreement. This raises the question, how might these themes be used in a reinterpretation of the role of political leadership during the Northern Ireland peace process?

The confusion and the contradiction of the roles

Overall, the peace process required that attention be paid to all of the political leaders' various roles. This was particularly true because 'the multiple actors, multiple levels of operation, multiple means of communication and multiple issues meant that the process was extraordinarily complicated'.[52] Ultimately however, the leaders seemed to struggle in terms of both understanding and effectively fulfilling all of their roles. This raises an obvious question: why?

Arguably, the political leaders were conditioned by the rather normative expectations of others in relation to what they should have actually been doing during the peace process. For example, one normative understanding was that the role of political leaders was to win the peace at all costs during the Northern Ireland peace process and that the leaders would say: 'I shall do the right thing, no matter what its effect on me and the parochial interests I represent, even if the effect on us is adverse'.[53] A second understanding of their role was that it was necessary for leaders to step down from earlier rhetoric and accept an agreement which was likely to be far below the leaders' original expectations and wishes, and in which the immediate benefits were not always obvious. In such an instance, the leader would say: 'I shall do the right thing, even though it is not, at this moment, in my interest or in the interest of those I represent; inasmuch as my vision does not permit me to see what will be in our interest in the future, I shall choose those arrangements I can live with, come what may'.[54] A third understanding was that the role of political leaders was to suffer short term pain for long-term gain in a process and to encourage their constituents to do likewise. In such instances, the leader would say: 'I shall do the right thing, because although its effects will be negative on us in the short run, I can see that they will be positive in the long run'.[55] These messages of the need for leaders to 'do the right thing' were delivered at different times by various international actors, the British and Irish governments, the churches, the business community and the media.

Additionally though, and in contrast to the above, the political leaders were also conditioned by the realities of 'real politik' and their own selfish interests. Taking heed of the calls to 'do the right thing', might well have resulted in winning the peace but could equally have resulted in losing the party. Certainly, making peace at any price could have cost the leaders their positions within their respective political parties. Making historic compromises with political opponents would have required a great deal of explanation with constituents and followers. Delivering constituents towards acceptance of a deal would have required emphasis on the various gains that had been made in the process as opposed to any mention of the concessions that had been made. Assisting opponents in the deliverance of their own constituents would have required that the aforementioned emphasis of gains that had been made in the process was not emphasized too much lest the political opponent's constituency only saw the gains of their adversaries as opposed to the gains that they themselves had secured. Maintaining party cohesion and unity required a two pronged approach. At times, it required leaders to negotiate firstly with their own people. At other times it necessitated being rather more economical with the truth. All of this resulted in a degree of role confusion for the political leaders insofar as the roles to be played often seemed to be contradictory in nature. Indeed, delivering peace and maintaining party unity required different role priorities with different effects and yet both were equally important in terms of the long term sustainability of any agreements made.

There was confusion over whether their role was to do the 'right' thing during the process or whether it was to protect their constituents in instances where the two roles seemed mutually exclusive. There was confusion over their role as figureheads and statesmen, in terms of their liaisons with other external political leaders. Were their roles comparable to that of Mandela and de Klerk, for example and, if so, was the purpose of their roles simply to emulate the Mandela's and de Klerk's of other peace processes? There was confusion over whether the role priority was to establish sound interpersonal relationships with followers or whether to try to establish sound interpersonal relationships with political adversaries. There was confusion over whether their role was to stick to previously articulated objectives or whether their role was to condition others into accepting a departure from original objectives. The role confusion led to an inconsistent approach towards the various roles of political leadership where, at times, some roles were prioritized over others without apparent rationale.

Conclusions

Most people have a clear understanding of the nature of their job, and of their particular role within their organization. Indeed, it is commonplace in most professions for an employee, at whatever level, to be provided with a list of roles and responsibilities or, in other words, a job specification upon taking up their post. Job specifications provide clarity to the employee about the expectations of their superiors in terms of their role and, equally, provide a measuring stick against which employers can gauge the success or otherwise of the employee in undertaking the tasks assigned to him or her. Unfortunately, political leaders are provided with no clear list of the specific roles and responsibilities associated with their positions. For the most part, it is deemed unnecessary, since in theory at least, political leaders know that their responsibilities lie within three spheres. There is the responsibility to wider society, the responsibility to those constituents who have elected the leader and, finally, there is the responsibility to those who work with them in the party. During a peace process, however, the responsibilities to society, constituents and party members can become complicated and the leaders' roles often vary according to the different political circumstances from moment to moment and according to the political leaders' own interpretation of what is or is not most important to deal with.

Political leaders in Northern Ireland had multiple roles to play in the peace process rather than any one specific role. Some roles were prioritized over others at different junctures of the process. The effect of this was that those who prioritized informational roles often had a better informed electorate as to an understanding of their aims and objectives and positions and those who prioritized their interpersonal roles often built better relationships and, by extension, trust during the process. Both roles were equally necessary to any progression of the peace process but the fact that multiple roles were necessary during the peace process led to a degree of role confusion among leaders in terms of which things to prioritize, rather than provided any clarity. The fact that some of the roles seemed to contradict one another, or at least, sat rather uneasily with one another, further compounded the role confusion. For example, some of the perceptions which existed included that it was a political leader's role in relation to his/her constituents to protect them; a political leader's role within a peace process was to deliver constituents to an agreed deal; a political leader's role within wider society was to endeavour that such a deal was acceptable to broader society; and a political leader's role among other political leaders was to engage with one another. The point, in reality, was that the roles needed to be fulfilled in tandem with one another. When a political leader focused on one at the expense of the others then his overall potential role in the peace process was severely diminished.

5
The Capacity of Political Leadership

Introduction

The roles of political leadership during the Northern Ireland peace process were inextricably linked to the leaderships' potential capacity to fulfil their roles. While an examination of the roles of political leaders focused on a variety of actions and activities expected of them, any examination of their capacity must then focus on their ability and aptitude to deliver on the same. Thus, the purpose of this particular chapter on understanding the capacity of political leadership during the Northern Ireland peace process is to explain the sources of influence available to the political leadership, as a way of opening up a discussion on their potential capacity to influence the shape and direction of the peace process. The sources of influence considered here are threefold: the influence of office, the influence of events and the influence of the personal.

At the outset, however, it must be acknowledged that there were significant influences other than leadership which contributed to the development of the peace process in the 1990s.[1] Moreover, it is worth stressing that the macro-political context was very much created by the British and Irish governments in terms of access to the talks, the agenda on the table and the deadlines imposed. Quite simply, the Northern Ireland political parties had to fit into the predetermined macro-political context. Despite this, mono-causal interpretations persisted for much of the process. These usually consisted of explaining the process as the 'Adams and Hume Show' or the 'David and Gerry Show'.[2] Such interpretations emphasized the role of leadership, or agency, in the process and, as one would expect, these interpretations were more often contradictory than complementary. For example, the traditional republican narrative 'involved historic compromises and magnanimous gestures in the face of obdurate opposition from truculent unionists and ungenerous British governments'.[3] One unionist narrative communicated how key unionist objectives were secured by the leadership and how the eventual agreement was 'as good as it gets'.[4] Another unionist narrative highlighted the continued capitulation of pro-agreement unionism to an overtly nationalist and republican agenda.[5] A more 'exogenous' narrative emphasized the drive, will and determination of the British, Irish and American governments above all else, complemented by the occasional and timely assistance from key personnel engaged in peace processes of their own, most notably from South Africa.[6] The Irish government saw itself as having begun the process through its Irish peace initiative under the tutelage of various Taoiseachs in Ireland since the 1970s.[7] Republicans have also claimed the mantle as the main architects of the process and point to their *Scenario for Peace* document in 1987 as the public launch of their developing peace strategy.[8] Those in support of the SDLP influence over the peace process have emphasized Hume's centrality to everything.[9]

Within such contradictory narratives, there is but one complementary aspect. Each of the narratives, in some way, emphasized the political leaders' capacity to influence the peace process. In other words, all of the narratives deemed the capacity of leadership to be significant and often explained the peace process through the actions and reactions of the various leaders engaged within in it. Although simplistic in the extreme, not least because of the often relative inattention to the various constraints on the leaders' ability to act and to react, such a narrative is still important for our understanding of the political leaders' capacity to influence the process. However, although the agency oriented narratives emphasized the political leaders' capacity to influence the peace process, these narratives tended not to deconstruct where that capacity actually lay. This gives legitimacy to the purpose of this chapter which seeks to analyse more systematically the phenomenon of political leadership during the Northern Ireland peace process and, thus, the following section turns towards an examination of the theory of influence, as a means of finding a way to systematically deconstruct the potential sources of capacity and influence upon which the political leaders in Northern Ireland could draw.

The theory of influence

There exists the tendency to use the terms power, authority and influence interchangeably. Thus, almost all of our perceptions of leadership are intricately bound up to concepts of power. Such power is usually explained as the leader's ability to produce effects on others or the ability to influence others. Power, however, is not the sole preserve of leaders. The actions of followers and the impact of situations can affect leaders' behaviour and therefore power is equally a function of leaders, followers and situations.[10] The power school of thought began with the work of Machiavelli and his approach and advice to the Prince, the elite theorists of Mosca, Pareto and Michels, and the creation of the 'political man' based on the wealth maximizing 'economic man' model. In many ways such approaches reduced politics to the seeking and exercise of political power, when the realities of history have sometimes shown leaders to rise above personal or party considerations. Gandhi is a case in point. Moreover, this power approach fails to explain what leaders do, or are expected to do once they have attained power and authority. In other words, the power-school theorists do not really explain *why* leaders choose to influence others.

Burns described the problem as viewing politics *as* power, and this skewed our understanding of the crucial role of power *in* politics.[11] Burns sought to study leaders on the basis of how they used their power, making the distinction between power wielders and leaders, with the former motivated to use their power to further their own ends and the latter motivated by both its own and its followers' needs and goals.[12] Essentially, Burns made the distinction between power as the capacity to influence others and the influence tactics actually used.[13]

As well as understanding political leader's power as the capacity to influence others, it is equally important to understand that political leaders are themselves little more than the product of different sets of influence. As Elcock points out in this respect, there are three sets of influence worthy of note, which explain a political leader's capacity to influence others.[14] First, there is the power and influence which has been derived from his or her office by virtue of the various constitutional provisions and the ability of a leader to control his/her voters.[15] Secondly, there are the events and circumstances which have led to the leader's election and period in office. For example, it is argued that those leaders brought into power as a result of a crisis can be assured more compliance from supporters than those who hold office in relatively peaceful times.[16] This is often because followers generally seem to be more willing to accept greater direction, control and structure from leaders in crisis situations.[17] The third influence stems from the abilities conferred on political leaders as a consequence of the leader's personal characteristics.

Using Elcock's analysis, the influence of office, events and personality will now be examined in the context of the peace process in Northern Ireland to ascertain how these might have contributed to the various leaders' capacity to influence the overall shape of the peace process and in order to identify whether the most potent sources of influence were more structural or personal in nature. This is particularly important because both the structural and personal sources of influence had the potential to be undermined, though often in very different ways, with the potential consequence of necessitating that the political leaders acted in different ways at different points in the process. This is particularly important to the development of the overall argument here insofar as it highlights yet another example of the contradictions and inconsistencies inherent with the political leaders' approach to the peace process.

The influence of office

One's position within a political party can be a source of power and influence with a person's 'ranking' within the party hierarchy the most obvious indicator of the source of power and influence. In general terms, 'the hierarchical context of leadership has profound effects on the personal, interpersonal, and organizational choices that can be made'.[18] However, centrality, unlike rank, does not require the same degree of hierarchy, but it is often the case that a leader with a central position of authority, as opposed to a hierarchical position of authority, is more likely to have greater access to resources and to other well connected people. Office holders of both distinctions were apparent in Northern Ireland.

There were clear distinctions between the positions of authority that the different key players held and how these positions related to their potential influence during the peace process. In the most obvious example, such distinctions are evidenced in an overview of the various mechanisms used to elect party leaders from the four main political parties and how this impacted upon their leadership capabilities. For example, the Ulster Unionist Council is an umbrella council which consists of the UUP and also representatives from the Orange Order, the Young Unionist Council, the Ulster Unionist Councillors's Association, and the Ulster Women's Unionist Council. It is this umbrella council which elects the leader of the UUP. The Executive Committee of the DUP elects the leader of its party. This Committee consists of four members from each of the Westminster Constituency Associations plus the leader and the deputy leader of the party. The leader and deputy leader of the

SDLP face annual re-election at their party conference, which consists of delegates from local branches, the General Council, District Councillors, the Women's group and the Youth Commission. For Sinn Féin, the annual party conference delegates elect the President of the party. This conference is made up of delegates from constituent branches and regional councils.[19]

Of these four electoral bodies, only the UUP's election body is made up of a completely hybrid group that has, on occasion during the peace process, appeared to have been difficult to manage. Such difficulties meant that predicting the outcome of the Council's elections was not always an easy task. Consider the illustrative example of Lee Reynolds, the 21 year old student who challenged Molyneaux's leadership in an UUC meeting in March 1995. Reynolds managed to obtain 15 per cent of the total Council votes and thus, on this occasion, Molyneaux retained the leadership of the party. Nonetheless, such a challenge at a critical period within the peace process severely undermined Molyneaux's authority in office. Consequently, Molyneaux began to command less respect from within his party and Reynold's challenge, arguably, precipitated his eventual departure from politics. The demise of Molyneaux's influence in office eventually led to his resignation on 28 August 1995.

The election of David Trimble as Molyneaux's successor was a shock and surprise for many in the field. Early indications suggested that Molyneaux himself would have preferred Willie Ross as his successor.[20] John Taylor and Ken Maginnis were heralded as the favourites by the media, given their seemingly pragmatic nature.[21] While Trimble had not entered the leadership race until only a week before the Council were due to vote on the matter, he managed to win. Much of his success in the election was put down to his decidedly hard-line ticket.[22] Although Trimble's election as leader of the UUP was a clear win for the leader, many commentators saw him as 'the leader no-one wanted'.[23] It was argued that his MP colleagues within the party did not want him as leader and his seemingly weak internal position suggested that he, at least initially, did not 'enjoy the affection that other Northern leaders inspire among their supporters'.[24] Such comments were a marked departure from those that saw Trimble's leadership as 'a positive, assertive leadership'.[25] Whilst the vote at the Council afforded Trimble considerable influence of office in electing him as their leader, the Council's attitude towards the leadership of the party did not dramatically improve after Trimble's election. Indeed, there were no less than ten leadership contests since his initial election in 1995. It is clear, that in comparison to the other political party's processes, the make-up and composition of the UUC has played a significant role in limiting the influence of office for any Ulster Unionist leader since its membership has been long fragmented and thus prone to dissension at decidedly inopportune moments. In terms of how this might have influenced the leadership of the party, it is surprising that the effect was not more pronounced.

A second distinction between the positions of authority that the different key players held and how these positions related to their potential influence during the peace process was evidenced in the different attitudes of party leaders to their positions of office. This was first touched upon in Chapter 3 with the emergence of the idea of 'reluctant leadership' among Northern Ireland's political leaders. Only Paisley seemed to be completely happy in his position as leader of the DUP. In contrast, Adams claimed not to have wanted to become President of Sinn Féin.[26] This offers a possible explanation for his willingness to delegate responsibilities of discussions and decision making to other key personnel throughout the peace process period. Trimble's attitude to becoming leader of the UUP has been described as somewhat ambivalent to begin with.[27] His eventual election was remembered as little more than a blur for Trimble and it was claimed that part of him did not want to assume the mantle of leadership at all.[28] More importantly however, was that Trimble's election was not the landslide win that Adams had experienced. Indeed, the result of the run-off ballot between the two remaining candidates, Trimble and Taylor, was 58 per cent of the vote for Trimble and 42 per cent for Taylor. This did indicate that a significant number of the Council were unhappy with the idea of affording the influence of office to Trimble at that point in the peace process, when Unionists were rather unsure about how best to approach and handle a process which they were not in control of. While Hume, as leader of the SDLP, did not face any overt challenges to his leadership of the party during his tenure of office, it has been suggested that he was subject to significant dissension within the leadership of the SDLP in relation to the strategy and approach that Hume had adopted during the peace process. However, the influence of office was not something that was alleged to have appealed to Hume anyway. Instead, Hume saw his office of leadership as a tool which he used to promote influence with other political players when necessary.[29] Moreover, it has been consistently reported that during the peace process Hume operated outside of the confines of his office and in some instances without the knowledge of other leaders within the party's elite. This led to considerable tensions within the SDLP party leadership. Indeed, the political triumph of the first IRA ceasefire for Hume was marred by the critics who accused him of being 'too autocratic, of holding too much power in his own hands, [and] of failing to bring his party colleagues along with him'.[30] Such criticisms were indicative of some loss of influence for Hume as a consequence of his earlier Hume-Adams dialogue.

The third distinction between the various positions of authority that the different key players held and how these positions related to their potential influence during the peace process, is apparent in the examination of the probability/possibility of a 'leader-in-waiting' within each of the parties. Clearly, the potential for influence and persuasion within the different political parties could have been diminished by the sound of dissenting voices within the party leadership and/or the possibility of any alternative vision during the peace process. This was more obvious in some parties than in others. It would have been unthinkable for there to have been any alternative leadership within the DUP such was the strength of character of their leader. However, the deputy leader of the DUP, Peter Robinson, was also considered to be a powerful influence within the party. An illustrative example of this was in his resignation as deputy leader of the party in 1987, after disagreements about the direction of the anti Anglo-Irish Agreement protests at that time.[31] He took up the post of deputy leader again about three months later without giving a detailed explanation as to why but his re-election to the post was indicative of the fact that he was a highly influential character within the DUP party structure.[32] For Sinn Féin, an heir apparent was not obvious. As one senior party leader said, 'Gerry is the obvious leader and on the contrary rather than people trying to take over the thing, people are probably trying to avoid it because it is such a hard task'.[33] Again, the UUP seemed to suffer most in respect of 'leader-in-waiting' syndrome. While Lee Reynolds was hardly conceived of as a 'leader-in-waiting', his leadership challenge was indicative of the wider malaise within the party and allowed for the genuine 'leaders-in-waiting' to emerge soon afterwards. Fortunately for Trimble, the numerous challenges to his leadership did not take place until after the Agreement was signed in 1998.

A final distinction between the positions of authority that the various political leaders held was that the different types of office structure also had the potential to affect the influence of leaders in office. For example, Trimble did not have the support of many of the party officers. Indeed, the Ulster Unionist leader was in a rather weak position in relation to the party organization. Despite his position as leader of the party, his influence over the party structure was limited. In his own analysis of his capacity to influence the party, Trimble noted:

The leader has no capacity to hire and fire the chief executive, which is in the hands of the officers and the UUP Executive collectively, of whom the leader is just one.[34]

Trimble's capacity to influence other leaders was stunted at the initial stages by the fact that he was 'supported by the grassroots of his party, as the most hard line of the candidates, but not by the party hierarchy or fellow MPs'.[35] Trimble therefore struggled with influence both internally and externally.

Within Sinn Féin's party structure, criticisms were made that there was no room for debate outside of the narrow band of leaders at the top of the organization and that it was reminiscent of Michel's 'iron law of oligarchy'.[36] The crux of Michel's 'iron law' involves working class leaders of workers' parties becoming transformed eventually into clones of their bourgeois counterparts, putting their own personal interests and organizational interests above the party's original ideology.[37] One party leader noted of the Sinn Féin leadership:

> Sinn Féin manages so well, they have got a thought police who don't let people say and do things. When people try to move against the leadership, they move in and remove them, and I don't mean take them away and bury them, I mean they remove them by making sure that they don't have any influence.[38]

However, another argued: 'I often wish at times that we had the capacity for executive leadership because democracy gets in the way'.[39] In other words, it was often too difficult to make dramatic moves forward because of the constraints on the leadership from constituents and party officials.

Overall, the differences between the various party leaderships in terms of the mechanisms used to elect party leaders, the attitudes of party leaders towards their positions of office, the plausibility of a 'leader-in-waiting', and differences within the party structures, all had an impact on the potential capacity of leadership to use their influence of office to shape and direct the peace process. Put simply, the influence of office and the parameters of influence within that position of office were not uniform between the various parties during the peace process. That much is clear. One point, however, stands out for further elucidation. While the influence of office can be substantial, any challenges to positions of office can seriously undermine the influence of a leader in office. For example, Reynolds's challenge to Molyneaux's leadership, in 1995 was a challenge from which Molyneaux failed to recover. In addition, the fact that Trimble was elected to office with 58 per cent of the vote in a two way ballot was directly relational to his subsequent difficulties with his party officers and fellow MPs. The result of any undermining of influence of a leader in office was, often, an inconsistent approach by leaders, in terms of handling their parties. At times, this was manifested in both the desire and attempts to operate outside of the confines of office and beyond the constraints of other leaders within the party's elite, as illustrated in the example of Hume and his engagement with Adams in the early 1990s, despite the legitimacy that his office afforded him on the world stage, not least with the various US administrations. Taken as a whole, the parameters of influence afforded by the positions of office were not stagnant and subject to change as the process moved along, even within parties. This was usually as a consequence of the influence of events that took place during the peace process.

The influence of events

Which events and particular circumstances occurred during the peace process that might have allowed for a strengthening of influence for the leadership? Obviously, the events and circumstances which led the various political leaders in Northern Ireland into office seemed to have considerable influence on their ability to engage and deliver during the process. On the one hand, given the context of Northern Ireland, it is fair to say that each leader was elected in a period of crisis. This strengthened their influence considerably, and serves as the only comparable factor between the various party leaderships. On the other hand, numerous specific events during the peace process have both enhanced and damaged the influence of leaders.

First, the Framework Document and the events which encapsulated that period of time amounted to a betrayal for James Molyneaux and was evidence of his declining influence on the political landscape. It was reported that until the time of the documents Ulster Unionism's policy was simply one of 'trust Jim'. 'Jim' had told party colleagues that he had indeed been consulted on the Framework document by British officials, as a measure of the documents acceptability to the wider unionist community. Critically though, 'the critics sensed that consultation did not mean influence'.[40] As Aughey said:

> To have played the card of the subtle, patient, behind-the-scenes, person-to-person diplomacy once – in 1985 – and to have failed was unfortunate. To have played the same card twice and to have

failed a second time seemed very like incompetence. Implicit in the criticism was the view that the task of good leadership is to ensure that history does not repeat itself. On that count, Molyneaux failed miserably... the performance of the party in the aftermath of the publication of the Frameworks was nothing other than ill-considered and ill-informed. Others, like the unfortunate Ken Maginnis, were left to pick up the pieces. This was an obvious failure of leadership.[41]

Overall then, the launch of the Framework documents, as a political event during the peace process, significantly undermined the leadership of Molyneaux and the influence of this particular event on his leadership limited his capacity to direct both his own party and the wider political process considerably.

Secondly, and as a contrast to the first example, the first IRA ceasefire in 1994 gave the Sinn Féin leadership considerable influence in the peace process not least in terms of how it propelled the republican leadership centre stage and allowed for considerable relaxing of previous restrictions on the leadership's physical movements both within the UK and internationally, and also in terms of the broadcasting restrictions which had been in place for a number of years. The subsequent breakdown of the IRA ceasefire in 1996, however, raised questions about Sinn Féin's leadership and the degree of actual influence that it wielded over the republican paramilitaries. It raised a striking contradiction. How could the leadership have been so influential in helping to secure the first ceasefire in 1994 and then wielded seemingly little to no influence in the decision made by the IRA to go back to war in 1996? In an overall analysis, it seems clear that the first event enhanced the influence of the Sinn Féin leadership while the second event seriously undermined it.

The third example is of the 'incident' which took place in Drumcree in July 1995, two months before Trimble's election as leader of the UUP, and subsequently regarded as an event which contributed significantly to the election of David Trimble as leader of the UUP. A deal had been reached between members of the Orange Order and local nationalist residents from the Garvaghy Road area to allow the Drumcree Orange Order parade to pass along the nationalist Garvaghy Road. Initial thoughts that the deal had amounted to a compromise gave way to perceived triumphalism on the part of Ian Paisley and David Trimble who joined the parade once it had reached the town centre. Both men were broadcast holding hands and dancing along the street in what were regarded, by many, as rather gleeful scenes. This was an event marked as a 'defining moment' for Trimble and was, in part, responsible for

his subsequent electoral success and all of the related influence associated with that position.[42] Indeed, many of the UUC members contacted
in the run up to the leadership election in 1995, by Trimble's election agents, also recalled Drumcree as an event in his favour. It was,
according to one election agent, 'referred to positively more than any
other issue'.[43]

Trimble's own speeches also indicated the significance that he,
himself, placed on how events influenced the nature and direction of the
peace process. Quoting from Harold Macmillan's response to a question
regarding the most difficult thing to contend with in politics, Trimble
noted that it was 'events, dear boy, events'.[44] Perhaps more importantly, Trimble further argued that 'while we wish to influence and to
shape events, while we wish to bring things about, we have to bear in
mind that we are not the only actor and we have to deal with what
happens elsewhere as well'.[45] Trimble's realization that there were other
'actors' to consider, in terms of the potential influence that they may
have had over the peace process, was an important one. Indeed, as a
potential source of influence, the capacity of the personal was not to be
underestimated in the context of Northern Ireland.

The influence of the personal

Personality matters in Northern Ireland as elsewhere. The plethora of
books, both biographies and autobiographies of the various political
leaders, is evidence of an interest in personalities, their own interest
in themselves, and their interest in conveying to us their story, their
truth, their reality.[46] The important question is why does it matter? As a
consequence of conflict and violence, perhaps there is simply a need to
believe in the power of individuals to find a way through the malaise.
This is not as far fetched as it might seem given the wealth of academic
literature on this subject.[47]

The earliest theory of leadership from this perspective is obviously the
'Great Man' theory, which is often linked to Thomas Carlyle who noted
that: 'the history of the world is but the biography of great men'.[48]
Another example from the literature which endorses the 'personality
matters' thesis is to be found in the theory of charismatic leadership,
a theory developed by Max Weber, which conceptualized one type of
authority as resting with individuals on the basis of their 'superhuman'
qualities.[49] In theory, charismatic leadership is a trait or aspect of an
individual's personality which sets that person as distinct and separate
from all others. Critically for Weber, charismatic leaders usually emerged

in times of social crisis when potential followers might be seen to be under stress from threats, oppression, or adverse social and economic conditions. Moreover, Jacobsen and House argue that it has been consistently shown that 'under conditions of threat and stress followers seek and respond positively to individuals who are bold, confident, and appear to have clear solutions to existing social problems'.[50] More cynically, it is also argued that some leaders actually purposely create crises in order to foster desire among followers for a charismatic leader to appear.[51]

It is questionable whether the characteristics noted by Jacobson and House were in evidence among political leaders in Northern Ireland during the peace process. In many respects, it is simply a matter of interpretation as to whether the political leaders were bold, confident and full of answers. Such interpretations have been the forte of the political commentators and journalists in Northern Ireland, and also leaders' interpretations of each other and of themselves. Some of these have already been discussed in Chapter 3. Others are presented here.

One interpretation has been that the political leaders in Northern Ireland during the peace process suffered from a lack of the intellectual ability necessary in order to see a way through the political process at hand. One author went so far as to ask explicitly whether the political players involved in the peace process 'contain[ed] the critical mass of moral commitment and intellectual capacity to achieve a settlement?'[52] Importantly, the crux of this debate about the charismatic and intellectual capabilities of political leaders masked a fundamentally more important question which was what leverage did personality based political leadership afford the peace process? At one level, it did give considerable leverage to the individual political leaders in terms of their ability to influence and persuade. Obviously, whether this transpired in a positive or negative context was directly relational to the individual leaders concerned. There were many examples of this. Firstly, Hume's near 'iconic' status in the US allowed him to use his 'personal' influence to press the US administration into helping Northern Ireland during the peace process. Indeed, McKittrick and McVea noted that: 'by the early 1990s he was, in sum, the most influential nationalist politician in Northern Ireland'.[53] Secondly, Adams' transition from terrorist to near statesman afforded him the opportunity to wield influence on US audiences, as well as influencing the growing interest in the south of Ireland much to the annoyance of his adversaries.[54] Thirdly, Trimble's 'proactive' approach to the leadership of the UUP was a marked departure from the leadership of the past, was seen as something of a 'refreshing change and saw Trimble try to influence the international stage also'.[55] Finally, Paisley's personality and influence has always been practically legend in Northern Ireland.[56]

There were, however, downsides to the personalization of politics, despite the level of influence that it afforded different players. The downsides were felt most sharply by the political leaders themselves. Because of the high-profile nature of many of those involved in the peace process, issues had a tendency to become personalized when, often, they were not so. Much was made of the first historic handshake between Adams and Albert Reynolds in 1994, and of Trimble's refusal to shake Adams' hand at any point during the peace process, at least prior to the eventual Agreement.[57] Similarly, much was made of Blair's decision to shake hands with Adams to such an extent that even Trimble accused the media of 'exaggerated reports of the significance of the occasion'.[58] Quite obviously, the issues at stake extended far beyond symbolic gestures between individuals; however, attention towards the latter rather than the former always seemed to dominate media coverage.

There are many contradictions to be noted in understanding the power and influence of the personal and the capacity that such power and influence afforded the political leaders at different points in the peace process. Perception and reality are two issues at the heart of the seeming contradictions. For example, while John Hume had, on the one hand, 'managed to develop the power of influence and has walked with more useful people than princes', on the other it was clear that while he was turning into an icon outside of his party, the party itself effectively lacked leadership during critical stages of the peace process.[59] The perception was that Hume had the capacity to lead his own party towards a peace process as well as the capacity to influence other actors at the international level. The reality, at least for many senior political actors within the SDLP, was that Hume was better at the latter than the former. What is most critical to any understanding of the capacity of political leadership to affect the overall peace process through their personal influence is that the perception of their personal influence often mattered as much, if not more, than the actual reality. While the perception was often that the various personalities wielded considerable influence on the nature and direction of the peace process (with the agency oriented accounts of the peace process standing as testament to this point), the reality was one of alternative sources of influence which acted as a considerable constraint on the political leaders and served, at times, to undermine the capacity to deliver during the peace process.

The perception and the reality of influence

For some, much of the peace process has been about perception as opposed to reality. Dixon identified a variety of political skills, or manipulatory practices which, he argued, were used to drive the process forward. He commented that: '. . . the choreography of the peace process may reflect a trend among politicians to emphasize the importance of "appearance" over "reality" '.[60] However, political leaders in Northern Ireland had a considerable burden placed upon their shoulders in terms of the expectations that they could, and would, deliver on a settlement. Concepts of leadership were bandied about between the various political parties in ways that were highly pejorative.[61] Even those on the outside looking in had their own distinctive notions of what political leadership and its influence was all about. Not long after the Agreement was signed, Trimble and Hume were honoured as Nobel peace prize winners. In his presentation speech to the two leaders, Professor Francis Sejersted, the Chairman of the Nobel Committee said:

> Political leadership is not to trim your sail to every wind; it is to initiate movement, and to act at the right time. Like other political leaders, the two Laureates have both helped to build confidence that it is possible to arrive at reasonable compromises by peaceful means. As political leaders, they are guarantors to their constituents that peaceful methods will lead to solutions which both sides can live with, and live better than if a state of war had continued. In a tense situation, such exposed positions require large amounts of both wisdom and courage. Today's Laureates have shown both.[62]

The awarding of the Nobel Prize to Trimble and Hume raised all sorts of questions about the accepted scripted narrative of leadership in Northern Ireland and its relationship to the 'truth' as perceived by others. There are a number of points worth mentioning in this regard. First, the definition of political leadership by Sejersted raises some concerns since it was not necessarily a definition which was inclusive of all of the different political positions in Northern Ireland. Clearly, not all leaders initiated movement and acted at the right time. Indeed, questions could be raised as to whether or not this could even legitimately have been said of Hume and Trimble. Secondly, the speech indicated that both winners had acted as guarantors within their constituencies, which ran contrary to the wisdom that not only does a leader have to bring along his or her own constituency base but equally must help deliver their enemies' constituency base also in a peace process. This did not seem evident in Northern Ireland. This then leads to the third and final point. Even within their respective acceptance speeches, Trimble and Hume had very different conceptions of what leadership meant, and where the capacity of leadership lay within the context of Northern Ireland. Consequently, each seemed to speak only to their own constituents rather than tangentially. Reading into his acceptance speech, it could be argued that Trimble did not want to attempt to influence others, and preferred to deal in actualities rather than in possibilities. He remarked:

> I am personally and perhaps culturally conditioned to be skeptical of speeches which are full of sound and fury, idealistic in intention, but impossible of implementation; and I resist the kind of rhetoric which substitutes vapour for vision. Instinctively, I identify with the person who said that when he heard a politician talk of his vision, he recommended him to consult an optician.[63]

Contrast this to Hume's requests for unionists to talk in the early days of the negotiations which was loaded with normative undertones.[64] Indeed, the normative approach towards political leadership during the peace process was such as to expect from all of the leaders a degree of 'peacemaker' in their behaviour rather than 'broker', representing a clear synonymy with that traditional argument in leadership studies that leaders will do right. One could argue whether such a role is ever possible to fulfil.

Conclusions

The influence which stemmed from the elected office of the political leaders, the influence which stemmed from events and incidents relating directly to their leadership, and the influence which came from the personalities themselves, were the influences which had most impact on the capacity of political leadership during the Northern Ireland peace process to fulfil its various roles. However, these sources of influence were not necessarily similar in terms of the impact that they actually had.

For the two governments, the influence of office was almost certainly one of the most critical for the peace process, in so far as the governments did not want to be seen to be negotiating with those without an electoral mandate, given that such an electoral mandate further endorses the political leadership of a particular political party. This, perhaps, explains the decision of the British government to use a list system for elections to the Forum and multi-party talks in 1996 since this system would ensure an electoral mandate for the loyalist parties with whom the governments had begun to engage with already.

For political leaders themselves, the influence of the personal appeared more dominant. What is particularly interesting is that political leaders focused as much on their personal capacity to influence other political leaders during the peace process as they did on their personal capacity to influence followers. In interviews, many spoke of the interaction and effects of interaction between political leaders at critical junctures of the peace process. This appeared to have as much importance for political leaders as did the interactions and effects of their interactions with followers during the peace process. While Chapter 4 has already touched upon the nature of the relationship with constituents and followers, Chapter 6 will now look specifically at the nature of the relationship between the political elites during the peace process and how, if at all, political leaders were able to have an effect on other political leaders during the process.

6
The Effect of Political Leaders on Other Political Leaders

Introduction

An anecdote is often told of a group of political leaders from Northern Ireland, standing together in a conference room in South Africa. A smaller number of these leaders are huddled together, making polite small talk as they wait for their hosts to arrive. They stand beneath a ceiling fan which has seen better days. It seems loose, as if it is ready to fall. Rather worriedly, one leader comments that it might fall down and hit them. Another responds: 'You're right – and this could be the first time that the fan hits the shit'![1] This anecdote is revealing in many ways. First, there is the tacit acknowledgment that political leaders in Northern Ireland did come together during the peace process, albeit outside of the parameters of Northern Ireland. Secondly, that in doing so they were then able to discuss matters completely unrelated to broader political events in Northern Ireland. Thirdly, that some of them showed a self-deprecating humour and others appreciated the humour enough to carry the story back to Northern Ireland and this is evidence of a trait which might ultimately help the peace process in its darker periods.[2]

Another anecdote is less encouraging. A group of somewhat similar political leaders from Northern Ireland are staying in a secured conference facility in Arniston, South Africa, as guests of the South African government. The purpose of their visit is to consider the lessons from the South African peace process in the context of their own. They arrive at South Africa separately, having departed from separate airports on different aircrafts. For the duration of their visit, they sleep in separate quarters and eat in separate canteens. An unexpected visit from Nelson Mandela is announced. He has made time in a busy schedule to meet with these political leaders to discuss their peace process. Some of the party leaders refuse to meet with Mandela if it means sharing communal space with the political adversaries they are so anxious to avoid. Mandela is forced to tolerate an apartheid type situation for three hours, first talking to one group and then to the other. His message is exactly the same to both groups.[3] The unspoken message that emanated from this display of self-imposed apartheid by some of the political leaders was first that, there was nothing more important than preserving the façade of moral superiority, even if such moral views necessitated behaviours that others might have consider immoral. Secondly, there existed an inflated sense of the leaders' own importance and grandeur in demanding that the President of South Africa accommodate them. Thirdly, there was a palpable acknowledgement that such behaviour was not 'becoming' and hence this anecdote was not relayed with the same enthusiasm as the first story, once the participants returned to Northern Ireland.

Both incidents took place during the period between 1994 and 1998, after the first IRA ceasefire and before the eventual Agreement. Told in isolation, they convey very different messages about the political leaders' attitudes and behaviours during the peace process. One is a story of hope and humour, the other a story of hardened attitudes and self-importance. Told together, they illustrate the rather 'schizophrenic' nature of the peace process and the relationships therein. Overall though, the potential effect of political leaders on other political leaders is critical to both our understanding of the peace process in general, and of political leadership in particular.

The nature of the relationship

To note that relationships between the majority of political leaders in Northern Ireland, during the early part of the peace process, were not good is an understatement. At the time of the first ceasefire in 1994, relations between the leadership of Sinn Féin and the leadership of unionism, both mainstream and fringe, were nonexistent.[4] Relations between the leadership of Sinn Féin and the leadership of the SDLP barely stretched beyond the fledgling association to John Hume.[5] Relations between Hume, in particular, and mainstream unionism were often sour with these unionists holding Hume in decidedly low esteem.[6] Relations between the unionist party leaderships had soured considerably in the period after the production of a joint-party report, *An End to Drift*, in 1987 which was critical of the party leaders' response to the Anglo-Irish Agreement.[7] Relations between mainstream unionism and loyalism emulated the fragile nature of the relationships on the nationalist side. The rise in prominence of the PUP and the UDP as a direct consequence of the loyalist ceasefire in October 1994 meant that they suddenly represented a real threat to the political careers of mainstream unionism.[8] The establishment of the Women's Coalition in 1996 was beset with significant hostility from many unionist leaders though not for electoral reasons but rather as a consequence of overt conservatism and reluctance to afford women a place at the negotiating table.[9] For their part, the Women's Coalition members made a conscious effort to build relationships with all of the political parties.

Overall, it cannot be stressed enough that the nature of inter-party relations in Northern Ireland was dysfunctional in the extreme. Many of the party leaders did not talk to one another and/or had no contemporary experience of dealing with one another. Clearly, much effort was needed if the fragile relationships between the various party leaderships were to improve as a necessary prerequisite to a holistic negotiation process. These efforts were to take place in both public and private arenas. Following the IRA ceasefire, the ensuing period bore witness to many of the first public interactions between some of the political players. While these interactions almost always happened at the individual level, it was clear that the meetings were sanctioned at party level. For example, in October 1994 Gerry Adams and Ken Maginnis (UUP) participated in a television debate in the US.[10] Mitchell McLaughlin (Sinn Féin) and Gary McMichael (UDP) shared a platform in September 1995 during a Liberal Democrat party conference in Glasgow.[11] Ken Maginnis and Pat McGeown (Sinn Féin) took part in a radio discussion in Belfast, in January 1996.[12] Pat McGeown and Gary McMichael took part in a live television debate for the first time in February 1996.[13] Mitchell McLaughlin and David Trimble shared a platform during a debate on Northern Ireland at the World Economic Forum in Switzerland in February 1996.[14] Martin McGuinness and Ken Maginnis participated in a BBC debate programme in August 1997.[15] Eventually, the individual interaction gave way to more collective interaction. This was illustrated when the UUP and Sinn Féin sat down at the same conference table for the first time during the all party talks in September 1997.[16]

It is interesting that these public interactions began outside of Northern Ireland, first in the US, and then in Britain and Europe before finally taking place in a local forum. Arguably, this was carefully choreographed and was not a case of 'by accident rather than by design'. The importance of the venue was such that public opinion could be tested in terms of the viability and acceptability of public interactions without the general public having to bear witness to the substance of these interactions initially. Also of importance was the identity of the particular leader who would represent the party. The pre-eminence of Mitchell McLaughlin at the meetings with unionists was explained by Adams, who argued that McLaughlin was: 'an innovative thinker who was described as being able to get to parts of unionism other republicans couldn't reach'.[17] The subtext of this was that McLaughlin was not perceived to have 'dirty hands' from previous paramilitary activities. He had never been in the IRA, nor had he been a political prisoner, therefore it was likely that the unionists would have slightly less difficulty in engaging with McLaughlin than with some of the leaders considered to have had more 'colourful' pasts. A more cynical interpretation was that McLaughlin was also more dispensable than Adams if things went 'wrong' for Sinn Féin during the course of such interactions with unionists.

In addition to these tentative first steps in public however, the various political leaders had been meeting together in various private forums. These private forums acted as a mechanism in which the leaders could engage in some type of 'pre-negotiation' activity. However, despite the argument that 'the beginning of the process of pre-negotiation is generally marked by a turning point in the relationship between the parties', this was very clearly not the case in Northern Ireland.[18] Indeed, the very point of these private forums was designed to help facilitate a turning point in relationships. One key objective, from the perspective of those hosting events, was to try to improve the poor relations between the political leaderships, and thus by extension, was an attempt to improve the prospects of the peace process more generally.

Changing the relationship among political leaders – the events

Track-two type work was not a new phenomenon in Northern Ireland. During the conflict and the early period of the peace process, much effort was made to engage with others. From a political leadership perspective, the cover of track-two work facilitated much needed dialogue. While 'traditional' track-two is normally reserved for interactions between middle ranking officials, non-political players, and private citizens to come together, it could be argued that the track-two forums were used to bring track-one players together in a different context. Arguably, this approach could best be described as the engagement of 'track one actors in a track-two context', or alternatively 'track one and a half'.[19] Given the necessarily discreet nature of such forums, there may have been a significantly higher number of 'track one and a half' initiatives than those which have been publicly acknowledged.

It is impossible to know all of the different initiatives undertaken in an attempt to engage the different party political leadership in a dialogue outside of the parameters of the normal peace process, such that they were during the early and latter parts of the peace process. Within the public domain, the South African initiatives are perhaps the most well-known of the various endeavours, and yet little has been documented about these. In 1994, the Institute for Democracy in South Africa (IDASA) hosted separate groups of political leaders from Northern Ireland to come to South Africa in order that they could study the South African experience of negotiations.[20] The political representatives came from the four main constitutional parties at that time, the UUP, the SDLP, the DUP and the Alliance Party. All of the representatives took part in the visit in a private capacity rather than as accredited representatives of their parties.[21]

In 1995, the Project on Justice in Times of Transition organized a conference in Belfast on 'Reconciliation and Community: The Future of Peace in Northern Ireland'. This conference hosted most of the key political leaders in Northern Ireland either as speakers or as conference delegates. The purpose was to highlight some of the important lessons from the experiences of other countries which held resonance for the Northern Ireland peace process.

Following this in 1996, a workshop was organized for political leaders from Northern Ireland, the Republic of Ireland and Great Britain by the Foundation for a Civil Society, a part of The Project on Justice in Times of Transition, and the J.F.K School of Government and Public Policy at Harvard University. A goal of the project was: 'to provide the participants with a unique and valuable opportunity to form personal linkages and develop mutual trust across faction lines – the foundations for effective negotiations and political co-operation'.[22] One of the objectives was: 'to increase the confidence and comfort level of the participants, who as political leaders must make difficult decisions, by providing practical advice on leadership and governance within a heterogeneous society'.[23] In fact, the subject of leadership was one of the central areas of discussion throughout the week-long workshop. In particular, the workshop was designed to examine the challenge of leadership in divided communities by looking at the policy aspects of leadership; the dynamics of leadership; political frameworks for leadership; and the relationship between leadership and the process.[24]

The various political parties were invited to choose their own representatives to the workshop, rather than direct approach by the conference organizers. This was a marked departure from previous initiatives whereby approaches were made to individuals within the different parties to ask them to take part in the initiatives. With the notable exception of the Women's Coalition, not one party chose to send their party leaders to the event, despite the fact that leadership was to be one of the central areas of discussion. The position and status of those in attendance could best be described as variable, with some parties choosing to be represented by key spokespersons and 'would-be' leaders and others choosing to send less well-known or obvious personalities.

In 1997, during a period of impasse in the multi-party talks, a group of senior level politicians from Northern Ireland travelled to South Africa at the invitation of the South African government, for the second of the South African initiatives. The event was convened by the National Democratic Institute (NDI), the John W. McCormack Institute of Public Affairs of the University of Massachusetts in the US and the Department of Provincial Affairs and Constitutional Development in South Africa who headed up the arrangements. The trip was purposely low key lest the confidential arrangements for the event be jeopardised.[25] That such a cross section of political leaders from Northern Ireland attended this event was significant. However, the caveat for the mainstream unionist political leaders was that they were not prepared to share space with Sinn Féin during the trip to South Africa, either professionally or socially.[26]

An overview of the various events raises a number of points which warrant further articulation. First, progress was made between 1994 and the eventual Agreement in terms of the inclusion of participants and the profile of participants. In 1994, the DUP leadership was reluctant to engage with initiatives that were inclusive of Sinn Féin, but by 1997 one participant had joined with other unionist leaders at the South African indaba, in a bizarre scenario which allowed them to be together but yet still separate from Sinn Féin. Secondly, the status of some participants became significantly higher as more events took place and as the multi-party negotiations gathered momentum. In 1994, those who travelled to South Africa as guests of IDASA were there in a personal capacity only. By 1997, the key negotiators from all of the political parties were in South Africa. The smaller political parties were the most consistent in their representation at events. For example, David Ervine, of the PUP, was in attendance at every event. Conversely, Sinn Féin and the UUP varied their participants the most. Arguably, there are benefits to both approaches – on the one hand a varied participant list ensured wider exposure for a greater number of people, but on the other hand a more limited participant list allowed for in-depth exposure of a smaller number of people. Thirdly, the apparent readiness of Ulster Unionism, in particular, to engage with Sinn Féin in a public arena was not met by a similar readiness to engage with the party leadership in a private arena. This ran contrary to the expectation that in politics, political leaders would grandstand against their political adversaries in public, but would behave with a degree of propriety in private. Certainly, it was the case that the more public interactions between the unionist leaders and Sinn Féin leaders were highly charged, but the fact that such debates took place at all was regarded as political progress. One key observation can be made here. Contradictions and inconsistencies were apparent in almost every example. The DUP leadership contradicted its stance on not sitting down with members of Sinn Féin in any capacity through its decision to take part in the 1997 South African initiative, regardless of the protestations, that they did not actually share the same space with Sinn Féin during that trip. Sinn Féin and the UUP were wholly inconsistent in terms of their representation at the different initiatives. Moreover, the UUP took an overtly contradictory stance in terms of readiness to engage with Sinn Féin in one set of circumstances but yet not in another. Such inconsistencies seem impossible to justify or explain at first glance. However, they might be best explained by an examination of the motivating factors which encouraged the various political leadership to take part in the events organized.

Relationship building among political leaders – the motivations

The motives that lead political leaders to reach an accommodation, according to Nordlinger, are the existence of a common external threat; recognition that conflict distracts from economic wellbeing; a drive for power when incentives are so structured; and avoidance of bloodshed or suffering.[27] However, the various events and exercises which took place between 1994 and 1998, did not necessarily seek to find accommodation. Simply, they sought to bring the various leaders together to hear one another's perspectives, to begin then to understand one another's perspectives, and then eventually to begin to respect one another's perspectives. Thus, it raises the question, what were the motivating factors which led the various political leaders to engage in these exercises? Clearly, the objective of those organizing the events was to build and develop relationships between the players, but can the same be said of the leaders themselves? Did they avail of the opportunities presented in order that they could hear and understand the perspectives of their political adversaries? Or were their motives more self-serving?

It would be naïve to assume that the motivations of the leadership necessarily matched the motivations of those organizing the events. Indeed, some of the more intransigent leaders did not see the need for alternative, informal approaches, tended to be dismissive of such initiatives and refused to engage at all. Of those who were less dismissive, the motivating factors varied. In total, the motives which led political leaders to engage in track-two type processes during the peace process could be defined as the opportunity to go junketeering (albeit a rather cynical view); a genuine curiosity about other leaders given that interactions at home were usually limited; fear of being perceived as the intransigent or unwilling partner in a peace process; fear of positive relations developing between political adversaries in the absence of other leaders' disapproval; seeking affirmation or legitimacy from other political leaders; and finally, seeking to influence other party leaders. Such motivations varied from individual to individual more so than from party to party.

Junketeering or 'political tourism', while cynical, is one reason for a leader's engagement with the track-two process.[28] Otherwise known as 'visititis', this chronic condition worked on the assumption that leaders could not turn down the prospect of just about any foreign trip.[29] This point could not have been lost on the organizers of the various initiatives. If the fact that an event was held in a luxurious, sought-after, interesting spot, the likelihood of participants accepting would always be higher than if the venue was closer to home. Hence, the appealing locations might have been used as bait with which to hook participants. It appeared to work. In interview, one party leader noted of the South African trip in 1997, that 'it was luxury and was good craic'.[30] Another leader was reported to have been concerned about how his voters would react to his 'unseasonally bronzed visage' after the 1994 South African trip and vowed to stay away from the television cameras for a period afterwards.[31]

The second motivating factor was a genuine curiosity about other leaders on a personal level that could not be pursued on home territory. In the absence of television crews and constituents, these initiatives afforded the various political leaders the opportunity to indulge in such inquisitiveness. Despite the fact that in 1997, the South Africans had catered for the Northern Ireland participants in apartheid fashion with separate planes, separate dining halls, and separate bars, one unionist leaders noted: 'I made it quite clear that irrespective of the issue of a united Ireland which I was not likely to concede easily, I was likely to concede my position at the bar', and chose to drink in the same bar as the somewhat ostracized Sinn Féin representatives.[32] Another party leader chose to picnic with the Sinn Féin representatives, on a day trip, despite the 'apartheid' caveat. As the Sinn Féin leader recalled:

> We went on a day trip to the southern most tip of South Africa, and they [unionists] wouldn't go on the bus with us. The bus came, and they wouldn't get on it. So we got into a minibus, got the picnic in, and two of the South African Ministers came with us and had a great time, and in fairness to _____ [s] he also came with us. [S] he said 'this is nonsense, I'm going with them'.[33]

Indeed, it appeared that the bar and the social outings organized did make a difference towards satisfying the levels of curiosity that each might have held in respect of the other. Again, the social activities were consciously factored into arrangements by event organizers, who were aware of the potential such informal interaction afforded. This was clearly evident to the organizers of the 1996 Harvard event also. The various informal social events, purposely built into the programme in Boston:

> offered participants the opportunity to quietly discuss substantial issues related to the situation in Northern Ireland in a relaxed and non-confrontational atmosphere. Because of the climate of trust that had developed over the course of the day, discreet discussions between representatives of some of the key protagonists in the Northern Ireland conflict took place.[34]

Thirdly, the fear of being perceived as the intransigent or unwilling partner in a peace process is a motivation which might explain the rationale for the unionists' decision to attend these initiatives albeit with the proviso to remain separate from Sinn Féin. Not to take part could be perceived to be more intransigent than to take part with a number of provisions in place. Not all followed this rationale. The South African hosts were said to be 'almost mesmerized by the behaviour of the Northern Irish politicians, by the fear on the part of some of even occupying the same physical space as others'.[35] For the event organizers, sharing the same space separately is one step forward from refusing to share space at all. Therefore, the 'provisos' were noted as progress from previously held positions.

Fourthly, the fear of relations developing between erstwhile political adversaries in the absence of others may have propelled some of the participants to take part in events. In particular, the fear of secret negotiations taking place, and of subsequent deals being done by freezing out some players, was enough to convince some of the more 'conspiratorially minded' players to take part in the process.

Fifthly, some engaged in these initiatives as a way of seeking affirmation of their own political convictions. When asked about the learning experience of South Africa in 1997, one party leader noted: 'In lots of cases, we had our own opinions vindicated but we also learned from the negotiations out there'.[36] The trips to South Africa were particularly 'easy' for the Sinn Féin leadership to undertake, given the strength of affinity that the leadership felt for South Africa.[37] Others engaged as a way of seeking affirmation of themselves from other party leaders. In other words, some took part in order that they became legitimized through the process. One Ulster Unionist representative was adamant that Sinn Féin did not seek to meet with the UUP because they had something important to discuss, but more simply because of the legitimacy that Sinn Féin would be able to garner as a result of that meeting.[38]

Finally, there was the notion that some of these events would afford political leaders the space and the opportunity with which to try to influence or even 'pressure' other political leaders. In most instances, this was an implicit rather than an explicit motivating factor. Again, referring to South Africa in 1997 and the apartheid situation therein, one party leader noted:

> Unionism would not sit in the same canteen there and they ended up being pressured. Not pressured in a very direct way, but being pressured because they knew that here were these black South Africans who had been oppressed in great magnitude. Hatred was absolute. Yet here they all were in Arniston and they were capable of having been through all of this and being able to sit down and talk it out. Here, on the other hand were the unionists, who were supposed to be much more sophisticated, coming from an alleged first world democracy and they could not even say hello or sit in the same canteen.[39]

These various motivating factors betrayed a range of attitudes by the political leaders in relation to notions of relationship building between them. The simple reality was that the majority of leaders did not

attend events in order to proactively build relations with their political adversaries, or even to try to influence other political leaders. The
converse of this point is no less true however. The majority of political
leaders did not attend events because of some bizarre 'visititis' condition. It can be safely concluded that most leaders' motives fitted on the
continuum somewhere beyond mild curiosity and before active seeking
to influence others.

Relationship building among political leaders – the impact

The impact of the various initiatives and events that took place between
the various political leaderships needs to be examined in different
contexts. First at the personal level, what was the impact of the initiatives
on improving the poor relations between the political leaders? Secondly
at the micro-political level, what was the impact of the initiatives in
terms of the lessons learned from other case studies and experiences?
Finally at the macro-political level, what was the impact of the initiatives
in terms of the development of the overall peace process, and in particular, of the talks process? It should be noted that measuring the actual
impact of the initiatives is a difficult if not impossible task. Neither eval-
uations, interviews, monitoring over time of political and social developments, nor counter factual tests have enough scientific precision to
prove a direct correlation between the initiatives and subsequent formal
political developments.[40]

Overall then, how useful were the relationship building exercises at
actually improving the poor relations which existed between the political leaders? In terms of how the initiative contributed to improving
the poor relations between the political leaders, there is both a short
term and a longer term analysis. In the short term, some incremental
changes were noted in relationships. After one other trip to South Africa,
Tom Hartley, Sinn Féin's National Chairperson said that the event had
allowed him to learn 'imaginative ways of co-operation, compromise,
and the significance of personal contact and trust'.[41] The significance
of personal contact was not lost on the smaller political parties who
refused to tow the mainstream unionist line of no contact with the Sinn
Féin leadership, during the various initiatives, and in the subsequent
multi-party talks process. The PUP, UDP, the Women's Coalition and
the Alliance Party all made progress with each other and with Sinn Féin
during this period. A key distinction was made between personal contact
and political contact and the smaller parties were more than willing
to engage in the former as a precursor to the latter. These incremental

shifts in relations were often difficult for the outside eye to see. Indeed, O'Malley said that the South African hosts were astounded by the degree of division between the parties during their 1997 trip, despite earlier initiatives.[42] Coming together separately might seem something of an oxymoron to the outside observer, but yet coming together in whatever capacity was significant progress from previous events.

The longer term impact is more difficult to analyse. For David McKittrick, a political journalist and commentator on Northern Ireland, the eventual agreement owed nothing to an improvement in personal relations between political leaders. He argued in the week leading up to the Agreement:

> This is not to assert that some new bonds of friendship and fellowship have been forged: It's not like that. This is Northern Ireland, and there remain vicious personal antagonisms, between unionism and nationalism and indeed within those two camps. If there was a change in the chemistry it is a political phenomenon, not a personal one.[43]

McKittrick, like the fringe leaders above, made a key distinction between the political and the personal except that he notes the shift in being the former rather than the latter. How can these two positions of the political and the personal be reconciled? Arguably, one is inconceivable without the other. It could be considered somewhat naïve to assume that political developments took place in Castle Buildings during the talks process in the absence of personal developments. Indeed, almost all accounts of the intense negotiations which took place in Castle Buildings in late 1997 and early 1998 mention the environment in which political decisions were taken and the other actors within that environment. For example, Adams remembered that there was no space for private 'off the record' meetings with other participants and that this was essential to progress, even in terms of simply initiating conversations with unionists.[44] However, unlike their trip to South Africa in 1997, negotiators at Castle Buildings did not have the luxury of dual dining rooms to eat in. Again Adams recalls:

> Even though all of the various factions ate in their own groups, sometimes we ended up in the non-segregated food line. I always said hello. The more rounded unionists would usually reply.[45]

Moreover, the Women's Coalition view seems to concur with the observation that personal hostilities were thawing during the negotiations.

The most obvious change in relationships was notable by the end of Easter week in 1998. Kate Fearon from the Women's Coalition made the point that much of the relationship building took place late at night between delegates. She said:

> It provided genuine opportunities to get to know other parties' delegates socially, on a human level, which had never happened before . . . the small bar area was the fullest it had ever been, late into the night, the squeeze making it impossible to ignore those around you . . . everyone would be in the bar or the canteen watching the wall to wall coverage of the negotiations . . . If someone made a strong, passionate statement and particularly if they scored a direct hit on Paisley . . . there would be loud cheering and laughter in the bar. Whenever the same hero or heroine of the airwaves re-entered the bar, there was sure to be a drink or applause awaiting them.[46]

On the other hand, some personal relationships, which did not seem hugely problematic during the various initiatives, had begun to deteriorate during the talks process as opposed to improve. David Ervine was said to have realized only during the course of the talks that many unionists hated him more than they hated Gerry Adams. He said:

> We were alien in so much as we were 'breaking the line'. Wee working-class boys, such as us, are not expected to have opinions that are, certainly, out of step with the Grand Democrats. But above all, Gerry Adams can't take their votes.[47]

Thus, it is clear that not all political leaders bought into McKittrick's analysis.

While acknowledging the huge political difference that existed between the leaders of unionism and nationalism, one unionist leader pointed out:

> I may not have any mutual consensus with other parties but I can have an affinity with those parties because they got up off their butts in the election year and got a mandate. I have a greater affinity with those people than those who say from the sidelines: do this, do that and the other, we're behind you . . . there was an affinity from when I met them the first time in the talks.[48]

In both the short-term and longer-term analysis, questions must be asked as to how much of the improvement in personal relations was genuine rather than contrived? Adams remarked that the unionists seemed to think Sinn Féin was in a 'love blitz' against them when they entered the talks in September 1997. The unionist complaint according to Adams was that:

> Smiling Shinners were always at hand to open doors and to greet them at every opportunity. We were behaving normally, and some of the more rounded unionists continued to respond in kind when they were on their own. But, in a group they returned to ignoring us again. The more decent ones still had the grace to look slightly embarrassed. With good cause. A genuine 'Good morning. How are you?' earlier was replaced by a sullen juvenile group stare later in the day, especially if the group included some of the harder elements.[49]

In the final analysis, it is impossible to unequivocally attribute any thaw in personal hostilities to the initiatives which took place. Whether they actually helped to cultivate them is still a matter of some speculation.

The second area of the potential impact of the various relationship building initiatives needs to be considered particularly in terms of the lessons learned from other case studies and experiences.[50] These ranged from specific lessons to the more general. In relation to the South Africa initiative in 1997, the lessons that the South Africans identified as having significant salience to the Northern Irish case study were: that there should be transparency and openness in the negotiating process but that some deals must be done in confidence although not in secret; there must be no fudge factors; progress only comes when negotiating parties learn to start trusting each other; parties must put themselves into the shoes of their protagonists; the level of trust that develops among negotiators is a function of their ability to communicate outside the formal settings of negotiating structures at crucial points; if political consensus is to emerge, then mutual trust and respect, tolerance of others, and a willingness to compromise must exist at all levels; party leaders should not act as their parties' chief negotiators; at every level, negotiations should involve the inherent risk of compromise since compromise is the essential ingredient of negotiations; the concept of sufficient consensus, rather than being defined in an arithmetical way, should be defined with more flexibility as that level of consensus that allows the process to move on to the next stage or does not result in the process breaking down; timetables are important but they should not be overriding; all parties must feel an equal ownership in the process; negotiations break down and during these times parties should establish backchannels to each other; technical committees are probably the most underestimated but indispensable tool of the peace process; negotiators must recognize that it might not be possible to reach compromise on some issues and will need to employ a deadlock breaking mechanism; only win, win settlements work; process is everything; when your party knows that an issue is 'non-negotiable' as far as the other party is concerned, never turn your knowledge of that into a demand that you know the other cannot meet; know thine enemy; trust should not be confused with friendship or with the kinds of trust that build friendships'.[51] Additionally, O'Malley said that he hoped that participants had learned 'the depth of commitment, compromise, and leadership required in negotiations'.[52] These were the lessons offered by the South Africans. The lessons that different participants learned are inclusive of some of those offered but not all.

Martin McGuinness claimed that a lesson learned was: 'I could learn to love my enemy'.[53] Perhaps, in a novel way, this explains the Sinn Féin 'love-blitz' during the negotiations. The lesson for Gregory Campbell was that 'the process was in the ownership of the participants'.[54] Perhaps this explains the DUP's decision to become part of the process once the agreement had been reached rather than continue to abstain from participation in the process. David Ervine commented: 'I think the constitutional unionist politicians were very affected by South Africa. Trimble and Robinson were. Robinson's own admission to me on the way back in the airport at Johannesburg made it very clear that he found it a very significant journey and a very significant experience'.[55]

Not all participants concurred with this analysis however. One of the biggest disappointments for one loyalist leader was how quickly the lessons had been forgotten.

> The DUP had learnt [in South Africa in 1997], like the rest of us, that you don't walk away from the process . . . you should always be there fighting your corner. I thought Peter Robinson learnt that lesson, but when he came back here the party overturned the decision.[56]

This particular leader saw the limitations of the party structures as the main difficulty with learning from elsewhere in so far as a personal transition does not equate to a party transition. The question is about how much influence a person has on his or her party. He goes on to discuss this in the context of Harvard in 1996:

I don't mean to be disrespectful but there were people there from the SDLP and the Alliance Party and from the Ulster Unionists and they were never going to have any impact on the party when they got back. At least the Ulster Unionist woman admitted that when she came back . . . it wouldn't make one iota of a difference to her party.[57]

Importantly, this was a point which had clear resonance with that of the sometimes restrictive nature of the party structures on the potential influence of leaders in office, as discussed in Chapter 5. The other lessons not learned were also highlighted:

Maybe we didn't learn some of the lessons that we might have learned about keeping contact and developing contact and sustaining contact between the parties here when difficulties arose. We didn't learn those lessons in the way we should have from the South African experience.[58]

In the final analysis of the impact in terms of particular lessons learned, it seems that a common lesson from the different initiatives was that of developing trust. To briefly reiterate the lessons from South Africa 1997, the main point was that progress would only come once parties started to trust each other. All other progress would necessarily flow from this one development. Roelf Meyer made a similar point earlier in 1995 at the Managing Diversity Conference. He said that even when you disagree, negotiators can still respect and trust one another.[59] Jeffrey Donaldson, at the same event in 1995, took this notion of trust among negotiators a step further and argued that trust must be built at the broad political level, not just among politicians.[60] It seems clear that by the time of the agreement in 1998, this lesson had only been learnt in theory but not yet in practice and that the actions of political leaders contradicted their understandings of the theory. This was most obvious in the often fractious nature of the multi-party negotiations, a point which will be examined in greater detail in the following chapter. For now, it is sufficient to say that much of the trust building work which had begun under the auspices of the various relationship building initiatives was, to an extent, undermined by the particularly adversarial nature of the talks process with the consequence of negating some of the potential effect that political leaders had on other political leaders.

The last area of potential impact emanating from the relationship building exercises was in terms of the development of the overall peace process, and in particular, the intense negotiations from late 1997 to

Easter week in 1998. The ultimate question is, did the initiatives, and the relationships developed therein, help to contribute to wider political progress? In other words, did the prenegotiation matter? For Monica McWilliams from the Women's Coalition, this was clearly the case in terms of South Africa 1997. She said:

> It was probably a critical turning point in our negotiations and it happened at the right time which was gratuitous inasmuch as it couldn't have been planned to have happened at the critical turning point.[61]

The more cynical view would be that the initiatives did not matter, as illustrated in some of the motivations of other participants. However, the important point here is that while it might be difficult to prove in measurable terms the actual impact on wider political developments, it is equally difficult to disprove the analysis. The transfer of learning from the micro-level to the macro-level is more likely plausible when one considers the range of actors engaged in some of the initiatives. In general, it is fair to assume that if participants represent the top leadership and include their likely negotiators then transfer is more likely. This was clearly the case in Northern Ireland. Influence is thus dependent on both the status of participants and the lessons learned. One without the other will not have the same degree of impact.

In distilling again the most important points of all of this for the development of the overall argument, a number of issues stand out which sit easily with the contention that political leadership during the Northern Ireland peace process was often necessarily contradictory and inconsistent in both style and substance. First, a contradiction was detected in terms of the attitudes and actions of some of those involved in the relationship building exercises. One leader summed this point up rather succinctly when they noted that they had taken part in one initiative and found that it was good, but yet would not concede that it had the potential to make a difference in terms of the overall peace process. Secondly, the inconsistency of participation throughout the various initiatives, whilst often for fairly valid reasons such as that the smaller parties did not have enough 'senior' political players' through which to rotate participants, undermined some of the potential of political leaders in terms of their influence on other political leaders. Thirdly, the behaviour of the various political leaders was often demonstrably different beyond the confines of Northern Ireland in comparison to their behaviour at home. Many anecdotal stories were revealed during the course of this research which indicated the softer side of the personalities involved, though it was made explicitly clear that these stories were not for citation. Fourthly and finally, the contradictory nature of the (limited) developing relationships beyond the immediacy of the relationship building initiatives was apparent in examples such as the nature of the relationship between the UUP and the loyalist parties. At some points in the process, the relationship between the two seemed to be positive and resulted in the parties' leaderships standing shoulder to shoulder when returning to the talks process after the departure of the DUP and the UKUP in 1997. At other points in the process, the relationship was alleged to have deteriorated with Ervine pointing out that during the course of the talks he discovered that many unionists disliked him more than they disliked Adams. Collectively, these contradictions and inconsistency of behaviour served to negate the potential of personal influence during the peace process.

Conclusions

Mo Mowlam drew very positive conclusions about the impact of relationship building initiatives such as those mentioned here.[62] Indeed, she believed that progress could be made in the final weeks of the talks process in 1998 by taking the various party leaders away from the television cameras, which had camped outside Castle Buildings at Stormont, to somewhere more remote. The argument in support of this was that while the political leaders were making some progress behind closed doors during the talks, their inevitable, subsequent grand standing to the awaiting media was not helpful. She was alleged to have joked about holding the final talks on an island in the Arctic.[63] In drawing more substantial conclusions about the extent to which political leaders can influence other political leaders in a peace process, a number of points can be made. The most obvious point has to be the schizophrenic nature of the peace process and the relationships therein during the period from 1994 to 1998. This was demonstrated implicitly rather than explicitly throughout the course of the chapter. Political leaders veered between only engaging publicly, to only engaging privately, to not engaging at all with other leaders. Equally, in terms of their attitudes they veered between placing significant emphasis on track-two initiatives, to placing no emphasis on it at all. Such changes in behaviour and attitudes could be attributed to the influence of other leaders. By way of conclusion, the contradictory nature of the relationships and the shifts in those relationships are reviewed in order to illustrate how they ultimately served to negate at least some of the potential of personal influence during the peace process.

First, it seems clear that the public arena provided the opportunity for political leaders to talk at each other. Private space provided the opportunity for political leaders to talk to each other. Whether political leaders availed of the opportunity to talk to others in the private arena was in no way relational to their decision to engage each other publicly and was an evidence of an obvious contradiction of political leadership. There were numerous examples of Sinn Féin leaders and the Ulster Unionists debating on television in the period prior to 1997. However, this did not negate the request for separate facilities in a private capacity and therein lay the schizophrenic nature of their relationship. Some political leaders, thus, seemed to be more concerned about the possibilities of the private than the public. In a convoluted sense, this meant that the private interaction was considered to have much more potential influence and impact than the more public interaction, hence the potential 'fear' factor associated with engaging in this type of work.

Conversely though, there were no examples of Sinn Féin and the DUP engaging on a public platform in the period between 1994 and 1998. A number of tentative steps were taken in private however. The DUP chose to participate in the initiative in South Africa 1994 with the assurance that Sinn Féin would not participate. They chose not to take part in the initiative in Harvard 1996 because Sinn Féin had been included. They then chose to take part in the initiative in South Africa 1997 despite the fact that Sinn Féin had been included, albeit with the proviso that they would be kept separate from their perceived political adversaries. While the policy on public interaction was absolute, the policy on private interactions seemed to be more fluid and did shift during that four year period. In this respect, it is clear that track-two processes with track-one leaders yielded more beneficial returns than the more public encounters between the different leaders. The benefits, however, could have been greater had a more consistent approach been taken in terms of the political leaders' engagement in the various initiatives since it would have allowed a longer time for relationships to have developed and become established before the critical stages of negotiation.

The second conclusion is that it appeared that the motivation for engagement in a private arena did not have to be altruistic in order for progress to be made. While some case study evidence suggests that pren-egotiation is 'triggered by an attempt to prevent a crisis or to manage a relationship in the wake of a recent crisis', these were not the motivating factors for engagement of Northern Ireland's political leaders.[64] Altogether, the motivating factors propelling Northern Ireland's political leaders towards such initiatives were more self-serving. At worst, they were for pure junketeering purposes; at best was a sense of curiosity about the other. The fact that they were motivated by more selfish than selfless reasons did not necessarily negate the potential for influence, once the initiative had taken place and the political leaders had actually engaged with them.

Thirdly and finally, the change in relationships, whilst critical to the peace process, took time, predated even the most tentative pre-negotiation initiatives and were not deflected by the often apparent contradictions and inconsistent behaviour of some of the political leaders. There were ten steps in all towards developing relationships which were of potential benefit to the peace process in Northern Ireland, though these may also be applicable more broadly. Dealing with a situation where relationships were poor or non-existent, the first step was to create the context for sharing the same space, albeit a large space; secondly, to create the context for sharing the same smaller space separately; thirdly, sharing the same space together (even if dialogue does not take place); fourthly, dialogue through another conduit (for example, a chairperson) in the same room; fifthly, direct confrontational dialogue; sixth, genuine dialogue; seven, the development of understanding; eight, the development of respect; nine, the development of trust; finally steps towards negotiations. While, in theory, it is probably best that these steps take place sequentially, it was obvious, at least in the context of Northern Ireland, that there were many instances of 'two steps forward and one step back' type behaviour. The stagnated progress made among Northern Ireland's political leaders stand as testament to this point though clearly there were other militating factors at play which could explain the stagnating progress and the stop start approach by political leaders towards engagement with one another, not least that the very ethos of the relationship building exercises sat in direct contradiction to the adversarially structured nature of the multi-party negotiations. These militating factors will be discussed in much detail in the following chapter, as the limitations on the role, capacity and effect of political leadership during the Northern Ireland peace process.

7
The Limitations of Role, Capacity and Effect

Introduction

In summary thus far, the purpose of this book has been to analyse more systematically the phenomenon of political leadership during the peace process in Northern Ireland using three interconnected foci – that of the role, capacity and effect of political leadership. Beginning at a very general level, it has sought to both explain and define the nature of political leadership during the period between 1994 and 1998 in Northern Ireland, as perceived by both the political leaders themselves and also those commentators and analysts following the peace process. While some of the definitions discussed in Chapter 3 were revealing, it was clear that a more robust definition was needed which could put clear water between the more general concepts of political leadership, as articulated in Chapter 2, and those which were more specific to the context of a conflicted society. Hence, political leadership as a concept, in the context of the Northern Ireland peace process, was deconstructed into its constituent parts of role, capacity and effect for further examination. Collectively, these chapters on role, capacity and effect have illustrated some of the difficulties in grasping the various contours of political leadership in the context of a peace process.

This chapter seeks to expand on some of the difficulties facing political leaders during that time. Its starting point is the presentation of an argument that has been drawn from an overall analysis of the previous three chapters. The crux of this argument is that political leadership suffered, at times, from confused roles, undermined capacity and negated effects. At the heart of the role confusion for political leaders were two key issues: the first was whether their ultimate role in the peace process was to do the right thing for the greater good and whether this was, in the context of the needs and demands of their own constituents, the right thing to do; and the second point of role confusion was apparent in the frequent comparisons of Northern Ireland's political leaders with those from the context of other peace processes. The undermined capacity of political leadership was evidenced in the usual manner not only through internal wrangling, intra-party politics and broader political events, but also through the over-personalization of the entire peace process, and the problems associated with that. The negated effect of political leaders on one another, despite some of the more positive developments of the relationship building exercises illustrated in Chapter 6, was evidenced and exacerbated by the often adversarial nature of the multi-party talks process.

Whilst some of these difficulties facing the leadership have already been touched upon in the relevant chapters, the focus of this chapter is to present them here more explicitly, as four key issues which affected the potential role, capacity and effect of political leadership during the pre-agreement process. Thus, the four issues for consideration are: the moral and ethical dimension of political leadership; the issue of borrowing lessons from other leaders and the 'impersonation' of other leaders in the peace process, both of which contributed to the likelihood of confused roles; the personalization of the peace process, which tended to diminish leadership capacity; and the nature of relationship building in an adversarial process, a process which sometimes caused a negated effect on developing leader–leader relations. Each will be considered in turn.

Moral and ethical dimensions of political leadership

The morality and ethics of leadership is an issue which has been the subtext of much of the preceding chapters. In this chapter then, there are two fundamental questions to be considered: what were the various moral and ethical dimensions of political leadership? How did these issues of morality and ethical or unethical behaviour ultimately affect the role, capacity and effect of political leaders during the peace process? The overall position here is that though moral arguments were often used to both persuade and dissuade political leaders from talking to one another during the peace process, and more fundamentally, to both persuade and dissuade political leaders from even taking part in the peace process, there was an inconsistency in even adhering to the moral arguments and positions that the political leaders themselves had put forward.

Questioning the various moral and political dimensions of political leadership is necessary not least because of the significant divergence of opinion on the issue of what is moral and what is not. To use a general example by way of illustration first, many people believe capital punishment is immoral, yet others do not.[1] In the context of Northern Ireland during the peace process, many people believed that support for violence was immoral, others did not. Many people believed that ignoring a democratically elected mandate was immoral, others did not. Many people believed that having a criminal conviction was immoral, others did not. Many people believed that talking to previously convicted 'terrorists' was immoral, others did not.

A similar point can be made in relation to the analysis of political leadership's capacity to influence the nature and direction of the peace process. Attempting to understand a political leader's capacity and influence in the absence of any moral or ethical dimension can make for a rather weak argument. In some cases, it could be argued that political influence was directly relational to issues of a distinctly moral, or otherwise, nature. For example, it can be argued that much of the Sinn Féin leaderships' influence, both with their constituents and with the British and Irish governments, was derived from their alleged links to the IRA. The influence which had been derived from 'office' in so far as they had had an electoral mandate for a considerable number of years was clearly less important than the influence which was derived from their paramilitary connections. A similar argument can be made in respect of the loyalist parties. The influence that the loyalist parties were able to garner as a result of their paramilitary links was substantial. This was clearly indicated in the British government's decision to use a list system to the 1996 Forum elections in so far as this was the electoral system most likely to secure seats at the table for the loyalist parties since their popular support was much less significant than either of the mainstream unionist parties but their paramilitary support was considerable. In both of these cases, 'dirty hands' equated to a greater political influence.[2] Finally, in terms of building relationships during the peace process, ideas about one's own and others' morals, ethics, values and practices were considered to be one of the biggest barriers to the development of relationships between key protagonists during the peace process. For example, Ken Maginnis was quoted as saying on a regular basis 'I don't talk to terrorists' when approached by Sinn Féin leaders intimating that it would have been immoral to do so.[3]

Despite the obvious differences of opinions on what constituted moral behaviour or otherwise by the leaders themselves, the nature and direction of the peace process was more identifiably shaped by some clear assumptions that were made about what was 'ethically right' by those other than the local elite. The normative expectation that Northern Ireland's political leaders would, and more importantly, should 'do the right thing' was evidenced in much of the language used by both the British and Irish governments and the different international actors. At the macro-level, the assumption was that the right thing to do was to 'make peace'. At the-median level, 'doing the right thing' in the peace process meant conforming to a British and Irish government agenda that was both statist and plural. At the micro-level, the right thing to do was to engage in the various forums and initiatives which had been designed to bring political parties and leaders together outside of the confines of the track-one process.

As a consequence of the different interpretations about what was moral and what was not for both the local political leaders and the governments and others, the moral high ground, during the course of the peace process, became 'a very crowded place indeed' with key players all operating from positions of principle – paramilitary organizations on account of calling their ceasefires, the two governments on account of their role as honest brokers rather than players, and unionists on account of their refusal to engage with those linked to terrorism.[4]

If the difference of opinion about what was moral and what was not constitutes one key dimension of the morals and ethics of political leadership, then a second dimension must be the moral contradictions which can be evidenced in the behaviours and actions of a number of political leaders during the peace process. For example, while the mainstream unionist leadership used moral reasoning in its refusal to meet with Sinn Féin, citing links to terrorism and political convictions as its reasoning, the same leadership appeared to suffer from no moral dilemmas in meeting groups and individuals 'guilty' of the same offences within their own community. An often cited example, in this respect, had been Trimble's meetings with the then leader of the Loyalist Volunteer Force (LVF), Billy Wright, during the standoff in Drumcree 1996.[5] Similarly, the Ulster Unionist leader appeared to have no moral dilemma in associating his party with the loyalist paramilitary linked political parties during the talks process whenever he felt it politically expedient to do so. In September 1997, when the UUP returned to the talks process after the final walkout by the DUP and the UKUP, Trimble surrounded himself with forty delegates from the other pro-union parties, which included the PUP and the UDP, linked to the UVF and the UDA respectively, in order to strengthen his own political hand. However, in

November 1997, when a pan-unionist conference had been organized by the Friends of the Union group and had chosen to specifically exclude the PUP and the UDP from the conference on the grounds of their links to loyalist terrorism, Trimble failed to protest at their exclusion from the conference.[6]

A third dimension to moral and ethical leadership in the peace process was raised by one interviewee, who felt that 'movement forward in a divided society is [often] held back by moralists'.[7] He argued that moralists constrained the capacity of leadership and rendered it ineffective at critical junctures of the peace process:

> I think that the nervousness of political parties is not necessarily about what happens among themselves, it is about how they perceive their position to be with the electorate and moral arguments which trap Prime Ministers, Taoiseachs and Presidents also trap the general population.[8]

In a sense, the argument presented here was that the issues of morals and ethics amounted to little more than a smokescreen during the peace process to mask some the real reasons for lack of engagement at elite level. This was, in fact, discussed during the 1997 trip to South Africa, as mentioned in Chapter 6, albeit in a rather inadvertent fashion. One of the lessons learned by the South African negotiators, which was presented to the Northern Ireland political leaders assembled was that you must afford your enemy legitimacy within the peace process and that respect for the other positions was germane to the whole process.[9] Obviously, affording such legitimacy would necessitate moving away from the moral and ethical arguments which had stunted any substantial political progress at that time. As one leader, who was in South Africa in 1997, noted of the South African lesson:

> When we went to Arniston we were nowhere near affording our enemy legitimacy. Unless you do that you cannot create a level playing field in which you can have dialogue. Moral arguments and moral debates are a waste of space because they are seen as another way to defeat, another way to wrong foot, another way to shaft.[10]

Mandela's approach was to highlight the futility of some of the moral arguments made by some of the political leaders from Northern Ireland during the same visit. An anecdote of one interaction between Mandela and these leaders noted:

Approaching the Ulster Unionist table Mandela spotted General Masondo of the South African Defence Forces, a former leader of the ANC's military wing who had been incarcerated with him on Robben Island. 'I don't know what this country is coming to', Mandela quipped to the Not-an-Inchers. 'Up at the other end of the table is an ex-convict. He calls himself a general. If I had known I was going to have to share a room with an ex-convict I would not have come here at all. I have my reputation to think of'. A toe-curling moment for the Unionists who had the good grace to look embarrassed. All except David Trimble, who didn't turn a hair.[11]

Nonetheless, whilst highlighting the futility of some of the moral arguments through the use of humour, Mandela still spoke to the group of Northern Irish political leaders assembled in South Africa separately, at their request, rather than collectively. The arguments can be made then that this, in fact, gave further legitimacy to the contradictory moral arguments rather than exposing them for their futility.

The fourth and final dimension of moral and ethical leadership was the issue of realpolitik and the tensions between normative and realist understandings of the peace process. While claiming the moral high ground by 'doing the right thing', however subjective an interpretation that might have been, the various political leaders faced the problem of realpolitik. 'Doing the right thing' sat uneasily with reality of whether doing the right thing was actually the right thing to do for the different political leaders, in terms of their relations with the constituents and followers and in terms of their relations with other party leaders. The latter was a much more Machiavellian approach to the peace process since primarily it was about protecting oneself, protecting one's constituents and delivering on previous electoral promises. Moreover, doing things right was an entirely relative concept – what was right for one person was wrong for another.[12] Darby and MacGinty saw such 'realpolitik' as not only inevitable, but the priority in a peace process. They proposed that 'during peace negotiations the primary function of leaders is to deliver their own people' and argued that while it was true that most leaders could understand and empathize with the difficulties that their opponents faced they could not necessarily risk assisting opponents for fear of alienating their own supporters.[13] Indeed, for Darby and MacGinty 'the loss of followers is a greater threat to party leaders than the collapse of the process'.[14] From this perspective then, protecting oneself is of paramount significance.

The reverse proposition was presented by O'Malley. He argued that not only should parties put themselves into the shoes of their protagonists but they must help their protagonists to bring their communities with them: 'In the end successful negotiations are not so much about bringing your community along with you as helping your protagonist bring their community along with them'.[15] O'Malley's normative thesis was not lost on some of those who went to South Africa in 1997. One leader said:

> In a round robin sense, the leadership of all of the parties were going through the same thing. I believe that the only formula that could take them through it is collectively. It is actually the responsibility of Gerry Adams to tell David Trimble's constituents to calm down and it is David Trimble's responsibility to tell Gerry Adams constituents to calm down. Now that is alien to the concept of western politics but it is like the poles of a wigwam. Take one leader away and they all fall. If one leader is in trouble, we're all in trouble.[16]

There are examples from the peace process which are illustrative of both leaders who did try to help opponents and of those who helped themselves. For example, Hume's attempts at engaging Adams in the process was undertaken at the expense of declining support among senior party elites within the SDLP and, more importantly, at the expense of the SDLP's electoral success in later years. Hume would argue that this was because he cared more for the peace process than the party.[17] Cynics argued that he had his eye firmly on a prize greater than anything his party could offer – the Nobel peace prize and helping his opponent would ultimately lead to helping himself.

There is much to reconcile within the various dimensions of the understandings of moral and ethical leadership during the peace process. Whether it is possible to do so is debatable and illustrates the divisions between the absolutist, realist and democratic realist approaches towards morals and ethics during a peace process. Dixon describes three perspectives on the dilemma of 'dirty hands' in politics; the absolutists, realists and democratic realists.[18] Absolutists argue that political leaders should and can be honest and ethical. Realists argue that it is unrealistic to expect political leaders to behave ethically. By its very nature, politics is a 'dirty business', thus those involved cannot help but get their hands dirtied. Democratic realists find such behaviour unpleasant but necessary.

Overall, it is clear that issues of morality and ethics affected the typical understandings of political leadership during the peace process. Moral arguments were often used in equal measure to both persuade and dissuade political leaders from talking to one another even informally. They were used in equal measure to defend and berate the decision to engage in the peace process in general and the talks process in particular. Ultimately, they were used to both undermine and encourage the potential of political leadership during the peace process. Much like the various dimensions of morals and ethics discussed here, the effect has been often contradictory. More than anything, the dilemma facing the leadership over the doing the right thing, and whether this was compatible with whatever might have been the right thing to do in the peace process as far as constituents and followers were concerned, meant that the issue of morals and ethics contributed to a rather confused understanding of political leadership during the peace process.

The international dimension and borrowing lessons from other leaders

Adding further confusion to the understanding of political leadership was the constant reference throughout the peace process to the examples of political leaders in the context of other peace processes and the positive roles, or otherwise, which they had played in their own respective peace initiatives. This issue of borrowing lessons from other leaders, is the second one which affected the potential role, capacity and effect of political leadership during the peace process in Northern Ireland. Though probably not intended to confuse the role of political leaders, the comparisons between Northern Ireland's political leaders and leaders from the South African peace process, for example, were primarily designed as a method of explaining progress in peace processes by using the concepts of lending, borrowing and exchange between them.[19]

In Northern Ireland, it was clear that the involvement of external 'third party' political leaders during the peace process, amounted to more than simply lending support and offering advice. Indeed, the suggestion that Northern Ireland's politicians should take their lessons from the success of the South African case study was implicit in the visits to Northern Ireland by leading South African negotiators at varying points in the process. De Klerk was invited to the Forum for Peace and Reconciliation in Dublin in November 1995 to extol the virtues of the South African example. Dr Fredrick Van Zyl Slabbert, co-founder of IDASA and former leader of the South African Progressive Party, gave a lecture in Northern Ireland in 1997 at Parliament Buildings in

Stormont.[20] On another occasion, a team of senior ANC negotiators were dispatched to Northern Ireland to speak to republicans in the immediate aftermath of the Agreement. The purpose of their visit was to help develop the internal debate among republicans in relation to accepting the terms of the Agreement or otherwise.[21]

The visiting traffic was not all one way. As illustrated in Chapter 6, numerous trips were made by Northern Ireland's leaders abroad to meet, greet and possibly learn from the experience of other case studies. As with the visits to Northern Ireland, some leaders were more open to the possibility of learning than others. For example, Adams regarded his own visit to South Africa in 1995 at the invitation of the ANC, to learn the lessons of South Africa's approach to conflict resolution, as extremely influential.[22] He said: 'Of all the political leadership I had met up to then and since, never have I met a group as cohesive, articulate and far-seeing as those in the ANC leadership'.[23] Of Mandela personally, he said: 'Madiba [Mandela] remains one of my heroes and in my view the greatest political leader of our time'.[24]

The rationale at the heart of borrowing lessons from other leaders, by either inviting them to Northern Ireland or by making trips to their home country to learn first-hand of their experiences was obviously that there was a lesson to be learned. For McGarry, though, this rationale was decidedly weak. He argued that this amounted to little more than a lazy theory of conflict resolution and that the analogies between the leaders in different countries were often misleading, superficial or inappropriate.[25] However, the theory that leaders learnt from others is both verified and dismissed in equal measure by the leaders in Northern Ireland. The argument between those who endear themselves to the virtues of borrowing lessons from other leaders and those who do not is the most obvious problem. Nonetheless, there are other problems to consider.

A second problem is that borrowing and lending aspects of leadership are neither straightforward nor measurable unlike the more structural aspects between processes. How can one prove that paradigmatic shifts of behaviour, attitudes and influence are attributable to the mimicking of other leaders in other peace processes? Arguably, one cannot. Moreover, the argument has already been put forward that we should not even try to prove that such shifts are as a consequence of imitating other leaders, since this would amount to little more than McGarry's lazy theory of conflict resolution. More recently though, he has argued that: 'If actors in one conflict come to identify sufficiently with actors in another the latter's behaviour many influence the former's. There is evidence of both in Northern Ireland'.[26] However, the fact that many comparisons were made between leaders from Northern Ireland and leaders from other peace processes is evidence enough of the *awareness* of behaviours and attitudes and potential influence of such leaders. Perhaps it was expected that the interactions would produce a shift in the approach to leadership in Northern Ireland by a process of osmosis. Not only would such an assumption be wrong, but it also tends to suggest an equally dubious assumption that there is, in fact, a leader for all seasons.

The third problem with borrowing lessons from other leaders is that although it has been claimed that 'Mandela-ism is not exportable' and that it leads to greater confusion than clarity in a peace process, this did not prevent comparisons being made.[27] The notion of a unionist de Klerk predated the actual peace process and was referred to at length by Hume.[28] This was refuted by Trimble who argued that such comparisons were wholly incorrect not least because de Klerk came from the minority population in South Africa and he [Trimble] was leader of the majority party in Northern Ireland.[29] The disagreement between unionism and nationalism on the issue of de Klerk reveals a more malign disagreement over which side needed to make the greater concessions.[30] Equally, comparisons were often made to the fate of previous leaders within Northern Ireland and Ireland which further confused rather than clarified, and worse still, acted as a crude forecaster of current leaders' fates.

A fourth and final problem associated with the multiple comparisons that have been made has been the self-elevation of stature in the eyes of some players. For example, O'Connor, commenting on the behaviour of Martin McGuinness, mentions McGuinness's response to a journalist who questioned his motivation in the peace process:

> It ill behoves anybody to call into question my motivation, or Gerry Adams, in South Africa at this minute meeting Nelson Mandela, a good friend to the peace process. If Nelson Mandela was sitting in this chair, would you even dare to ask him these questions? I think not.[31]

Similarly, when Adams was reminded by a journalist that most people in the UK questioned whether or not he had killed anyone, or had merely led a movement whose members had killed people, he argued: 'I presume they wouldn't think of a leader of the Tory or Labour party in the same terms'.[32] Adams had also compared himself with Mandela and Arafat quite directly back in 1994. When asked in an interview to renounce violence by a journalist prior to the first IRA ceasefire, Adams replied:

I don't remember Nelson Mandela renouncing violence or Arafat genuflecting. It's a two way process to bring about demilitarisation, to get those involved in armed conflict to stop'.[33]

In terms of lesson drawing, there are a number of things to consider. First, whilst borrowing from other peace processes has been a common theme in peace process literature, comparisons and borrowing between different political leaderships has provided no answers. Comparisons at the nation state level have been difficult enough. When this method is derived down to the individual level it becomes so complicated as to render it useless as a deductive tool.[34]

Secondly, it appears that leaders are as much in tune with the experiences and historical antecedents at home as they are with learning lessons from leaders abroad. For example, Trimble referred to Adams as a 'Michael Collins' figure – someone who could make a settlement, but also acknowledged Adams' concern with the eventual fate of Collins given that he was shot by those who refused to accept a Free State.[35] Trimble himself saw parallels between his own position and that of James Craig who had met with Michael Collins, despite being aware of IRA sectarian murders at the time. Like Adams, there were historical precedents which Trimble would have preferred to avoid, not least the fate which befell his predecessor, Brian Faulkner, who lost control of the UUP in 1974.

The third lesson which can be drawn is that there is no leader for all seasons in the context of a peace process and any attempts to create such a leader by cherry picking qualities from other leaders will inevitably lead to failure. Nonetheless, the building of relationships between leaders from one jurisdiction to another can serve as a positive mentoring experience for those involved. This was highlighted in particular in Chapter 4 which looked at the roles of political leadership during the Northern Ireland peace process and highlighted the nature of interpersonal relationships between political leaders from Northern Ireland with their counterparts from elsewhere. Related directly to this though is a final point which is of a more cautionary note:

> There is a real danger in effect that people have been rewarded for their intransigence by getting to meet all kinds of influential and important people on the world stage and they've had a grossly inflated idea of the importance of a small corner of the off shore island, of the off shore island of Western Europe.[36]

Taken together, these lessons illustrate that borrowing lessons of leadership from other peace processes and from the experiences of predecessors at home, has contributed significantly to the role confusion facing Northern Ireland's political elite. Such role confusion was aptly displayed by Trimble, in his defence against being called Northern Ireland's de Klerk. He said of the often cited de Klerk analogy: 'Oh, I would much rather be the Mandela. Absolutely. De Klerk was the leader of a minority group that was frustrating the rights of the majority'.[37] Importantly, the role confusion emanating from borrowing and lending between different peace process helps to further develop one of the assertions of this book which surmised that the multiple roles which political leaders had to undertake during the peace process were often incompatible with one another, thus leading to possible contradictions and inconsistencies within those roles. In addition to the multiple roles which cause contradictions and inconsistencies in terms of the political leaders' approaches must be added the concept of 'pseudo roles' of emulating political leaders from other peace processes, causing a similar degree of confusion for both political leaders and analysts alike.

The personalization of the process

The third overall issue which affected the potential role, capacity and effect of political leadership during the Northern Ireland peace process was the issue of personalization. The personalization of politics is not unusual. In politics, personalities are just as significant as the policies and events that are taking place.[38] This point is as true in the context of the peace process in Northern Ireland as it is elsewhere. It is interesting that while this book has not been about understanding political leadership in Northern Ireland in any individual sense, it has been completely impossible to discuss the concept of political leadership without making that reference 'personal' by contextualizing it in an example of one of a number of political leaders. One of the most fundamental problems with doing so, as Arthur points out, is that it ignores the role of the bureaucratic machines and the key players within it during the peace process.[39] In other words, it ignores the backroom players. Additionally, the total personalization of the peace process had the unfortunate consequence of undermining the potential capacity of political leadership to deliver a peace agreement. How did this happen? There are four main reasons to consider.

First, attacks on the substance of the peace process often gave way to attacks on the personalities involved. For example, the issue of the decommissioning of paramilitary weapons, which was a substantive issue during the peace process, became an issue of whether or not to shake the hand of Gerry Adams. At a broader level, it became an issue of whether or not to even talk to Adams and the other members of the Sinn Féin leadership. The fact that for the entire peace process even informal dialogue between the Sinn Féin leadership and the Ulster Unionist leadership was more monologue from Sinn Féin than dialogue, undermined the capacity of the Sinn Féin leadership to directly influence their political adversaries within the UUP.

Secondly, since the peace process was often portrayed as the 'David and Gerry Show', as one interviewee pointed out, then it was likely that David [Trimble] and Gerry [Adams] would want to be involved in all aspects of that show.[40] Arguably, the peace process demonstrated that some of the political leaders got carried away with the potential kudos and glory that a peace agreement might bring them and wanted to remain as intricately involved in the process as possible. This point was highlighted in Trimble's case by David Brewster, one of Trimble's negotiators. Brewster remarked that Trimble seemed unable to delegate control of the various strands of negotiations to others but rather tried to do absolutely everything himself.[41] The reverse was argued in Hume's case. It was alleged that he had taken a back seat to much of the actual negotiations in the multi-party talks, and had been there only 'physically but not mentally'.[42]

Both approaches were equally culpable of undermining the political leaders' capacity to influence the political process. Those involved in every single part of the negotiation process could have been accused of spreading themselves too thinly to have enough impact; those involved in only specific parts of the negotiations ran the risk of having no influence over other crucial aspects of the negotiations. Neither approach seemed to take into consideration the lesson taught during the relationship building exercise in South Africa in 1997 that the most significant progress can often be made by those players who are not referred to so 'personally' in relation to the conflict and the peace process. As O'Malley noted: 'Party leaders should not act as the party's chief negotiator' but rather should appoint people to negotiate on their behalf.[43] The point was made again by another South African negotiator in Belfast in 1997 who told those assembled: 'Both Mandela and de Klerk did not negotiate directly with one another but did so at arm's length through appointed negotiators in their ranks'.[44] The rationale behind such a lesson was similar to Lederach's argument, as discussed in Chapter 2, which indicated that high-profile leaders often found it difficult to retreat from previously held positions without appearing weak, whereas non-named entities did not tend to suffer from this as much.[45] The personalization of the Northern Ireland peace process was indicative of the fact that the lesson from elsewhere had not been learnt.

The third drawback of personalization was that it ran the risk of placing too much faith in a single person's ability to deliver. While much of the peace process was referred to as the 'David and Gerry Show', only one of the two political leaders was perceived to have had the sufficient capacity to help deliver on the paramilitary dimension of the peace process. The lesson that appeared not to have been learned in the Northern Ireland context was that just because a person had a high profile does not necessarily mean that the person had the ability to deliver. This was critically important in the context of delivering the loyalist paramilitaries in support of the eventual Agreement. Divorcing the personalities of Ervine, McMichael and so forth from the peace process at times, especially at the point where the UDP were excluded from the talks in early 1998 because of UDA violence on the streets, ignored the fact that only the loyalist political parties had the capacity to influence the loyalist paramilitary organizations. The mainstream unionist parties did not. Any agreement reached in the absence of support from the loyalist paramilitaries would not have been as likely to hold and yet the personalities from the loyalist parties engaged in the talks were never afforded the same degree of exposure as the Ulster Unionist leaders.

Overall, the personalization issue has highlighted yet another contradiction. There was a sizable contradiction between the need to build relationships between individuals in the peace process, in other words, to actually make the process personal, as demonstrated in some of the activities undertaken in Chapter 6 through the various relationship building initiatives, and the need to leave the big personalities out of the actual negotiating process since this could have diminished their potential for selling the Agreement afterwards. The contradiction was not one that could be easily solved and further clouded the understanding of political leadership. Moreover, relationship building and the potential effect of political leaders on other political leaders suffered from other problems. It is to these particular problems that the chapter now turns.

Relationship building and the adversarial nature of the process

For Lederach, cultivating long-term authentic relationships should be the main priority in any peace process.[46] This is an orientation which found some currency in the context of the relationship building exercises which took place in Northern Ireland, as detailed in the previous chapter. The argument put forward in support of such exercises is that progress only comes when negotiating parties learn to start trusting one another.[47] The logic behind this argument is that negotiating parties cannot trust each other when they do not know each other. In attempting to convince players to 'do the right thing', attention was placed on building trust between the players involved in the Northern Ireland peace process. The perceived logic was that building trust would lead to a greater propensity for shared learning among key political protagonists. Shared learning would lead to a greater propensity to make compromises. Compromise would, inevitably, lead to agreement. Thus, developing relationships between the key players was seen to be the natural conduit for producing a peace agreement. As O'Malley argued:

> The discovery of common interests – music, books, sport, similar hobbies, children and the problems you have with them, the worries they unwittingly give you, the difficulties they have to deal with, and the fact that their futures rest in the decisions you mutually take – humanize the negotiating process and create bonds that go beyond the bonds that protracted negotiations themselves create.[48]

There is anecdotal evidence, beyond Northern Ireland, to support such claims, however altruistic they may seem. For example, mention is often made of a fly fishing incident in South Africa, when Cyril Ramaphosa and Roelf Meyer, two key negotiators for the ANC and the National Party, took time out to fish together during the negotiation process. Ramaphosa was unfortunate enough to get a fish hook embedded in his finger which only Meyer was able to remove and a trust between the two was built on the basis of this one incident. In Oslo, during the talks process between the Israeli and Palestinian negotiators in 1993, attention was paid to the dynamic between the various negotiators which began formally and full-suited. By the end of the first day, relations had thawed enough that the negotiators took to removing their ties, rolling up shirt sleeves, and engaging with one another wholeheartedly. The limited physical space in which those particular negotiations took place was said to have contributed to the breaking-down of barriers between those involved.[49]

In Northern Ireland though, the humanization of the process was to prove more difficult than in the South African or Israeli/Palestinian examples. There are a number of reasons which can be attributed to this. First, the fact that mainstream unionism refused to share space, either in a formal or an informal capacity, with Sinn Féin was considered an immovable impediment to any notions of humanization. Secondly, while attempts were made at promoting consistency in terms of invitations to the same actors to attend organized events and workshops through the various relationship building initiatives, this did not always happen in practice. Consequently, a series of one-off meetings between players was much less significant, in terms of its possible impact. Thirdly, during the peace process a number of new political actors came onto the scene. These actors had not been courted by event organizers to the same extent as some of the main players and some had only limited exposure to the other political players. This was certainly the case with the Women's Coalition, the PUP and the UDP.

Nonetheless, attempts at cultivating relationships persisted and persisted beyond the confines of the events organized. Adams discusses the influence of Fr Alex Reid, a Redemptorist Priest from Clonard Monastery in West Belfast, on his own political journey.[50] Fr Reid had been involved in attempts to bring various leaders and other influential people together, to discuss the way forward in the conflict since the early 1980s. He facilitated discussion between Sinn Féin and the SDLP, and between Sinn Féin and the Irish and British governments through various back channels. Additionally, Chris Hudson, a trade unionist from Dublin who had been involved in the Peace Train organization, forged a relationship with David Ervine and representatives from the UVF, and kept the Irish government informally informed of his liaisons with them during the early period of the peace process.[51]

While building relationships remains both a noble and important aspect of any peace process, there were significant problems with such an approach in the context of the Northern Ireland peace process. Four problems can be highlighted. First, there existed a sizable contradiction between the desire to build relationships between players and the adversarial nature of the talks process which the players were necessarily engaged in.[52] Guelke argued:

> The failure of negotiations to end protracted violent conflict is typically attributed to a variety of factors, including most commonly the pursuit of irreconcilable aims by the major antagonists, obdurate political leadership, and the stage of the conflict. The obverse of these propositions is that, successful negotiation depends on a readiness of the parties to compromise; political leadership capable of developing a relationship with the other side and the right timing.[53]

This approach amounts to a rationalistic and positive view of the role of negotiations in a peace process. However, Guelke claimed that it is equally possible to present the process of negotiations in a realpolitik fashion, with power politics and coercion as central features. At all stages of the negotiation process, there might exist suspicion of the other side, assumptions that the other side is pursuing a hidden agenda, and thus, any engagement in negotiations is purely tactical. Consequently, it is the issues of trust and good faith that take on significant importance in the progression of a peace process.

It is, however, reasonable to assume that any progress on issues of trust and good faith that came through the building of personal relationships during the peace process had the potential to be negated by the structure of the actual negotiation process. For example, in South Africa during the 1997 relationship building initative between Northern Ireland's political leaders much attention was paid to the idea of affording one's enemy legitimacy in the process. Once back in Northern Ireland again, the cut and thrust of the negotiations necessitated a different approach and mental attitude. In particular, a conspiratorial attitude was very evident. For example, the Ulster Unionist leadership feared being kept up all night by the two governments and then agreeing to some foolish concession in their exhaustion.[54] The Sinn Féin leadership noted of the location of the negotiations in Castle Buildings at Stormont that: 'There was nowhere for private, outside the room conversations – essential to progress or even for initiating conversation'.[55] Their own conspiracy theory was that the British intelligence had probably bugged the rooms to be used in the negotiations in an attempt to pick up information that might be useful to the British government's position in the talks.[56] Overall, harmonizing the need for relationship building in the process and the realities of negotiation was difficult.

A second problem with the relationship building approach was that it was difficult to guarantee whom the relationships might be developed between. For example, in instances where the peace process came up against different problems, attempts were made to engage the key political players with the issues at stake by bringing them together in a different context, and without explicit discussion of the issues. An obvious example of this was in terms of the invitation list to the annual St Patrick's Day event at the White House, under Clinton's administration, which included all of the key players from Northern Ireland. In such instances, the stage management was of paramount significance. For example, if the perceived wisdom was to build relationships between key players, how did those engaged in organizing the events manage to get the key players to come along? In essence, they did not. The actors engaged in the relationship building sessions varied widely from party to party with varying degrees of success, which was put down to the degree of commitment from the individual party.[57]

A third problem with the relationship building approach, which might have contributed to the lack of certainty in personnel represented at events, was the perception of some that the plethora of initiatives which took different political players outside of the country during the peace process was less helpful than initiatives which could have taken place locally.[58] This presented something of a conundrum for the relationship building initiatives. Clearly, it was easier to engage players outside of the confines of Northern Ireland away from the media spotlight, the shackles of their party political positioning and other work commitments, than it was to engage them in a similar fashion at home. A cynical analysis suggests that the attitudes and behaviours of the players involved and the relationships that might have developed holds synonymy with the concept of a holiday romance – wonderful at the time but less likely to work at home. Here lies the dilemma.

The fourth problem with relationship building in Northern Ireland stemmed from what did not happen rather than what did happen during the peace process. This is derived, in part, from the previous point. Much attention was given to building relationships between players for a substantial period of time during the peace process. Once the Agreement was reached in April 1998, this type of engagement was alleged to have subsided so significantly, that it almost no longer existed. One party leader said: 'There was no vehicle upon which the coming together of leaders could function', which was somewhat ironic since the machinery for 'normal' interactions was now in place through the establishment of the Assembly.[59] It was argued that more emphasis should have been devoted to developing and sustaining relationships after the deal had been reached because it was at this point that the political players became locked into consociational arrangements which necessitated the ability to work together.

In the final analysis of this, the impact of attempts at building relationships was more successful in some instances than in others. By the time of the Agreement in 1998, the leader of the UUP still refused to shake hands with the leader of Sinn Féin. However, they did sit in the same room together which was marked departure from the politics of old, when UUP politicians would not even share physical space with Sinn Féin for television broadcast purposes or for any other matter.[60] However, the effect of political leaders on other political leaders during the peace process was heavily conditioned by the problems associated with using relationship building initiatives as a mechanism for building potential influence within the peace process. Most importantly, was the glaring contradiction between attempts to build relationships and trust and the adversarial nature of the talks process which often negated the relationship building progress made.

Contradictions, inconsistencies and chameleonic leadership

Collectively, the various limitations on the role, capacity and effect of political leadership as discussed in this chapter confirms the original argument of this book that political leadership during the Northern Ireland peace process was often necessarily contradictory in both style and substance.

While Chapter 3 concluded with the description of political leadership as 'contradictory' in nature and allowed leaders to be both hard liner and moderniser; protagonist and pragmatist; transformational and transactional; reluctant and ambitious; innovative and pedantic; and charismatic and 'robot-like', this chapter comes to a somewhat similar conclusion in terms of understanding the political leaders' role, capacity and effect during the Northern Ireland peace process. In total, there are five key contradictions which exemplify the nature of the limitations on the role, capacity and effect of political leadership during the peace process. First, there was a contradiction in the confusing role and expectation placed on political leaders to do the 'right thing' on the one hand and to secure the best deal possible for their own constituents on the other hand. One, almost always, negated the other. Secondly, there was a contradiction between needing 'influential political leaders' to be engaged in the process, and wanting to work with political leaders untarnished by the 'politics of dirty hands'. Thirdly, there was a contradiction between the tendency to personalize the process by focusing on a very small cohort of political leaders and needing to broaden the number of political elites who would help shape and drive the peace process forward. Fourthly, there was a contradiction between the needs and the desire to build relationships between political players during the peace process, and the realities of the adversarial nature of the process which they were bound to engage within. Finally, there were the multiple contradictions of comparisons with other political leaders in other peace processes.

In summation then, deconstructing political leadership into its constituent parts of role, capacity and effect has merely further emphasized the complicated and contradictory nature of political leadership during the peace process in Northern Ireland. It is clear that matters were not as simplistic as some peace and conflict scholars would have had us believe. The research here has shown that progress in the Northern Ireland peace process was not as a result of two strong leaders with a motivation to make peace, as Rothstein argues of peace processes more generally.[61] It was more complicated than that. For a start, there were more than two leaders representing two political parties in the Northern Ireland case study. Each had their own strengths. There were leaders who had strong electoral support, as in the case of the Ulster Unionists, the SDLP and the DUP. There were leaders who had strongish electoral support coupled with additional strength garnered from their links with paramilitaries, as in the case of Sinn Féin. There were leaders who appeared relatively weak electorally, as in the case of the PUP and the UDP, but who gathered significant strength from their links and associations with paramilitaries. There were leaders who were strong in terms of gender representation, as in the case of the Women's Coalition and in standing for the 'silent majority', as in the case of the Alliance Party. The motivations for engaging in the peace process also varied. As illustrated in Chapter 6, the motivations for even meeting with political adversaries beyond the immediate context of the peace process varied from person to person and included motivations such as the opportunity to go junketeering, a genuine curiosity about other leaders, fear of being perceived as intransigent, fear of positive relations developing with other political leaders in one's absence, seeking affirmation from other political leaders and seeking to influence other party leaders.

As a further indication of the complicated and contradictory nature of political leadership, progress in the peace process was not necessarily made as a consequence of the actor transformation which amounted to either a change of character, a change of leadership, a change in the constituency of the leader or adoption of its goals, values and/or beliefs, as argued in a more general context, by Miall, Ramsbotham and Woodhouse.[62] Again, the reality was more complicated. The research on political leadership in the context of the Northern Ireland peace process has demonstrated that the 'transformations' of leadership in terms of a change in character have not been binding. So, while there might have been a change in character which allowed for some unionists to engage with Sinn Féin during the peace process, as illustrated in Chapter 6, this was not necessarily a change which was absolute. Indeed, the examples presented showed that some political leaders veered between only engaging publicly, to only engaging privately, to not engaging at all during the process. Equally, there was no change of party leadership during the 1994–98 period with the notable exception of the election of Trimble after the resignation of Molyneaux. In the three other largest political parties, the leadership had remained unchanged for nearly twenty years. The fact that the key political players remained the same in Northern Ireland and yet the political situation dramatically shifted is highly significant. The question is, what has allowed the political changes to take place, if it was not a change of leadership within the main parties?

Quite clearly, a different dynamic was created with the change of leadership in the UUP in 1995. Trimble's election as leader of the UUP cannot be ignored in this respect. However, the previously parochial nature of political leadership in Northern Ireland was overturned with the emergence of additional, new actors into the process. These actors did not represent a 'change of leadership' in terms of replacing an old party leadership. The political 'arrival' of the UDP, the PUP and the Women's Coalition onto the political scene brought a new dimension to the process, and may have been one of the most influential catalysts for change during the peace process. Therefore, in the context of Northern Ireland, a 'change of leadership' was probably no more important as a factor than the introduction of additional leadership to that process, alongside the already existing and established leadership.

How then is it possible to use these results from this examination of the role, capacity and effect of political leadership, and the limitations therein to contribute towards a new theory of political leadership during the peace process in Northern Ireland, and of political leadership in peace processes more generally? The multiplicity of contradictions that have been thrown up in the course of this research highlights the limited value of the creation of any new dichotomies, classifications and/or typologies to explain political leadership in Northern Ireland. Classifying individual leaders as either one type or another runs the risk of being disproved as a consequence of another shift in leadership behaviours dictated by broader political circumstances. Thus, a conscious attempt has been made throughout the course of this research not to identify particular traits with particular leaders but rather to consider political leadership in Northern Ireland as a collective entity. The argument that follows then is applicable to the collective.

In behavioural terms, the ultimate argument is that the multiple contradictions and inconsistencies inherent within political leadership in the context of the Northern Ireland peace process can best be explained as a form of 'chameleonic leadership'; an inconstant form of political leadership which shifted according to the opinions of others and the climate in which it existed, just as a chameleon can change its colour to blend with its background. The concept of 'chameleonic leadership' is based on the notion that, when political leaders find themselves in a position which compromises their intentions during a peace process, they seek to find an alternative position. Finding themselves in positions which compromise their intentions is usually dictated by broader political circumstances and changes in the political environment. It is this idea of environment which gives the concept of 'chameleonic leadership' its currency. Just as chameleons can change their colour rapidly in response to changes in the light, or temperature or mood, political leaders can change their positions in response to new issues coming to light during a peace process, the temperature of the peace process increasing or decreasing, and the mood of themselves, their followers, and/or their political adversaries.

For example, in the context of Northern Ireland, the admission of Sinn Féin to the talks process in September 1997 resulted in a shift in position for the DUP and the UKUP from involvement in the peace process to withdrawal from it. It also saw a shift in the position of the leadership of the UUP from one which refused to engage with those with links to paramilitarism to one which used the loyalist political parties, complete with their links to paramilitarism, in an attempt to garner further legitimacy from its decision to continue to stay in the talks process despite the arrival of Sinn Féin and the departure of the DUP and UKUP. At a later point, the peace process saw a shift in position again by the DUP and the UKUP once the Agreement had been signed, at least insofar as they decided to engage with the process once again by contesting the Assembly elections in 1998, rather than remain withdrawn from the process. The shift in position by the UUP was more contradictory. Moreover, as the British and Irish governments turned up the heat on the peace process by fixing absolute deadlines for an Agreement to be signed, the positions of the various political parties shifted considerably to allow for the eventual compromises inherent within the Agreement. At other times, when the peace process appeared to have been put 'on ice' when there was virtually no political activity, as was considered to be the case during the last year of John Major's premiership, the cooler temperature afforded the political leaders the opportunity to shift their positions to become more hard-line than compromising.

The concept of 'chameleonic leadership' gives us a new understanding when applied to the particular chapters of this book. In particular, 'chameleonic leadership' serves to explain the perceived dichotomy between collective and individual leadership styles. It explains the perceived dichotomy between reluctant leadership and a leadership that remained quite consistent for the duration of the peace process. Sometimes it was one, sometimes the other. In terms of Chapter 4 which focused on the role of political leadership during the peace process, the concept of 'chameleonic leadership' explains how political leaders were able to shift between their multiple roles during the peace process, at times prioritizing a minimalist role which tended towards the maintenance and protection of existing benefits for followers; at times prioritizing a more moderate role which sought small changes within the political system; and at times prioritizing a maximalist role which sought more fundamental transformations of existing institutions and policies. From the perspective of Chapter 5 on the capacity of political leadership during the peace process, 'chameleonic leadership' clearly is identifiable with the perceptions of capacity and influence, especially in relation to Dixon's point that politicians often chose to emphasize the importance of appearance over reality.[63] And finally, in the context of Chapter 6 on the potential effect of political leaders on other political leaders during the peace process, the concept of 'chameleonic leadership' illustrates just how political leaders changed in relation to the political climate. For example, the Ulster Unionists saw fit to engage with Sinn Féin in public but not in private, and while the DUP were absolute in their refusal to engage with Sinn Féin in public, their attitudes towards private interactions seemed to be more fluid.

Overall, this idea of 'chameleonic leadership' can be used to contribute towards a new understanding of much of the collective political leadership behaviour during the peace process. This new understanding, in itself, does not necessarily amount to a theory of political leadership however. The various attributes which make up a political theory of leadership, as discussed in Chapter 3, have been touched upon implicitly throughout the course of this research.[64] They are drawn together here by way of a final conclusion.

8
Conclusion: Towards a New Understanding of Political Leadership

Summary

One of the more memorable images from the day that the Good Friday Agreement was signed was when the leadership of the Women's Coalition, on the steps of Castle Buildings, threw their negotiating papers high into the air to the delight of the international media assembled there, in a scene similar to students throwing their mortar boards into the air for graduation photographs. The symbolism suggested that the political leaders finally graduated from war to peace. Such symbolism was easy for us to understand. Indeed, much of our understandings about political leadership during the peace process in Northern Ireland have been symbolic rather than substantive, where progress in the process was illustrated by handshakes and meetings with Prime Ministers, Presidents and Taoiseachs. This book has sought to move away from the symbolism of political leadership towards an understanding grounded in knowledge of their role, capacity and effect. The results presented here have attempted to move the narrative of political leadership during the peace process in Northern Ireland beyond the personalized accounts offered in the various biographies and autobiographies produced, and also beyond the analysis which focused on who shook hands with whom, and where, and the significance of this for the broader peace process.

Consequently, this book sought to find an alternative way of explaining political leadership in the context of the Northern Ireland peace process. It began generally, by introducing a number of different ways to define and explain the phenomenon of leadership at that time. When leaders themselves were asked to explain their leadership, they struggled to do so, indicating something of a lack of self-awareness among the political elite. The reverse was true of those political journalists, commentators and academics on the outside of the process and demonstrated an ultra-awareness and opinion on the personalities involved in the peace process and their leadership styles therein. The contrasting assessments of leadership by both parties raised questions about the impartiality and objectivity of such assessments. The general analysis concluded that any definition of political leadership must not ignore the analysis of leaders themselves and others despite their often-contradictory nature, but rather must build upon them and interpret them in order to present a more definitive explanation of leadership at the time.

In doing so, it was necessary to deconstruct the concept of political leadership in the context of the Northern Ireland peace process into more manageable dimensions. It did so by focusing on the role of leadership in the peace process, the capacity of political leadership to shape and influence the nature and direction of the peace process and the effect of leadership in terms of the relationships that were built up between political leaders during the course of the process. Collectively, the chapters on role, capacity and effect demonstrated the confused roles, undermined capacity and negated effects of leadership which were compounded by a number of leadership 'difficulties'. The role confusion for leaders was in the ultimate moral and ethical dilemma of doing the right thing in the peace process versus the right thing to do in terms of constituents and followers. Their capacity to influence the nature and direction of the peace process was somewhat stunted by the very personalized nature of that process, especially in terms of the attention focused on particular individuals by both the media and the two governments. The potential effect of political leaders on other political leaders involved in the peace process, through the various humanizing processes within which they were engaged, were often negated by the adversarial nature of the talks process itself, and the difficulties in consistently engaging the 'key players' with the relationship building exercises on offer.

Overall, the depth of the complications and contradictions inherent within the phenomenon of political leadership during the peace process in Northern Ireland have been consistently demonstrated. Against such a backdrop, and in light of the criticisms of 'false dichotomies', it was unlikely that the creation of any new dichotomies of leadership or classifications of leadership would be absolute. Moreover, creating multiple classifications of leadership, which could be used in the context of Northern Ireland, would only serve to identify individuals, something which this book did not set out to do. Instead, it has sought to present a definition of the more collective political leadership experience, all the while realizing that there would be possible and probable exceptions to every definition presented. Ultimately though, it saw the political leaders practicing a type of chameleonic politics whereby they said one thing and did another, or said different things to different audiences in different places for different purposes. In other words, it has argued that at different points in the peace process the majority of political leaders practiced some form of 'chameleonic leadership'. It further contends that through this interpretation of political leadership as 'chameleonic leadership' we can move towards the development of a broader understanding of political leadership in the context of the Northern Ireland peace process than that which currently exists.

How then might we use the concept of 'chameleonic leadership' to contribute towards a new understanding of political leadership in the context of Northern Ireland's peace process, as contended? Much of what has been discussed during the course of this book make up the building blocks of a theory of political leadership and the notion of 'chameleonic leadership' is central to that theory. According to House and Aditya, a general theory of political leadership needs more than a definition of political behaviour. It also needs a specification of the conditions that enhance or impede the exercise of political behaviour; a specification of the sources of influence on which leaders can draw; a specification of the countervailing forces that exists in the context discussed; a specification of the motives and personality traits relevant to the exercise of power and political behaviour in organizations; a description of the kinds of behavioural tactics enacted in the pursuit of political objectives; a description of when such tactics will be used; a description of how politically motivated behaviour becomes legitimized; the moderating effects of organizational contexts on relationships between politically motivated behaviours and their effects; and the ultimate effects of politically motivated behaviour on organizational performance and survival.[1] Moreover, developing a theory of political leadership in the context of a peace process requires all of the above plus the added dimension of the particularities of peace processes. The various building blocks are stacked together here as a way of tentatively moving us towards a theory of political leadership in the context of the Northern Ireland peace process.

Towards a theory of political leadership in the Northern Ireland peace processes

The focus of this book was to find a way of explaining the phenomenon of political leadership during the Northern Ireland peace process, though the building blocks presented here can obviously be applied beyond the confines of Northern Ireland to the context of other peace processes. Beginning with a definition of political leadership in Northern Ireland, it is recalled from Chapter 3 that existing definitions of leadership behaviour were ill-suited to the case study presented. After deconstructing the concept of political leaders down to its role, capacity and effect it was argued that their behaviour could, at best, be described as 'chameleonic leadership' undertaking confused roles, with limited capacity and negated effects.

The conditions likely to enhance or impede such chameleonic behaviour, which involved saying different things to different audiences at different times for different purposes, and the role, capacity and effect of leadership, were almost entirely environmental. There were at least five such conditions to note: the likelihood of elections during the peace process; the frequency of violent incidents during the peace process; the emergence of alternative, viable leadership within a particular community; the formation of alliances or allegiances between different political leaders; and/or potential allegations of a personal or professional nature against specific political leaders.

In terms of the impact of these conditions on the role, capacity and effect of political leadership, it is arguable that the likelihood of elections during the peace process could lead to either the loss of an electoral mandate or the gaining of an electoral mandate for some leaders. In the case of the 1996 Forum Elections, the PUP, the UDP and the Women's Coalition, all benefited from a new electoral mandate as a result of the elections. This gave them a clearly defined role in the more specific political process, as well as in the broader peace process. In addition, for all of the political parties, there was the likelihood that the possibility of elections would enhance chameleonic attitudes and behaviour since the leadership's message usually became more hard line during an election period. The frequency of violent incidents during the peace process temporarily diminished the capacity of both Sinn Féin and the UDP. This was apparent in early 1998 with the forced exclusion of both parties, at separate times, as a consequence of their perceived links with paramilitaries undertaking violent activities. The emergence of an alternative, viable leadership contributed to a loss of influence for some of the more established political parties. This was particularly true in the case of the emergence of the PUP and the UDP and the slight slackening of support for mainstream unionism. The formation of alliances and allegiances during the process contributed to a more limited effect on the leadership of those beyond the alliance. While it would be completely misleading to suggest that those engaged in negotiations from the late 1997 period onwards had any allegiance to one another, the fact that they were part of the same process, negotiating on the same issues forced some degree, however detached, of interaction between them. This degree of inter-action afforded the potential for leaders to affect other leaders during the process. For those who had withdrawn from the talks process in September 1997, namely the DUP and the UKUP, the potential for others to affect their leadership was severely diminished. Finally, allegations of a personal or professional nature during the peace process had the potential to lead to a loss of personal influence over the process.

The sources of influence from which leaders could draw were examined in Chapter 5. There were three sources detailed: the influence of office, the influence of events and the influence of the personal. The countervailing political forces which existed in Northern Ireland were two fold – those leaders involved indirectly in the process such as the Clinton administration in the US, and those leaders seen as superior to the local political elite in Northern Ireland, in particular the British and Irish government leaders and associated officials.

The motives and personality traits relevant to the exercise of power and political behaviour during the peace process were in dispute. Most political leaders claimed their own motives as being entirely altruistic and all others as entirely dubious, though the predominant motives tended to vary from leader to leader, and from circumstance to circumstance.

This book has been most interested in the sources of power which afforded leaders the capacity to influence the peace process rather than the specific tactics that they used in order to do so. However, some of the kinds of political tactics enacted by political leaders in the pursuit of political objectives, and when such tactics are used, have been loosely examined by Dixon's work on the choreography of the peace process.[2] He argued that tactics and techniques used by many political leaders included choreography and playacting; creating smokescreens of hostile rhetoric to mask more conciliatory actions; salami-slicing their positions from the extremes towards the centre ground under the cover of the aforementioned smokescreens; playing a game of hard cop/soft cop by sending out different messages from two different leaders within the same party to two different audiences at the same time; using leaks as means of gauging the measure of public acceptance of issues; and engaging in constructive ambiguity with constituents to allow room for manoeuvre at a later stage.

In reviewing how politically motivated behaviour became legitimized during the peace process, the relationship building exercises were critical to the process that would afford legitimacy to one's enemy. Such exercises were critical, in particular, as an avenue through which some degree of peer learning could take place between the political leaders. This idea of peer learning is tangentially linked to John Hume's notion of political leadership as something like being a teacher. He said: 'It's about changing the language of others. I say it and go on saying it until I hear the man in the pub saying my words back to me'.[3] Hume's entire political style was considered distinctly pedagogic.[4] Indeed, it is argued that much of Hume's language (which supporters refer to as his 'single transferable speech',[5] and his detractors refer to as 'Humespeak') became the language of the peace process. The eventual Agreement in 1998 seemed to represent Hume's political thinking more than any other politician in Northern Ireland.[6] Hume's teaching analogy, however, could be considered as somewhat flawed. If political leadership is like being a teacher, and the man on the street is the student, how do political leaders learn? Upon reflection, it is as equally true to suggest that political leadership is like being a student. Their sources of learning are threefold. First, there are those leaders who are conditioned by the historical antecedents of their predecessors. Secondly, there are those leaders who can be susceptible to the influence of their political peers and political adversaries. Thirdly, there are those leaders predisposed towards the actions of other leaders from other peace processes. What is common to each strand of political leadership is the capacity of leaders to learn from other leaders.

This learning capacity forms the basic rationale of the various attempts to bring key political players together at different junctures of the peace process in Northern Ireland. The assumption was also made that building relationships between key players would make a positive difference to the peace process. In particular, the assumption was made that the interactions which took place between the various political elites outside of the confines of the normal talks process would be likely to accomplish two things. One was to allow for the building and development of personal relationships between the key players. Another was to create a quality of leadership among the elite which would be more predisposed towards a political settlement than otherwise. In a sense, the focus was on developing a 'peace' process as opposed to a 'political' process.[7]

There are two interpretations to such an approach. On one hand, bringing leaders together to build relationships between them could be considered an incredibly naïve approach. Michael Gove referred to the 1997 South African trip as having 'an element of patronising naivety' about it.[8] On the other hand it could be considered a calculated risk with more to gain than to lose in terms of the overall process. Padraig O'Malley is an advocate of the latter analysis. From his perspective, it is argued that:

> The outcome of the Indaba (the zulu word for 'gathering of the minds') was a series of historic events. Seven weeks after the conference, Sinn Féin declared a ceasefire that paved the way for negotiations and ultimately the fragile Good Friday Agreement to share power, still in place today. A year later, Trimble and Hume, leader of the Social Democratic and Labour Party, were awarded the Nobel prize for peace. And most recently, in fall 2001, the IRA mustered the courage to destroy its weapons to further the cause of peace. That stunning announcement came two weeks after Gerry Adams of Sinn Féin once again visited former President Mandela in South Africa.[9]

Clearly, the assumption was made that these historic events were directly relational to the 1997 Indaba. The difficulty with both interpretations is simply a matter of measurement. There exists only a very limited capacity for proving or disproving the usefulness of peer learning, building relationship and leadership development initiatives. Despite the limitations of measurement, the possibility of their impact cannot be discounted. For example, in the absence of any other reason presented by the DUP for taking their seats in an administrative government which they had campaigned so vigorously against, it is not beyond the realms of possibility that Peter Robinson took home from South Africa in 1997 the lesson that you must never leave the process. O'Malley argues:

> In Northern Ireland the right wing (DUP) learned assiduously from the mistakes of the South African right wing. Although it walked out of the assembly when Sinn Féin was admitted, it never left the process. It learned that once abandoning a process, your power of control over its direction becomes nonexistent...[10]

That said, the DUP did leave the negotiation process prior to the Agreement's final negotiation. As another party leader said:

> I thought that Peter Robinson had learnt that lesson that you don't walk away from the process. That you should always be there fighting

your corner. When he came back here the party overturned the decision. That's the difficulty. You can send people on these things and then they come back and it's really about how much influence they have in their party.[11]

In terms of the moderating effects of contexts on relationships between politically motivated behaviours and their effects, it is sufficient to simply acknowledge that the eventual Agreement in Northern Ireland was more than 'the sum of a clutch of very able leaders'.[12] As Smith points out: '. . . even the most agile, perceptive and courageous leader operates in a specific cultural, economic and political context'.[13] While political leaders may have behaved in a rather chameleonic fashion and while the effects of such behaviour may have increased the suspicions of other leaders on the one hand, and/or broken down the barriers between them on the other, the context in which these leaders operated was critical, though not always insofar as it always moderated behaviours and effects. As was often the case during the Northern Ireland peace process, the political context could serve to adversely affect the behaviours, and the role, capacity and effect of political leaders. These have already been demonstrated, to an extent, in terms of the various environmental conditions and context as mentioned above.

Finally, the theory should consider the ultimate effects of politically motivated behaviour on performance and survival. A 'chameleonic leadership' style, in the final analysis, was critical to the survival of those leaders involved in the peace process. It was a style of leadership which allowed them the opportunity to adapt and shift their behaviours, attitudes and convictions, whether temporarily or permanently. This, in turn, was perceived as evidence of a more pragmatic leadership in the context of the Northern Ireland peace process. It was the very idea that such pragmatism existed which encouraged those driving the process from outside Northern Ireland, in particular the British and Irish governments and the US administration, to assume that a peace agreement was actually possible and to engage with the political leaders on that basis.

More than anything, this book has sought to find a new and alternative way to define the phenomenon of political leadership during the peace process. The building blocks which can be used to build a fuller theory of leadership have been touched upon implicitly rather than explicitly during the course of the research and have been tied together here. Naturally, this only helps to take us *towards* a theory of political leadership during the Northern Ireland peace process. It does not constitute a holistic theory yet. Greater attention would need to be given to some of the latter building blocks mentioned above. In fact, each might constitute a research project of its own. It is, hopefully, a start.

Implications beyond Northern Ireland

Though this book has focused on the peace process in Northern Ireland, there do seem to be wider implications of this analysis for political leadership in other contexts. In almost every country and context, both the contradictions and inconsistencies of political leadership and examples of chameleonic leadership can be found. From the culture of chameleon politics in Malawi,[14] to the recent Labour party political broadcast for the 2006 UK local elections which pictured David Cameron, leader of the Conservative Party, as 'Dave the Chameleon' changing colour from red, to yellow to green, with a blue core; to Herbert Hoover's pronouncement on Franklin D. Roosefelt as 'a chameleon on plaid', illustrations abound. While the concept in such contexts is often used derogatorily, the scope and potential exist to use the concept in the manner in which it has been done here with no real value base, in so far as it does not judge whether the various shifts in behaviour and attitude make for 'better' leadership or not. In doing so, it also allows us all to move away from the perpetuation of often false dichotomies which have been used to explain the phenomenon of leadership. The dichotomies of heroes and villains, foxes and lions, positive and negative leaders, power wielders and power seekers, ignore the likely difficulties in assigning villainy in matters of politics. This is as true in the context of many of the world's current intractable conflicts as it is in Northern Ireland. Chameleonic leadership is grounded in the reality of politics which is much more complex and nuanced and therefore 'fits' with the multi-dimensional nature of all politics and the political leaders therein. Consequently, as a way of understanding the realities of leadership, as opposed to the normative ideals of how leadership ought to be, it has much to offer.

Conclusion

By way of a final conclusion, the arguments presented here make a modest contribution to the scholarly literature of both peace and conflict studies and political leadership. It has done so by exploring an important topic which has, to a certain degree, been overlooked by the literature. This is important not only in academic terms, but also in terms of the real world where we seem to know more about the role of leaders in stimulating ethnic and communal conflict than we do about the role of leaders in diminishing it. The introduction of the concept of 'chameleonic leadership' in the context of the Northern Ireland peace process is a sound beginning in terms of explaining some of the issues around the role of leadership in diminishing conflict. It is a concept which all of those involved in current peace processes elsewhere might learn from. The potential impact of such learning on the nature and direction of other peace processes simply cannot be underestimated.

Notes

1 Introduction

1. For an understanding of the background to the Northern Ireland conflict see Paul Bew and Gordon Gillespie, *Northern Ireland: A Chronology of the Troubles 1968–1999* (Dublin: Gill & Macmillan, 1999); Brendan O'Leary and John McGarry, *Explaining Northern Ireland* (Oxford: Blackwell, 1995); and Jennifer Todd and Joseph Ruane, *The Dynamics of Conflict in Northern Ireland: Power, Conflict and Emancipation* (Cambridge: Cambridge University Press, 1996).
2. Inter-party talks were launched by the Secretary of State, Peter Brooke, in January 1990. These continued after the 1992 British general election under Sir Patrick Mayhew. See David Bloomfield, *Political Dialogue in Northern Ireland: The Brooke Initiative, 1989–1992* (London: Macmillan, 1998).
3. The Agreement was unofficially dubbed the 'Good Friday Agreement' because it was signed on Good Friday, two days before Easter Sunday. However, the Agreement is also referred to as the 'Belfast Agreement' because it was signed in Belfast. The official document is simply titled 'The Agreement'.
4. Hugh Miall, Oliver Ramsbotham and Tom Woodhouse, *Contemporary Conflict Resolution* (Oxford: Polity Press, 1999) p. 154.
5. See Cynthia Arnson, ed., *Comparative Peace Processes in Latin America* (California; Stanford University Press, 1999); John Darby and Roger MacGinty, eds, *The Management of Peace Processes* (Basingstoke: Palgrave Macmillan, 2000); John Darby and Roger MacGinty, *Contemporary Peace Making: Conflict, Violence and Peace Processes* (Basingstoke: Palgrave Macmillan, 2003); Chester A. Crocker, Fen Osler Hampson, and Pamela Aall, eds, *Turbulent Peace: The Challenges of Managing International Conflict* (Washington DC: United States Institute of Peace Press, 2001); and Chester A. Crocker, Fen Osler Hampson and Pamela Aall, eds, *Managing Global Chaos: Sources of and Responses to International Conflict* (Washington DC: United States Institute of Peace Press, 1996).
6. These case studies, in particular, have been the subject of extensive research. For comparative analysis of Northern Ireland, South Africa and the Middle East, see Benjamin Gidron, Stanley Nider Katz and Yeheskel Hasenfeld, *Mobilizing for Peace: Conflict Resolution in Northern Ireland, Israel/Palestine, and South Africa* (Oxford: Oxford University Press, 2002); Hermann Giliomee and Jannie Gagiano, eds, *The Elusive Search for Peace: South Africa, Israel and Northern Ireland* (Oxford: Oxford University Press in association with IDASA, 1990); and Colin Knox and Padraic Quirk, *Peace Building in Northern Ireland, Israel and South Africa: Transition, Transformation and Reconciliation* (Basingstoke: Macmillan, 2000).
7. See Chester A. Crocker, Fen Osler Hampson and Pamela Aall, eds, *Grasping the Nettle: Analyzing Cases of Intractable Conflict* (Washington DC: United States Institute of Peace Press, 2005).

8. Michael E. Brown, 'Ethnic and Internal Conflicts: Causes and Implications', in Crocker, Osler Hampson and Aall, eds, *Turbulent Peace: The Challenges of Managing International Conflict*, p. 220.
9. *Ibid.*, p. 223.
10. *Ibid.*, p. 220.
11. For example, the majority of biographies that have been written about Northern Ireland's political leaders have been written by political journalists, rather than by academics. See Henry McDonald, *Trimble* (London: Bloomsbury, 2000); Liam Clarke and Kathryn Johnston, *Martin McGuinness: From Guns to Government* (Edinburgh: Mainstream, 2001); David Sharrock and Mark Devenport, *Man of War, Man of Peace?* (London: Macmillan, 1997); and Fionnuala O'Connor, *Breaking the Bonds: Making Peace in Northern Ireland* (Edinburgh: Mainstream, 2002). McDonald is the Northern Ireland political correspondent for *The Observer*. Clarke is the Northern Ireland political correspondent for *The Sunday Times*. Sharrock, at the time of publication of the biography, was the Northern Ireland correspondent for *The Daily Telegraph*. Devenport, at the time of publication of the biography, was the BBC's Ireland correspondent. O'Connor is the Ireland correspondent for *The Economist*.
12. O'Connor, *op. cit.*, p. 12.
13. O'Connor, *op. cit.*, p. 12.
14. For an introduction to this argument see, Paul Arthur, 'Multiparty Mediation in Northern Ireland', in Crocker, Osler Hampson and Aall, eds (1999), *op. cit.*
15. Katherine Hite, *When the Romance Ended: Leaders of the Chilean Left, 1968–1998* (New York: Columbia University Press, 2000) p. xvi.
16. Robert Elgie, *Political Leadership in Liberal Democracies* (London: Macmillan, 1995) p. 3.
17. Ed Moloney and Andy Pollak, *Paisley* (Dublin: Poolbeg, 1986); and Patrick Marrinan, *Paisley: Man of Wrath* (Tralee, Co. Kerry: Anvil, 1973).
18. Jean Blondel, *Thinking Politically* (London: Wildwood House, 1976) p. 107.
19. *Ibid.*
20. Lewis J. Edinger, 'Approaches to the Comparative Analysis of Political Leadership'. *Review of Politics*, 54, 4 (1990) p. 509.
21. See Thomas Carlyle, 'The Leader as Hero'; and Herbert Spence, 'The Great Man Theory Breaks Down', in Barbara Kellerman, ed., *Political Leadership: A Source Book* (Pittsburgh, Pa.: University of Pittsburgh Press, 1986).
22. For example see the introduction to Colin Barker, Alan Johnson and Michael Lavalette, eds, *Leadership and Social Movements* (Manchester: Manchester University Press, 2001). Not all are in agreement with this point however and see the construction and uses of political leaders as a way of deflecting from the underlying reasons of why changes take place. For a good critique of leadership from this perspective, see Murray Edelman, *Constructing the Political Spectacle* (Chicago: University of Chicago Press, 1988).
23. See Chris Brown, *Understanding International Relations* (Basingstoke: Palgrave Macmillan, 2001); Michael Nicholson, *International Relations: A Concise Introduction*, 2nd edn (Basingstoke: Palgrave Macmillan, 2002); and Steven Lobell and Philip Mauceri, *Ethnic Conflict and International Politics: Explaining Diffusion and Escalation* (Basingstoke: Palgrave Macmillan, 2004).

24. Stanley A. Renshon, 'Political Leadership as Social Capital: Governing in a Divided National Culture', *Political Psychology*, 21, 1 (2000) p. 202.
25. Jean Blondel, *Political Leadership: Towards a General Analysis* (London: Sage, 1987) p. 1.
26. See Alan Finlayson, 'Elements of the Blairite Image of Leadership', *Parliamentary Affairs*, 55, 3 (2002) p. 593; Michael Foley, *The British Presidency: Tony Blair and the Politics of Public Leadership* (Manchester: Manchester University Press, 2000); and Leo Abse, *The Man Behind the Smile: Tony Blair and the Politics of Perversion* (London: Robson Books, 2001).
27. Richard Heffernan, 'Prime Ministerial predominance? Core executive politics in the UK', *British Journal of Politics and International Relations*, 5, 3 (2003) pp. 347–372.
28. John Gaffney, 'Imagined Relationships: Political leadership in Contemporary Democracies', *Parliamentary Affairs*, 54, 1 (2001) p. 120.
29. Michael Foley, *John Major, Tony Blair and the Conflict of Leadership: Collision Course* (Manchester: Manchester University Press, 2002).
30. Robert C. Tucker, *Politics as Leadership* (Columbia: University of Missouri Press, 1981).
31. Darby and MacGinty 2003, *op. cit.*, p. 2.
32. *Ibid.*, p. 3.
33. *Ibid.*, p. 3.
34. *Ibid.*, p. 5.
35. David Hamburg, George Alexander, and Karen Ballentine, 'Preventing Deadly Conflict: The Critical Role of Leadership', *Archives of General Psychiatry*, 56 (1999) p. 971
36. Christopher Mitchell, 'Conflict Research', in A.J.R. Groom and Margot Light, eds, *Contemporary International Relations: A Guide to Theory* (London: Pinter Press, 1994) pp. 128–141. Mitchell presents a concise overview of the field, focusing on general textbooks, ethnic conflicts, psychology, peace processes, and third party involvement. With 111 books cited in the bibliography, this review is still one of the most informative in the field.
37. It is true that many academics see the leadership factors as one of significant importance in the context of a peace process. For example, Darby notes that timing, the quality of leadership and the cohesion of groups in negotiations are vitally important factors in peace processes. See John Darby, *Custom of Fell Deed: The Effects of Violence on Peace Processes* (Washington: United States Institute of Peace Press, 2001). The point is that the leadership factor is not isolated for in-depth analysis but rather touched upon in the context of all other things.
38. For example, see Hermann Giliomee and Janine Gagiano, *op. cit.*, Interestingly, there are just two references made to 'leadership' in the index of the book, and while arguing that if leaders fail to persuade their parties and followers to move from confrontation to accommodation then the societies will be confronted by even greater turmoil, the authors make no attempt to define further the central role of leaders in a peace process.
39. James Macgregor Burns, *Leadership* (New York: Harper & Row, 1978) p. 315.
40. Barbara Kellerman, 'Hitler's Ghost: A Manifesto', in Barbara Kellerman and Larraine R. Matusak, *Cutting Edge: Leadership 2000* (College Park, Maryland: James Macgregor Burns Academy of Leadership, 2000) p. 66.

41. Fran Buntman and Tong-yi Huang, 'The role of political imprisonment in developing and enhancing political leadership: a comparative study of South Africa and Taiwan's democratization', *Journal of Asian and African Studies*, 35, 1 (2000) pp. 43–66; and Kieran McEvoy, *Paramilitary Imprisonment in Northern Ireland: Resistance, Management and Release* (Oxford: Oxford University Press, 2001).

42. John Whyte, *Interpreting Northern Ireland* (Oxford: Clarendon Press, 1990).

43. *Ibid.*, p. 248.

44. John McGarry and Brendan O'Leary, *Explaining Northern Ireland: Broken Images* (Oxford: Blackwell, 1995) p. 1.

45. Fred Halliday, 'Peace Processes in the Late Twentieth Century: A Mixed Record.' in Michael Cox, Adrian Guelke and Fiona Stephen, eds, *A Farewell to Arms? From 'Long War' to Long Peace in Northern Ireland* (Manchester; New York: Manchester University Press, 2000) p. 285.

46. McGarry and O'Leary, *op. cit.*

47. McGarry and O'Leary, *op. cit.*

48. The author has already tentatively broached this particular subject in a previous paper. See Cathy Gormley-Heenan, *From Protagonist to Pragmatist: Political Leadership in Societies in Transition* (Derry/Londonderry: INCORE, 2001). In this report, I argue that there were a number of 'shifts' which took place at elite level which might explain some of the 'progress' in the peace process. These included the development of a leadership with a desire to actually hold power themselves rather than be ruled from Westminster; the development of a leadership which had become articulate in the knowledge of best and worst practice from other case studies; the development of a more broadly defined leadership which was inclusive of those previously excluded from politics; and the development of leadership as a profession which more people began to embrace.

49. Paul Arthur, *Peer Learning: Northern Ireland As A Case Study* (New York: Carnegie Corporation on Preventing Deadly Conflict, 1999).

50. *Ibid.*, p. 10.

51. Adrian Guelke, 'Comparatively Peaceful: South Africa, the Middle East and Northern Ireland' in Cox, Guelke and Stephen, eds, *op. cit.*, p. 224.

52. John Lloyd, 'Only the naïve believe that Nelson Mandela's magnanimity is a formula for politicians seeking to bring peace to other trouble spots'. *New Statesman and Society* (19 July 1996); and John Hume, *Personal Views: Politics, Peace and Reconciliation in Ireland* (Dublin: Town House, 1996) pp. 95–96.

53. Suzanne Breen, 'Rapture and Ecstasy – but not for Trimble', *Irish Times* (Dublin), 10 April 1998.

54. See Elgie, *op. cit.*, p. 3 for a series of definitions of political leadership.

55. Boutros Boutros-Ghali, George Bush, Jimmy Carter, Mikhail Gorbachev, and Desmond Tutu, *Essays on Leadership* (New York: Carnegie Corporation of New York, 1998) p. vii.

56. Robert C. Tucker, 'Nonconstituted Leaders', in Kellerman 1986, *op. cit.*, pp. 265–268.

57. Chong-Do Hah and Fredrick C. Bartol, 'Political Leadership as a Causative Phenomenon: Some Recent Analyses', *World Politics*, 36, 1 (1983) p. 107.

58. Fiona Devine, 'Qualitative Methods', in Marsh and Stoker, eds, *op. cit.*, p. 138.

59. Jay A. Conger, 'Qualitative Research as the Cornerstone Methodology for Understanding Leadership', *Leadership Quarterly*, 9, 1 (1998) p. 108.
60. *Ibid.*, p. 111.
61. David Richards, 'Elite Interviewing: Approaches and Pitfalls', *Politics*, 16, 3 (1996) p. 200.
62. *Ibid.*, p. 200.
63. Alan Finlayson, 'The Problem of the Political Interview', *Political Quarterly*, 73, 3 (2001) pp. 335–344.
64. Barney Glaser and Anselm Strauss, *The Discovery of Grounded Theory: Strategies for qualitative research* (Chicago: Aldine, 1967).
65. Ken W. Parry, 'Grounded Theory and Social Process: a new direction for leadership research', *Leadership Quarterly*, 9, 1 (1998) p. 89.
66. The potential for the rewriting of history by elite interviewees is discussed in more detail by Darren G. Lilleker, 'Interviewing the Political Elite: Navigating a Potential Minefield', *Politics*, 23, 3 (2003) p. 211.
67. Gary King, Robert Keohane, and Sidney Verba, *Designing Sound Inquiry* (Princeton: Princeton University Press, 1994) p. 15.
68. *Ibid.*, pp. 16–17.
69. David Marsh and Gerry Stoker, 'Conclusions', in Marsh and Stoker, eds, *op. cit.*, p. 289.
70. David A. Hamburg and Cyrus R. Vance, 'Foreword' in Boutros Boutros-Ghali, George Bush, Jimmy Carter, Mikhail Gorbachev and Desmond Tutu, eds, *Essays on Leadership* (New York: Carnegie Corporation of New York, 1998).

2 Conceptualizing Political Leadership in Peace Processes

1. For an extensive overview of existing leadership theory and practice, which spans a variety of academic disciplines, see Bernard M. Bass, *Bass & Stogdill's Handbook of Leadership: Theory Research & Managerial Applications* (New York: Free Press, 1990). See also Barbara Kellerman and James Macgregor Burns, eds, *Leadership: Multidisciplinary Perspectives* (Englewood Cliff, NJ: Prentice-Hall, 1984); and Joseph Rost, *Leadership for the Twenty-First Century* (New York: Praeger, 1991).
2. For an overview of political leadership literature sources, see Barbara Kellerman, ed., *Political Leadership: A Source Book* (Pittsburg: University of Pittsburg Press, 1986).
3. For an overview of the subject area, see David P. Barash and Charles P. Webel, *Peace and Conflict Studies* (London: Sage, 2002); and Ho-Won Jeong, *Peace and Conflict Studies: An Introduction* (Aldershot: Ashgate, 2000).
4. See Plato, *The Republic*, translated by Robin Waterfield, ed. (Oxford: Oxford World Classics, 2004); Niccolo Machiavelli, *The Prince* (Oxford: Oxford World Classics, 1998); and Max Weber, 'Politics as a Vocation', in *From Max Weber: Essays in Sociology*, translated and edited by H.H. Gerth and C. Wright Mills (London: Routledge & Kegan Paul, 1948).
5. For biographies of leaders grouped together around a common theme, for example, see Martin Westlake, ed., *Leaders of Transition* (Basingstoke: Macmillan, 2000).

6. See Anthony P. Ammeter, Ceasar Douglas, William, L. Gardner, Wayne A. Hochwarter and Gerald R. Ferris, 'Towards a Political Theory of Leadership', *Leadership Quarterly*, 13, 6 (2002) pp. 751–796; Jean Blondel, *Political Leadership: Towards a General Analysis* (London: Sage, 1987); Murray Edelman, *Constructing the Political Spectacle* (Chicago: University of Chicago Press, 1988) Lewis Edinger, 'Approaches to the Comparative Analysis of Political Leadership', *Review of Politics*, 52, 4 (1990) pp. 509–523; Howard Elcock, *Political Leadership* (Cheltenham: Edward Elgar, 2001); Chong-Do Hah and Fredrick C. Bartol, 'Political Leadership as a Causative Phenomenon', *World Politics*, 36, 1 (1983) pp. 100–120; Bryan D. Jones, ed., *Leadership and Politics: New Perspectives in Political Science* (Lawrence: Kansas University Press, 1989); Cedric J. Robinson, *The Terms of Order: Political Science and the Myth of Leadership* (Albany: SUNY Press, 1980); and Robert C. Tucker, *Politics as Leadership* (Columbia; London: University of Missouri Press, 1981).
7. For example, much of Robert Putnam's work on 'social capital' has been used in recent years to develop a new body of knowledge on political leadership. See John Kane, *The Politics of Moral Capital* (Cambridge: Cambridge University Press, 2001); and Stanley A. Renshon, 'Political Leadership as Social Capital: Governing in a Divided National Culture', *Political Psychology*, 21, 1 (2000) pp. 199–226. Similarly, John Gaffney has looked at the question of political leadership in relation to image and style and the relationship between leaders and the electorate. See John Gaffney, 'Imagined Relationships: Political Leadership in Contemporary Democracies', *Parliamentary Affairs*, 54, 1 (2001) pp. 120–133. Finally, see Glenn D. Paige, *To Nonviolent Political Science: From Seasons of Violence* (Honolulu: Center for Global Nonviolence Planning Project, Matsunaga Institute for Peace, 1993) which looks at moving towards non-violent global problem solving and the tasks that this presents to political leadership studies.
8. Blondel, *op. cit.*, p. 42.
9. Blondel, *op. cit.*, p. 44.
10. Paige, *op. cit.*, p. 90.
11. See Elcock, *op. cit.*, p. 21.
12. This is qualified and justified by Machiavelli's pessimistic view of human nature. In arguing that a prince need not adhere to previously made promises, he argues: '*If men were entirely good, this precept would not hold but because they are bad and will not keep faith with you, you are not bound to observe it with them*'. N. Machiavelli, *The Prince and The Discourses*, translated from the Italian by L. Ricci and revised by E.R.P. Vincent (New York: Modern Library, 1950) pp. 92–93.
13. As quoted in Paige, *op. cit.*, p. 90.
14. See Max Weber, 'Types of authority', in Kellerman, *op. cit.*, pp. 232–244.
15. Robert D. Kaplan, *Warrior Politics: Why Leadership Demands a Pagan Ethos* (New York: Random House, 2002).
16. David C. Nice, 'The Warrior Model of Leadership: Classic Perspectives and Contemporary Relevance', *Leadership Quarterly*, 9, 3 (1998) pp. 321–322.
17. See Oren Harari, *The Leadership Secrets of Colin Powell* (New York: McGraw-Hill, 2002); and Rudolph Giuliani and Ken Kurson, *Leadership* (New York: Hyperion, 2002).

18. Lewis J. Edinger, 'Political Science and Political Biography: Reflections on the Study of Leadership (1)', *The Journal of Politics*, 26, 2 (1964) p. 424.
19. Blondel, *op. cit.*, p. 39.
20. Edinger (1964), *op. cit.*, p. 426.
21. For example, see Peter J. Paris, *Black Leaders in Conflict: Joseph H. Jackson, Martin Luther King, Jr., Malcolm X, Adam Clayton Powell, Jr* (New York: Pilgrim, 1978).
22. Blondel, *op. cit.*, p. 26.
23. Blondel, *op. cit.*, p. 28.
24. See Blondel, *op. cit.*, p. 97.
25. Each of these definitions are explained in detail by Blondel, *op. cit.*, pp. 87–96.
26. Edinger, *op. cit.*, p. 510.
27. Edinger, *op. cit.*, pp. 510–512.
28. Edinger, *op. cit.*, p. 512.
29. See Stephen Ryan, 'Peace and Conflict Studies Today', *The Global Review of Ethnopolitics*, 2, 2 (2003) p. 80.
30. Mostafa Rejai and Kay Philips, *Loyalists and Revolutionaries: Political Leaders Compared* (New York; London: Praeger, 1988) p. ix.
31. *Ibid.*, p. xix.
32. Kane, *op. cit.*
33. Renshon, *op. cit.*
34. Barbara Kellerman, 'Hitler's Ghost: A Manifesto', in Barbara Kellerman and Lorraine R. Matusak, eds, *Cutting Edge: Leadership 2000* (College Park, Maryland: James Macgregor Burns Academy of Leadership, 2000) p. 66.
35. Giacomo Chiozza and Ajin Choi, 'Guess Who Did What: Political Leaders and the Management of Territorial Disputes, 1950–1990', *Journal of Conflict Resolution*, 47, 3 (2003) p. 253.
36. Todd S. Sechser, 'Are Soldiers Less War-Prone Than Statesmen?', *Journal of Conflict Resolution*, 48, 5 (2004) pp. 746–774.
37. Michael E. Brown, 'Ethnic and Internal Conflicts: Causes and Implications', Chester A. Crocker, Fen Osler Hampson and Pamela Aall, *Turbulent Peace: The Challenges of Managing International Conflict* (Washington DC: USIP Press, 2001) p. 220.
38. See Barbara Kellerman, *Bad Leadership: What it is, How It Happens, Why It Matters* (Harvard: Harvard Business School Press, 2004).
39. See James MacGregor Burns, *Leadership* (New York: Free Press, 1978).
40. See Arnold M. Ludwig, *King of the Mountain: The Nature of Political Leadership* (Lexington: Kentucky University Press, 2002).
41. See Michael Colaresi, 'When Doves Cry: International Rivalry, Unreciprocated Cooperation, and Leadership Turnover', *American Journal of Political Science*, 48, 3 (2004) pp. 555–570.
42. Blondel, *op. cit.*, p. 24.
43. See Betty Glad, 'Passing the Baton: Transformational Political Leadership From Gorbachev to Yeltsin; From De Klerk to Mandela', *Political Psychology*, 17, 1 (1996) pp. 1–28; and David Welsh and Jack Spence, 'F.W. de Klerk: Enlightened Conservative', in Martin Westlake, ed., *Leaders of Transition* (London: Macmillan, 2000) pp. 29–52.
44. Author interview, 22 March 2000.
45. Rejai and Philips, *op. cit.*, p. xix.

46. See David P. Barash, *Introduction to Peace Studies* (Belmont, California: Wadsworth, 1991).
47. See Johan Galtung, *Violence, Peace and Peace Research* (1969); and John Burton, *Deviance, Terrorism and War* (1979).
48. For example, see Hugh Miall, Oliver Ramsbotham and Tom Woodhouse, *Contemporary Conflict Resolution: The Prevention, Management and Transformation of Deadly Conflicts* (Oxford: Polity, 1999); and Louis Kriesberg, ed., *Intractable Conflicts and their Transformation* (Syracuse, New York: Syracuse University Press, 1989).
49. For example, see John Darby and Roger MacGinty, eds, *The Management of Peace Processes* (Basingstoke: Macmillan, 2000).
50. Barash, *op. cit.*
51. See John W. Burton, ed., *Conflict: Human Needs Theory* (Basingstoke: Macmillan, 1990).
52. John Paul Lederach, *Building Peace: Sustainable Reconciliation in Divided Societies* (Washington DC: United States Institute of Peace Press, 1997).
53. *Ibid.*, pp. 38–40.
54. *Ibid.*, p. 45.
55. *Ibid.*, pp. 45–46.
56. Paul Dixon, 'Political Skills or Lying and Manipulation? The Choreography of the Northern Ireland Peace Process', *Political Studies*, 50, 4 (2002) pp. 725–741.
57. Arthur Aughey, 'The Art and Effect of Political Lying in Northern Ireland', *Irish Political Studies*, 17, 2 (2002) pp. 1–16.
58. Eric A. Nordlinger, *Conflict Regulation in Divided Societies* (Harvard: Center for International Affairs-Harvard University, 1972) p. 40.
59. *Ibid.*, pp. 20–29.
60. *Ibid.*, p. 40.
61. *Ibid.*, pp. 43–51.
62. *Ibid.*, p. 119.
63. Miall, Ramsbotham and Woodhouse, *op. cit.*, p. 157.
64. Miall, Ramsbotham and Woodhouse, *op. cit.*, p. 157.
65. Burns, *op. cit.*
66. Stephen J. Stedman, *Peacemaking in Civil War: International mediation in Zimbabwe 1974–1980* (Boulder, Colorado: Lynne Rienner, 1990) p. 241.
67. Louis Kriesberg, ed., 'Introduction', in Louis Kriesberg and Stuart Thorson, eds, *Timing the De-escalation of International Conflicts* (New York: Syracuse University Press, 1991) p. 9.
68. Robert L. Rothstein, 'In Fear of Peace: Getting Past Maybe', in Robert L. Rothstein, ed., *After the Peace: Resistance and Reconciliation* (London: Lynne Rienner, 1999).
69. *Ibid.*, p. 9.
70. *Ibid.*
71. *Ibid.*
72. Gerry Adams, *Hope of a New Beginning – Opening remarks at strand two of the peace talks*, 7 October 1997. Accessed online at http://sinnfein.ie/peace/speech/24.
73. Daniel Lieberfeld, 'Conflict "Ripeness" Revisited: The South African and Israel/Palestine Cases', *Negotiation Journal*, 15, 1 (1999) pp. 63–82.

74. Ian S. Lustick, 'Ending Protracted Conflict: The Oslo Peace Process Between Political Partnership and Legality', *Cornell International Law Journal*, 30, 3 (1997) pp. 741–757.
75. See John Whyte, *Interpreting Northern Ireland* (Oxford: Clarendon, 1990) who made the point that Northern Ireland has been exhaustively researched.
76. See David McKittrick, *Endgame: The Search for Peace in Northern Ireland* (Belfast: Blackstaff Press, 1994); David McKittrick and Eamon Mallie, *The Fight for Peace: The Secret Story Behind the Irish Peace Process* (London: Heinemann, 1996); David McKittrick, *The Nervous Peace* (Belfast: Blackstaff Press, 1996); David McKittrick, *Making Sense of the Troubles* (London: Penguin, 2001).
77. For example, see Gerry Adams, *Hope and History: Making Peace in Ireland* (Kerry: Brandon, 2004); Bill Clinton, *My Life* (New York: Knopf, 2004); Kate Fearon, *Women's Work: The Story of the Northern Ireland Women's Coalition* (Belfast: Blackstaff Press, 1999); John Major, *John Major: The Autobiography*, 1st edn (London: HarperCollins, 1999); George Mitchell, *Making Peace* (London: Heinemann, 1999); Majorie Mowlam, *Momentum: The Struggle for Peace, Politics, and the People* (London: Hodder & Stoughton, 2002); and David Trimble, *To Raise up a New Northern Ireland* (Belfast: Belfast Press, 2001).
78. See Paul Bew and Gordon Gillespie, *The Northern Ireland Peace Process 1993–1996: A Chronology* (London: Serif, 1996); Chris Gilligan and Jonathan Tonge, eds, *Peace or War? Understanding the Peace Process in Northern Ireland* (Aldershot: Ashgate, 1997); Jennifer Todd and Joseph Ruane, *After the Good Friday Agreement: Analysing Political Change in Northern Ireland* (Dublin: University College Dublin Press, 1999); Thomas Hennessey, *The Northern Ireland Peace Process: Ending the Troubles* (Dublin: Gill & Macmillan, 2000); Roger MacGinty and John Darby, *Guns and Government: The Management of the Northern Ireland Peace Process* (Basingstoke: Palgrave Macmillan, 2002); Michael Cox, Adrian Guelkeand Fiona Stephens, eds, *A Farewell to Arms? From the Long War To Long peace in Northern Ireland* (Manchester: Manchester University Press, 2000): Marianne Elliott, *The Long Road to Peace in Northern Ireland* (Liverpool: Liverpool University Press, 2002).
79. O'Connor, *op. cit.*
80. Hennessey, *op. cit.*
81. David Trimble, 'The Belfast Agreement', *Fordham International Law Journal*, 22, 4 (1999) pp. 1145–1170.
82. Trimble (1999), *op. cit.*, p. 1149.
83. Trimble (1999), *op. cit.*
84. Trimble (1999), *op. cit.*
85. The other factors which Trimble highlighted that are not germane to the concept of 'leadership' were changes in Europe, the collapse of communism and unionist changes.
86. George Mitchell, 'Toward Peace in Northern Ireland', *Fordham International Law Journal*, 22, 4 (1999) p. 1138.
87. George Mitchell, *The Times* (London), 28 August 1998. As quoted in Henry Sinnerton, *David Ervine: Uncharted Waters* (Kerry: Brandon, 2002).
88. Keith Alderman, 'Setting the Record Straight', *Parliamentary Affairs*, 54, 1 (2001) pp. 134–138.

89. McGarry and O'Leary, *op. cit.*, p. 386.
90. Elena Mastors, 'Gerry Adams and the Northern Ireland Peace Process: A Research Note', *Political Psychology*, 21, 4 (2000) p. 839.
91. *Ibid.*, p. 842.
92. *Ibid.*, pp. 842–843.
93. Ken Heskin, Ed Cairnsand Deborah McCourt, 'Perceptions of Political Leaders in Northern Ireland: A Factor-Analytic Study', *Irish Journal of Psychology*, 11, 4 (1990) p. 364.
94. Morna Crozier, 'Good Leaders and "Decent" Men: an Ulster Contradiction', in Mrytle Hill and Sarah Barber, eds, *Aspects of Irish Studies*, (Belfast: Institute for Irish Studies, Queens University, 1990).
95. *Ibid.*, p. 83.
96. Hugh O'Doherty, 'Leadership and Developing Democracy Where There is None', in Adrian Guelke, ed., *Democracy and Ethnic Conflict: Advancing Peace in Deeply Divided Societies* (Basingstoke: Palgrave Macmillan, 2004) p. 118.
97. *Ibid.*, p. 119
98. *Ibid.*, p. 134
99. Warren G. Bennis and Burt Nanus, *Leaders: The Strategies of Taking Charge* (New York: Harper & Row, 1985).
100. Blondel, *op. cit.*, p. 24.

3   Explaining Political Leadership in Northern Ireland

1. Bernard Bass, *Bass and Stodgill's Handbook of Leadership* (New York: Free Press, 1990) p. 22.
2. Barbara Kellerman, *Political Leadership: A Source Book* (Pittsburg: University of Pittsburg Press, 1986) p. 193.
3. Margaret G. Hermann, 'Leaders, Leadership and Flexibility: Influences on heads of Government as negotiators and Mediators', *American Academy of Political and Social Science*, 542 (1995) pp. 148–167.
4. Robert J. House and Ram A. Aditya, 'The Social Scientific Study of Leadership: Quo Vadis?', *Journal of Management*, 23, 3 (1997) p. 439.
5. See Colin Barker, Alan Johnson and Michael Lavalette, eds, *Leadership and Social Movements* (Manchester: Manchester University Press, 2001); Betty Glad, 'Passing the Baton: Transformational Political Leadership from Gorbachev to Yeltsin; from de Klerk to Mandela', *Political Psychology*, 17, 1 (1996) pp. 1–28; John Kane, *The Politics of Moral Capital* (Cambridge: Cambridge University Press, 2001); Gabriel Sheffer, *Innovative Leaders in International Politics* (Albany: State University of New York Press, 1993); and Martin Westlake, ed., *Leaders of Transition* (Basingstoke: Macmillan, 2000).
6. See Kevin B. Lowe and William L. Gardner, 'Ten Years of the Leadership Quarterly: Contributions and Challenges for the Future', *Leadership Quarterly*, 11, 4 (2000) pp. 459–514. The authors estimate that one third of all published research over the ten year period analysed focused on transformational/charismatic leadership.
7. Burns, *op. cit.*
8. Terry L. Price, 'The Ethics of Authentic Transformational Leadership', *Leadership Quarterly*, 14, 1 (2003) pp. 67–81.

9. See James Macgregor Burns, 'The Difference between Power Wielders and Leaders', in Kellerman, ed., *op. cit.*, pp. 287–299, for a description of the distinctions made between leaders and power wielders.

10. Barbara Kellerman, 'Hitler's Ghost: A Manifesto', in Barbara Kellerman and Larraine R. Matusak, eds, *Cutting Edge: Leadership 2000* (Maryland: James MacGregor Burns Academy of Leadership, University of Maryland, 2000) p. 66.

11. *Ibid.*, p. 67.

12. Bernard Bass and P. Steidlmeier, 'Ethics, character and authentic transformational leadership behavior', *Leadership Quarterly*, 10, 2 (1999) pp. 181–217.

13. See Adele Bergstrom, 'An Interview with Dr Bernard M. Bass', Kravis Leadership Institute *Leadership Review*, Winter 2003; and Bass and Steidlmeier, *op. cit.*, for an introduction to the concepts of pseudo-transformational and pseudo-transactional leadership.

14. Notes from closed meeting with Bernard Bass, James MacGregor Burns Academy of Leadership, University of Maryland, 28 April 2000.

15. *Ibid.*

16. Burns, *op. cit.*

17. Notes from closed meeting with Bernard Bass, *op. cit.*

18. Gabriel Sheffer, 'Moshe Sharett: The Legacy of an Innovative Moderate Leader', in Gabriel Sheffer, eds, *Innovative Leaders in International Politics* (Albany: State University of New York Press, 1993) p. 85.

19. Gabriel Sheffer, 'A Final Overview', in Gabriel Sheffer, *op. cit.*, p. 245.

20. See Max Weber, 'Types of Authority', in Kellerman 1986, *op. cit.*

21. Robert J. House, 'A 1976 Theory of Charismatic Leadership', in Jerry G. Hunt and Lars L. Larson, eds, *Leadership: The Cutting Edge* (Carbondale: Southern Illinois University Press, 1977) pp. 189–207.

22. Peter G. Northouse, *Leadership: Theory and Practice* (Thousand Oaks, Calif.: Sage, 2004) p.171.

23. House and Aditya, *op. cit.*, p. 441.

24. David C. Nice, 'The Warrior Model of Leadership: Classic Perspectives and Contemporary Relevance', *Leadership Quarterly*, 9, 3 (1998) pp. 321–322.

25. *Ibid.*, pp. 321–332.

26. See note 5.

27. Author Interview, 24 March 2000. The use of the word 'collective leadership' in respect of the party has been taken on by political analysts also. See Fionnuala O'Connor, *Breaking the Bonds: Making Peace in Northern Ireland* (Edinburgh: Mainstream, 2002) p. 67.

28. Author Interview, 22 February 2000.

29. Author Interview, 22 March 2000.

30. Author Interview, 22 March 2000.

31. Author Interview, 22 March 2000.

32. A more sceptical interpretation of collective leadership can be related to the concept of 'groupthink' as introduced by Janis. He questions the notion of seemingly collective leadership when he said: '. . . the group's agenda can be readily manipulated by a suave leader, often with the tacit approval of the members so that there is simply no opportunity to discuss the drawbacks of a seemingly satisfactory plan of action. This is one of the conditions that foster groupthink'. See Irving L. Janis, 'Groupthink', in Kellerman, *op. cit.*, p. 336.

33. This was a phenomenon not unique to Northern Ireland however. See Fran Buntman and Tong-yi Huang, 'The Role of Political Imprisonment in Developing and Enhancing Political Leadership: A Comparative Study of South Africa's and Taiwan's Democratization', *Journal of African and Asian Studies*, 35, 1 (2000) pp. 43–66, which looks at the connections among prisoner resistance, politics in prisons, and post-imprisonment patterns of democratic leadership and elite formation.
34. As cited in *Vanguard Bulletin*, 2 (1976).
35. Author Interview, 22 February 2000.
36. Author Interview, 22 March 2000.
37. Mary Braid, 'The Protestant Pretenders', *The Independent* (London), 8 March 1995.
38. Author Interview, 22 March 2000.
39. Author Interview, 22 March 2000.
40. Author Interview, 22 March 2000.
41. Kieran McEvoy, *Paramilitary Imprisonment in Northern Ireland: Resistance, Management and Release* (Oxford: Oxford University Press, 2001) pp. 38–39.
42. See Arthur Aughey, 'Unionism and Self Determination', in Patrick J. Roche and Brian Barton, eds, *The Northern Ireland Question: Myth and Reality* (Aldershot: Avebury, 1991) p. 10.
43. Author Interview, 9 March 2000.
44. Author Interview, 22 February 2000.
45. Author Interview, 22 March 2000.
46. Comment made by David Trimble, *Irish News*, 2 September 1995. As cited in Fergal Cochrane, *Unionist Politics and the Politics of Unionism Since the Anglo-Irish Agreement* (Cork: Cork University Press, 2001) p. 340.
47. Author Interview, 22 March 2000.
48. Author Interview, 24 March 2000.
49. Author Interview, 22 February 2000.
50. Author Interview, 22 February 2000.
51. Author Interview, 22 February 2000.
52. Author Interview, 1 March 2000.
53. Author Interview, 22 March 2000.
54. Author Interview, 24 March 2000.
55. Decca Aitkenhead, 'Time and Gerry', *The Guardian* (London), 4 August 1997.
56. Jude Collins, 'Lessons in the Ignoble Art of Politics', *Irish News*, 21 August 2003. Collins argues that Hume was seen by supporters as 'a man suffused with goodness, shining Gandhi-like in the gloom of local politics'.
57. Jeremy Smith, *Making the Peace in Ireland* (Harlow: Longman, 2002) pp. 186–187; Michael Gove, 'Preface', in David Trimble, ed., *To Raise Up a New Northern Ireland: Articles and Speeches 1998–2000* (Belfast: The Belfast Press, 2001). Gove commented that Trimble *was* 'a remarkable politician. His gifts: of moral courage, intellectual power and personal persuasiveness elevate him above the ordinary ranks of most politicians in these islands. He has been likened to a prophet, insufficiently recognised in his own land but garlanded elsewhere'. p. i.
58. Braid, *op. cit.*
59. Jonathan Stevenson argues that the Clinton administration were willing to treat the leaders of various terrorist movements as virtual statesmen

in the hope of converting them into non-violent politicians. He uses and uses the case of Gerry Adams as a 'terrorist' to prove his point. See Jonathan Stevenson, 'Northern Ireland: Treating Terrorists as Statesmen', *Foreign Policy*, 105 (1996) pp. 125–140.

60. Ruth Dudley Edwards recalls: 'I sat listening in mingled amazement and horror as British and Irish officials, politicians and journalists and other movers-and-shakers denounced him as a hard-line, bad-tempered bigot'. See Ruth Dudley Edwards, 'Trimble and I', *Sunday Independent*, 12 March 2000.

61. Sinnerton, *op. cit.*, p. 9. Sinnerton mentions Professor Paul Arthur's comment that Ervine broke the perception of the humourless 'Ulster-Prod'. He quotes Arthur as saying: 'In terms of personality, he could almost be a nationalist politician'.

62. Sharrock and Davenport, *op. cit.*

63. Donald P. Doumitt, *Conflict in Northern Ireland: The History, The Problem and The Challenge* (New York: Peter Long, 1985) p. 113.

64. *Ibid.*, as quoted on p. 113.

65. David McKittrick, 'Unhappy Unionists Left feeling Outflanked', *The Independent* (London), 1 September 1994.

66. UDP Election Communication for the Forum Election, 1996. As cited in James White McAuley, 'Still "No Surrender"? New Loyalism and the Peace Process in Northern Ireland,', in John P. Harrington, and Elizabeth J. Mitchell, *Politics and Performance in Contemporary Northern Ireland* (Amherst: University of Massachusetts Press, 1999) pp. 57–81.

67. David McKittrick, 'Ulstermen march to a new drum', *The Independent*, 14 October 1994. McKittrick details a heated exchange between Billy Hutchinson from the PUP and Iris Robinson, wife of Peter Robinson from the DUP over whether the DUP leaders encouraged people to go out onto the street and fight republicanism. The subject of whether mainstream unionist party leaders encouraged others to terrorism is examined by Steve Bruce, 'Fundamentalism and Political Violence: The Case of Paisley and Ulster Evangelicals, *Religion*, 31, 4 (2001) pp. 387–405. Bruce claims that while Paisley's record in deliberately encouraging others to use political violence is mixed, there are two examples of Paisley giving public support to loyalist terror organisations in civil disobedience.

68. As quoted in Henry McDonald, *Trimble* (London: Bloomsbury, 2000) p. 201.

69. Cochrane, *op. cit.*

70. Cochrane, *op. cit.*, p. 342.

71. See O'Connor (1999), *op. cit.*, p. 26.

72. Eamon Mallie and David McKittrick, *Endgame in Ireland* (London: Hodder & Stoughton, 2001) p. 272.

73. Mo Mowlam, *Momentum: The Struggle for Peace, Politics and the People* (London: Hodder & Stoughton, 2002).

74. McDonald, *op. cit.*, p. 201.

75. See Paul Dixon, *Northern Ireland: The Politics of War and Peace* (Basingstoke: Macmillan, 2001) for a discussion on what is 'truth' and whose 'reality' we are talking about.

76. The most obvious example of this must be David Trimble's transition from his hardliner stance, evidenced in his behaviour at Drumcree in 1995, to

a more moderate approach in the period after his election as leader of the Ulster Unionists in September 1995.

77. Dixon 2002, *op. cit.*
78. Mo Mowlam was alleged to have grown particularly frustrated with this type of behaviour from the political leadership in the multi-party talks process which took the form of band standing in front of the cameras after making progress behind closed doors. See Colin Brown, 'Mowlam's Getaway for Party Leaders', *The Independent* (London), 4 February 1998.
79. Dixon 2002, *op. cit.*, p. 734.
80. See Anonymous, 'Calling John Hume', *The Economist*, 13 February 1999. It notes: 'Mr Hume and Mr Trimble may have clasped hands on public stages, colleagues point out, but they do not get along. Mr Hume asked his deputy, Seamus Mallon, to be Mr. Trimble's opposite number as deputy First Minister. This choice was welcomed by unionists, who had boosted Mr Mallon throughout the talks preceding the agreement. David could not work with John, it was said. John was short-tempered, openly contemptuous of unionists, devious. Seamus, on the other hand was pragmatic, decent. David and Seamus could work together'.
81. Robert L. Rothstein, 'In Fear of Peace: Getting Past Maybe', in Robert L. Rothstein, ed., *After the Peace: Resistance and Reconciliation* (London: Lynne Rienner, 1999).
82. Fionnuala O'Connor, *Breaking the Bonds: Making Peace in Northern Ireland* (Edinburgh: Mainstream, 2002) p. 31.
83. One political leader was clear as to the type of leadership that was needed during the peace process, irrespective of the type of leadership which actually existed: 'What leadership is needed? It's challenging your own people all the time, speaking to the best hopes of what you would like then to do, rather than reinforcing their fears, recognising your dependency on the other person in a negotiation process, that you are as dependent on that leader as he is on you, or she is on you, and also making a collaborative team effort, and all the time disseminating any decisions that you make, and finally obviously there's the element of being radical and risk taking, but that being made in the context of all the other things'. Author Interview, 22 February 2000.
84. House and Aditya, *op. cit.*, p. 455.

4   The Role of Political Leadership

1. John Darby and Roger MacGinty, *Contemporary Peacemaking: Conflict, Violence and Peace Processes* (Basingstoke: Palgrave Macmillan, 2003) p. 267.
2. *Ibid.*, p. 268.
3. David Bloomfield, Yash Ghai and Ben Reilly, 'Analysing Deep Rooted Conflict' in Peter Harris and Ben Reilly, eds, *Democracy and Deep-Rooted Conflict: Options for Negotiators* (Stockholm: IDEA – International Institute for Democracy and Electoral Assistance, 1998) p. 38.
4. *Ibid.*
5. *Ibid.*, p. 393.
6. *Ibid.*, p. 393.

7. See Mostafa Rejai and Kay Philips, *Leaders and Leadership: An Appraisal of Theory and Research* (Westport Connecticut and London: Praegar Press, 1997) for a more normative analysis in relation to the roles of leadership and Henry Mintzberg, *The Nature of Managerial Work* (New York: Harper & Row, 1973) for a more behavioural overview.

8. Martin Fletcher, 'Picture that was almost missed', *The Times* (London), 1 December 1995.

9. Alan Murdoch, 'Irish leaders shake hands across a 30 year divide', *The Independent* (London), 3 October 1995.

10. David Sharrock, 'McAliskey convinced the peace will prevail', *The Guardian* (London), 31 August 1995.

11. John Gray, 'Awful racket, this peace', *The Guardian* (London), 6 January 1996.

12. Dean Godson, *Himself Alone: David Trimble and the Ordeal of Unionism* (London: HarperCollins, 2004) p. 194.

13. *Ibid.*, p. 195.

14. *Building a Dynamic for Change*, Sinn Féin Westminster Election Manifesto, 1997, p. 2.

15. Henry McDonald, *Trimble* (London: Bloomsbury, 2001) p. 180.

16. *Ibid.*, pp. 190–191.

17. Fionnuala O'Connor, *Breaking the Bonds: Making Peace in Northern Ireland* (Edinburgh: Mainstream, 2002) p. 33.

18. Margaret G. Hermann, 'Leaders, Leadership and Flexibility: Influences on Heads of Government as Negotiators and Mediators', *The Annals of the American Academy of Political and Social Science*, 542 (1995) p. 160.

19. Harvey Waterman, 'Political Order and the "Settlement" of Civil Wars', in Roy Licklider, ed., *Stopping the Killings: How Civil Wars End* (New York: New York University Press, 1993) pp. 292–302.

20. Gerry Adams Presidential Address to Sinn Féin Ard Fheis, 1996.

21. Author Interview, 24 March 2000.

22. Author Interview, 22 February 2000.

23. Gary McMichael, *An Ulster Voice: In Search of Common Ground in Northern Ireland* (Boulder, Colorado: Roberts Rinehart, 1999) pp. 174–176.

24. Roger MacGinty and John Darby, *Guns and Government: The Management of the Northern Ireland Peace Process* (Basingstoke: Palgrave Macmillan, 2002) p. 80.

25. Kirsten Sparre, 'Megaphone Diplomacy in the Northern Irish Peace Process: Squaring the Circle by Talking to Terrorists Through Journalists', *The Harvard Journal of Press/Politics*, 6, 1 (2001) pp. 88–104.

26. Dean G. Pruitt, 'Flexibility in Conflict Episodes', *The Annals of the American Academy of Political and Social Science*, 542 (1995) p. 106.

27. Author Interview, 22 March 2000.

28. Henry Sinnerton, *David Ervine: Uncharted Waters* (Kerry: Brandon, 2002) pp. 178–181.

29. *Ibid.*, p. 181.

30. David McKittrick, 'Paramilitaries want peace to continue, says Trimble', *The Independent* (London), 19 October 1996.

31. Author Interview, 1 March 2000.

32. Author Interview, 22 March 2000.

33. Sparre, *op. cit.*

34. Author Interview, 1 March 2000.
35. Author Interview, 22 March 2000.
36. Paul Bew and Gordon Gillespie, *Northern Ireland: A Chronology of the Troubles 1968-1999* (Dublin: Gill & Macmillan, 1999) p. 350.
37. Gerry Adams, *Hope and History: Making Peace in Ireland* (Dingle: Brandon, 2004) p. 51.
38. Private information.
39. This role has clear resonance with Miall, Ramsbotham and Woodhouse's concept of 'actor transformation' as discussed in Chapter 2.
40. Jeremy Smith, *Making the Peace in Ireland* (Harlow: Longman, 2002) p. 210.
41. Martin Fletcher, 'Trimble Plots to Discredit Adams at Talks', *The Times* (London), 23 September 1997.
42. Nicholas Watt, 'Adams Rejects New Assembly', *The Times* (London), 28 October 1994.
43. O'Connor, *op. cit.*, p. 260.
44. Author Interview, 22 March 2000.
45. Rick Wilford, 'Introduction', in Rick Wilford, ed., *Aspects of the Belfast Agreement* (Oxford: Oxford University Press, 2001) p. 6.
46. *Building a Dynamic for Change*, Sinn Féin Westminster Election Manifesto, 1997.
47. *DUP Election Special*, DUP Election Manifesto, May 1996.
48. *Ibid.*
49. MacGinty and Darby (2002), *op. cit.*, p. 168.
50. Nicole Veash, 'Leaked Letter Sparks Unionist Row', *Belfast Newsletter*, 17 February 1998.
51. *Ibid.*
52. MacGinty and Darby (2002), *op. cit.*, p. 76.
53. Donald Horowitz, 'Explaining the Northern Ireland Agreement: The Sources of An Unlikely Constitutional Consensus', *British Journal of Political Studies*, 32, 2 (2002) p. 202.
54. *Ibid.*
55. *Ibid.*

5   The Capacity of Political Leadership

1. See Jeremy Smith, *Making the Peace in Ireland* (Harlow: Longman, 2002) p. 241. Smith points to a general war weariness pervading all groups and parties; the blurring of national boundaries and questions of sovereignty in the 1990s; and the influence of European 'post-modern' politics as influential factors which meant that Northern Ireland's problems were more likely to be accommodated in the1990s than at any other time previously.
2. Author Interview, 22 March 2000.
3. Roger MacGinty, 'From Revolution to Reform: Republicans and the Peace Process', in Michael Cox, Adrian Guelke and Fiona Stephens, eds, *A Farewell to Arms: From 'Long War' to Long Peace in Northern Ireland* (Manchester: Manchester University Press, 2006) pp. 124–138.
4. Arthur Aughey, 'The 1998 Agreement': Unionist Responses', in Michael Cox, Adrian Guelke and Fiona Stephens, eds, *A Farewell to Arms: From 'Long War'*

   to Long Peace in Northern Ireland (Manchester: Manchester University Press, 2000) p. 69.

5. Ian Paisley, 'A Talks Alternative', *Belfast Telegraph*, 25 June 1999.

6. Adrian Guelke, 'Comparatively Peaceful: South Africa, the Middle East and Northern Ireland', in Michael Cox, Adrian Guelke and Fiona Stephens, eds, *A Farewell to Arms: From 'Long War' to Long Peace in Northern Ireland* (Manchester: Manchester University Press, 2000) p. 230.

7. Martin Mansergh, 'The Background to the Irish Peace Process', in Michael Cox, Adrian Guelke and Fiona Stephens, eds, *A Farewell to Arms: From 'Long War' to Long Peace in Northern Ireland* (Manchester: Manchester University Press, 2000) p. 19.

8. Gerry Adams, *Hope and History: Making Peace in Ireland* (Kerry: Brandon, 2004) p. 51.

9. For example, James Loughlin, *The Ulster Question Since 1945* (Basingstoke: Macmillan, 1998) has been critiqued as rewriting some of the early history of the SDLP insofar as his arguments 'give the impression that Hume almost single-handedly persuaded London, Dublin and the republican movement into the peace process'. See Sabine Wichert, 'The Northern Ireland Conflict: New Wine in Old Bottles', *Contemporary European History*, 9, 2 (2000) pp. 308–309.

10. Richard L. Hughes, Robert C. Ginnett and Gordon J. Curphy, *Leadership: Enhancing the Lessons of Experience* (London: Irwin/McGraw-Hill, 1999) p. 138.

11. James MacGregor Burns, *Leadership* (New York: Harper & Row, 1978) p. 11.

12. James MacGregor Burns, 'The Difference Between Power Wielders and Leaders', Barbara Kellerman, ed., *Political Leadership: A Source Book* (Pittsburg: University of Pittsburg Press, 1986) p. 295.

13. These tactics include rational persuasion, inspirational appeals, consultation, ingratiation, personal appeals, exchange, coalition tactics, pressure tactics, and legitimizing tactics. The tactics used are directly relational to the relative power of the leaders. For example, leaders will tend to use 'soft tactics' such as ingratiation when they expect their own position is weak. Conversely, leaders tend to use 'pressure tactics' when their position is much stronger. See Gary A. Yukl, Richard Lepsinger, and Antoinette D. Lucia, 'Preliminary Report on the Development and Validation of the Influence Behavior Questionnaire', in Kenneth E. Clark, Miriam B. Clark, and David P. Campbell, eds, *Impact of Leadership* (Greensboro, NC: Centre for Creative Leadership, 1992) pp. 417–427.

14. Howard Elcock, *Political Leadership* (Cheltenham: Edward Elgar, 2001) p. 62.

15. A similar point is also made by Richard Heffernan, 'Prime Ministerial predominance? Core Executive Politics in the UK', *British Journal of Politics and International Relations*, 5, 3 (2003) pp. 347–372.

16. See Arjen Boin and Paul 't Hart, 'Public leadership in Times of Crisis: Mission Impossible?', *Public Administration Review*, 63, 5 (2003) pp. 544–553.

17. Hughes, Ginnett and Curphy, *op. cit.*, p. 145.

18. Stephen J. Zaccaro and Richard J. Klimoski, eds, *The Nature of Organizational Leadership: Understanding the Performance Imperatives Confronting Today's Leaders* (San Francisco, CA: Jossey-Bass, 2001) p. 12.

19. For a full analysis of the various political parties structures and platforms see Arthur Aughey, 'Political Parties: Structures and Platforms', in Arthur Aughey

and Duncan Morrow, eds, *Northern Ireland Politics* (London: Longman, 1996).

20. Nicholas Watt and Philip Webster, 'Four Unionists Join Contest to Succeed Molyneaux', *The Times* (London), 29 August 1995.

21. Afterward coming second to Trimble in the 1995 leadership contest, Taylor claimed: 'Leading the UUP is the hardest job in British politics . . . I actually felt a weight lifted off my shoulders when I lost. Anyone who wants to be leader needs their head examined. I think David is doing a great job and I have no ambitions to be leader'. See BBC Online, *'IRA Will Return to Violence'*, 6 October 1999. Available online at http://news.bbc.co.uk/1/hi/northern_ireland/467308.stm.

22. See Henry McDonald, *Trimble* (London: Bloomsbury, 2000) pp. 155–156.

23. John Mullin, 'The Hard Man of Peace', *The Guardian* (London), 3 July 1999.

24. Suzanne Breen, 'David's Dilemma', *Fortnight*, November 1997, p. 7.

25. Suzanne Breen, 'The Glacier Shifts', *Fortnight*, November 1995, p. 7.

26. After Ruairi O'Bradaigh's resignation as leader of Sinn Féin, in 1983, Adams was elected. He said: 'I was elected in his place as president of Sinn Féin, a job I did not want. I felt inadequate for the position. I also didn't know how I could fit everything in between elected responsibilities, efforts to build the party, the ongoing tensions of the conflict, my own life and family, as well as my own political view that Sinn Féin – as an all-Ireland party – should have a Southern-based leader'. See Adams, *op. cit.*, p. 20.

27. Dean Godson, *Himself Alone: David Trimble and the Ordeal of Unionism* (London: HarperCollins, 2004) pp. 147–148.

28. *Ibid.*, p. 152. Trimble's wife said of his election as leader: 'Part of David didn't want it at all; a part of him wanted a quiet life – to sit at home and listen to music and to go to the opera'.

29. See Fionnuala O'Connor, *Breaking the Bonds: Making Peace in Northern Ireland* (Edinburgh: Mainstream, 2002) p. 25.

30. Anne Cadwallader, 'A Political Triumph for the Derryman', *Irish Press*, 1 September 1994.

31. David Bloomfield, *Political Dialogue in Northern Ireland: The Brooke Initiative 1989–92* (Basingstoke: Macmillan, 1998) pp. 3–4.

32. Flackes, W.D. and Sydney Elliot, *Northern Ireland: A Political Directory 1968–1993* (Belfast: Blackstaff, 1994) p. 297.

33. Author Interview, 24 March 2000.

34. This was Trimble's own analysis of the situation as discussed in an interview with Godson, *op. cit.*, p. 181.

35. Paul Dixon, *Northern Ireland: The Politics of War and Peace* (Basingstoke: Palgrave Macmillan, 2001) p. 253.

36. Liam Clarke, 'Fall Out', *Sunday Times* (London), 9 November 1997.

37. Robert Harmel, 'The Iron Law of Oligarchy' Revisited', Bryan D. Jones, ed., *Leadership and Politics: New Perspectives in Political Science* (Kansas: University of Kansas Press, 1989) p. 161.

38. Author Interview, 22 March 2000.

39. Author Interview, 22 March 2000.

40. Aughey (1996), *op. cit.*, p. 161.

41. Aughey, *op. cit.*, p. 160.

42. Mullin, *op. cit.*

43. Godson, *op. cit.*, p. 154.
44. See Paul Dixon, 'Peace within the realms of the possible? David Trimble, unionist theology and theatrical politics', *Terrorism and Political Violence*, 16, 3 (2004) pp. 462–482.
45. *Ibid.*
46. Adams, *op. cit.*; Godson, *op. cit.*; John Hume, *Personal Views: Politics, Peace and Reconciliation in Ireland* (Dublin: Town House Press, 1996); Barry McCaffrey, *Alex Maskey: Man and Mayor* (Belfast: Brehon Press, 2003); Henry McDonald, *Trimble* (London: Bloomsbury, 2000); David Sharrock and Mark Davenport, *Man of War, Man of Peace? The Unauthorized Biography of Gerry Adams* (London: Macmillan, 1997); Henry Sinnerton, *David Ervine: Uncharted Waters* (Kerry: Brandon, 2002).
47. This is discussed in greater detail in Chapter 2.
48. Thomas Carlyle, 'On Hero's and Hero Worship', in Barbara Kellerman, ed., *Political Leadership: A Source Book* (Pittsburgh, Pa.: University of Pittsburgh Press, 1986).
49. Max Weber, 'Types of Authority', in Barbara Kellerman, ed., *Political Leadership: A Source Book* (Pittsburgh, Pa.: University of Pittsburgh Press, 1986).
50. Chanoch Jacobsen and Robert J. House, 'The Rise and Decline of Charismatic Leadership', Unpublished Paper, 26 January 1999.
51. Hughes, Ginnett and Curphy, eds, *op. cit.*, p. 307.
52. Robin Wilson, 'Asking the Right Question', Democratic Dialogue, *Reconstituting Politics* (Belfast: Democratic Dialogue, 1996) p. 43.
53. David McKittrick and David McVea, *Making Sense of the Troubles* (Belfast: Blackstaff, 2000) p. 186.
54. See David McKittrick, 'What are the options for peace?', *The Independent* (London), 14 February 1996.
55. David Sharrock, 'Preserving the Union', *Fortnight*, June 1996, p. 15.
56. Steve Bruce, 'Fundamentalism and Political Violence: The Case of Paisley and Ulster Evangelical', *Religion*, 31, 4 (2001) pp. 387–405.
57. David McKittrick, 'Sinn Féin returns to the fold; Britain quibbles, but Dublin hails a historic handshake as a new beginning', *The Independent* (London), 7 September 1994; and David McKittrick, 'Trimble and Adams Make History', *The Independent* (London), 12 September 1998.
58. David McKittrick, 'Ulster Talks: Blair Barracked after Historic Handshake with Adams', *The Independent* (London), 14 October 1997.
59. O'Connor (2002), *op. cit.*, p. 33.
60. Paul Dixon, 'Political Skills or Lying and Manipulation? The Choreography of the Northern Ireland Peace process', *Political Studies*, 50, 4 (2002) p. 739.
61. Author Interview, 1 March 2000.
62. Francis Sejersted, *Presentation Speech: the Nobel peace prize 1998*. Full text available online at http://www.nobel.se/peace/laureates/1998/presentation-speech.html.
63. David Trimble, *Acceptance Speech: the Nobel peace prize 1998*. Full text available online at http://www.nobel.se/peace/laureates/1998/trimble-lecture.html.
64. Michael Cunningham, 'The Political Language of John Hume', *Irish Political Studies*, 12 (1997) pp. 13–22.

6   The Effect of Political Leaders on Other Political Leaders

1. Private information from author interview.
2. This trait was identified by one party leader as being an important characteristic of leadership. Author Interview, 22 February 2000. See Chapter 3 and the section on soft-skilled leadership for a further explanation of this.
3. See Sue Denham, 'Unionists song remains the same', *Sunday Times* (London), 8 June 1997.
4. The exception to this was discreet contact that had been established between the politicians such as Billy Hutchinson from the PUP and republicans, often through their work on community groups. See David McKittrick and David McVea, *Making Sense of the Troubles* (Belfast: Blackstaff, 2000) p. 201.
5. Adams recall of their first meetings with the SDLP in 1989 that: 'apart from John Hume, they were hostile, confrontational, on occasion arrogant . . . right up to the end of the discussions, Seamus Mallon, Austin Currie and Sean Farren lectured and hectored us'. See Gerry Adams, *Hope and History: Making Peace in Ireland* (Kerry: Brandon, 2004) pp. 78–79. See also Gerard Murray, *John Hume and the SDLP: Impact and Survival in Northern Ireland* (Dublin: Irish Academic Press, 1998). Chapter 4 of Murray's work details the opposition among senior SDLP personnel towards the Hume/Adams dialogue.
6. Stephen King, 'The Tragedy of Hume', *Ulster Review*, 22 (1997).
7. David Bloomfield, *Political Dialogue in Northern Ireland: The Brooke Initiative, 1989–92* (Basingstoke: Macmillan, 1998) pp. 3–4.
8. Author Interview, 22 March 2000.
9. For a full narrative of the difficulties faced by the Northern Ireland Women's Coalition during both the Forum debates and the talks process. See Kate Fearon, *Women's Work: The Story of the Northern Ireland Women's Coalition* (Belfast: Blackstaff, 1999).
10. Ben Macintyre, 'Maginnis snubs Adams on American TV', *The Times* (London), 6 October 1994.
11. Patrick Wintour, 'Ulster Factions Share Platform', *The Guardian* (London), 19 September 1995.
12. Mark Simpson, 'Loyalist and Sinn Fein Man in Debate', *Belfast Telegraph*, 11 February 1996.
13. *Ibid.*
14. Home News, 'Round Table Discussion with Trimble and McLaughlin', *The Time* (London), 3 February 1996.
15. Jonathan Freedland, 'Democratic Power of Televised Debate', *The Guardian* (London), 13 August 1997.
16. Martin Fletcher, 'Unionists Meet Sinn Fein at Talks', *The Times* (London), 24 September 1997.
17. Adams, *op. cit.*, p. 51.
18. Janice Gross Stein, 'Getting to the table: The Triggers, Stages, Functions, and Consequences of Prenegotiation', *International Journal*, XLIV (1989) p. 475.
19. Paul Arthur, 'Multiparty Mediation in Northern Ireland', in Chester A. Crocker, Fen Olsen Hampson and Pamela Aall, eds, *Herding Cats: Multi party Mediation in a Complex World* (Washington DC; Great Britain: United States Institute of Peace Press, 1999) p. 495.

20. Helen Brocklehurst, Noel Stott, Brandon Hamber and Gillian Robinson, 'Lesson Drawing: Northern Ireland and South Africa', *Indicator SA*, 18, 1 (2001) pp. 89–94.
21. See Paul Arthur, 'Some Thoughts on Transition: A Comparative View on the Peace Process in South Africa and Northern Ireland', *Government and Opposition*, 30, 1 (1995) pp. 48–59.
22. *Managing Change in A Diverse Society*, Conference Report, 21–26 July 1996, p. 2.
23. *Ibid.*, p. 6.
24. *Ibid.*, p. 7.
25. For example, the Irish Times learned of the event a month before it was due to take place but agreed to delay reporting the story until after the participants had confirmed their attendance. See Joe Carroll, 'Northern Ireland Politicians to Visit South Africa', *Irish Times* (Dublin), 13 May 1997.
26. Private information.
27. Eric A. Nordlinger, *Conflict Regulation in Divided Societies* (Harvard: Center for International Affairs – Harvard University, 1972) pp. 42–53.
28. The term 'political tourism' was used by the SDLP's Alban Maginness in response to a unionist based study trip to South Africa in 2002. See William Scholes, 'Unionists accused of double standards', *Irish News* (Belfast), 1 November 2002.
29. Dean Godson makes this comment about David Trimble with particular reference to his decision to fulfil a speaking engagement at the University of Chicago in the US at a critical point in the peace process – the period between when the Agreement was signed in April 1998 and the ensuing referendum in May 1998. See Dean Godson, *Himself Alone: David Trimble and the Ordeal of Unionism* (London: HarperCollins, 2004) p. 363.
30. Author Interview, 24 March 2000.
31. James McKnight, 'Sidelines', *Fortnight*, No: 335, January 1995, p. 46.
32. Author Interview, 22 March 2000.
33. Author Interview, 24 March 2000.
34. *Managing Change in A Diverse Society, op. cit.*, p. 14.
35. Theresa Judge, 'SA hosts "mesmerised" by Northern intransigence', *Irish Times*, 16 June 1997.
36. Author Interview, 24 March 2000.
37. Adrian Guelke, *The International System and the Northern Ireland Peace Process* (Institute for British-Irish Studies, Working Paper 21, 2002).
38. Peter Weir, 'The Enemy Within', *Ulster Review*, Spring 1998, Issue: 25, p. 8.
39. Author Interview, 24 March 2000.
40. Ronald J. Fisher, 'Prenegotiation Problem-Solving Discussions: Enhancing the Potential for Successful Negotiations', *International Journal*, XLIV, 2 (1989) p. 472.
41. J. Masilela, 'SA Hailed as a Beacon of Hope', *Pretoria News*, 17 February 1995.
42. Martina Purdy, 'Leaders' Legacy of Confusion', *Belfast Telegraph*, 14 June 1997.
43. David McKittrick, 'Prospects for peace: Ulster moves towards its Mandela moment', *The Independent* (London), 6 April 1998.
44. Adams, *op. cit.*, p. 302.
45. Adams, *op. cit.*, p. 311.

46. Fearon, *op. cit.*, p. 109.
47. As cited in Henry Sinnerton, *David Ervine: Uncharted Waters* (Kerry: Brandon, 2002) p. 218.
48. Author Interview, 23 June 2000.
49. Adams, *op. cit.*, p. 321.
50. Padraig O'Malley, 'Northern Ireland and South Africa: Hope and History at a Crossroads', in McGarry, J., ed., *Northern Ireland in the Divided World: Post-Agreement Northern Ireland in Comparative Perspective* (Oxford: Oxford University Press, 2001) p. 284. O'Malley notes that the South African hosts to the 1997 Northern Ireland political delegate presented to the group what they felt were the 'common dominators' of any peace process.
51. O'Malley, *op. cit.* See pp. 285–293 for a full explanation of each of the salient points offered by way of potential lesson learning.
52. Purdy, *op. cit.*
53. As cited in O'Malley, *op. cit.*, p. 300.
54. O'Malley, *op. cit.*, p. 300.
55. O'Malley, *op. cit.*, p. 301.
56. Author Interview, 22 March 2000.
57. Author Interview, 22 March 2000.
58. Unpublished transcript. Interview undertaken by Dr Chris Farrington, 26 January 2004.
59. The Project on Justice in Times of Transition, *Reconciliation and Community: The Future of Peace in Northern Ireland* (Belfast, 1995) p. 6.
60. *Ibid.*, p. 21.
61. O'Malley, *op. cit.*, p. 300.
62. Colin Brown, 'Mowlam's Getaway for Party Leaders', *The Independent* (London), 4 February 1998.
63. *Ibid.*
64. Stein (1989), *op. cit.*, p. 476.

7   The Limitations of Role, Capacity and Effect

1. Joseph C. Rost, *Leadership, Leaders, and Sin*, Selected Proceedings: 1998 Annual Meeting: Leaders/Scholars Association (Maryland: Center for the Advanced Study of Leadership and the James MacGregor Burns Academy of Leadership, University of Maryland, 1999) p. 66.
2. The term 'dirty hands' has been taken from Daniel R. Sabia Jr, 'Weber's political ethics and the problem of dirty hands', *Journal of Management History*, 2, 1 (1996) pp. 6–20.
3. See Gerry Adams, *Hope and History: Making Peace in Ireland* (Kerry: Brandon, 2004) p. 332.
4. John Darby and Roger MacGinty, 'Imperfect Peace: The Aftermath of Northern Ireland's Peace Accord', *Ethnic Studies Report*, 17, 2 (1999) pp. 201–225.
5. According to Godson, Trimble met Wright twice: '. . . once in a room in the church hall and once in the vicinity of the digger [at Drumcree church]'. Dean Godson, *Himself Alone: David Trimble and the Ordeal of Unionism* (London: HarperCollins, 2004) p. 235.

6. Henry McDonald, *Trimble* (London: Bloomsbury, 2000) pp. 189–190.
7. Author Interview, 22 March 2000.
8. Author Interview, 22 March 2000.
9. Padraig O'Malley, 'Northern Ireland and South Africa: Hope and History at a Crossroads', in John McGarry, ed., *Northern Ireland and the Divided World: Post-Agreement Northern Ireland in Comparative Perspective* (Oxford: Oxford University Press, 2001) p. 287.
10. Author Interview, 22 March 2000.
11. Sue Denham, 'Unionists' song remains the same', *Sunday Times* (London), 8 June 1997.
12. Fionnuala O'Connor, *Breaking the Bonds* (Edinburgh: Mainstream, 2002) p. 71.
13. John Darby and Roger MacGinty, 'Conclusions: Peace Processes, Present and Future', in John Darby and Roger MacGinty, eds, *Contemporary Peacemaking* (Basingstoke: Palgrave Macmillan, 2003) p. 267.
14. *Ibid.*, p. 268.
15. O'Malley, *op. cit.*, p. 287.
16. Author Interview, 22 March 2000.
17. O'Connor, *op. cit.*, p. 24.
18. Paul Dixon, 'Political Skills or Lying and Manipulation? The Choreography of the Northern Ireland Peace process', *Political Studies*, 50, 4 (2002) pp. 725–741.
19. See John Darby, 'Borrowing and Lending in Peace Processes', Darby and MacGinty, eds, *op. cit.*
20. See 'Right Leaders' Solution', *Belfast News Letter*, 23 October 1997.
21. These included Cyril Ramaphosa, Mac Maharaj, Matthew Phosa and Valli Moosa. See Adams, *op. cit.*, p. 372.
22. Adams, *op. cit.*, p. 217.
23. Adams, *op. cit.*, p. 215.
24. Adams, *op. cit.*, p. 220.
25. John McGarry, 'Political Settlements in Northern Ireland and South Africa', *Political Studies*, 45, 5 (1998) p. 854.
26. McGarry, *op. cit.*
27. John Lloyd, 'Only the naïve believe that Nelson Mandela's magnanimity is a formula for politicians seeking to bring peace to other trouble spots', *New Statesman and Society*, 19 July 1996. One leader in Northern Ireland reiterated a similar point: 'Although there was an enormous call for leadership here, like for the equivalent of a Mandela and de Klerk, you can't do that. You can't transport it'. Author Interview, 22 February 2000.
28. John Hume, *Personal Views: Politics, Peace and Reconciliation in Ireland* (Dublin: Town House, 1996) pp. 95–96.
29. Deaglan de Breadun, Trimble Confident of doing business with Blair, *The Irish Times*, 29 April 1997.
30. Adrian Guelke, 'Comparatively Peaceful: The Role of Analogy in Northern Ireland's Peace Process', *Cambridge Review of International Affairs*, XI, 1 (1997) p. 37.
31. O'Connor, *op. cit.*, p. 87.
32. Decca Aitkenhead, 'Time and Gerry', *The Guardian*, 4 August 1997.
33. John Stacks and Barry Hillenbrand, 'Struggling to Make History', *Time*, 1 August 1994.

34. See Guelke, *op. cit.*
35. John Lloyd, 'Ulster's First Minister waits to see if Gerry Adams turns out to be Eamon de Valera or Michael Collins', *New Statesman and Society*, 28 August 1998.
36. Unpublished transcript. Interview undertaken by Dr Chris Farrington, 22 January 2004.
37. Paul Routledge, 'Apprentice for Peace', *The Independent* (London), 5 April 1998.
38. James Prior, *A Balance of Power* (London: Hamish Hamilton, 1986) p. 52.
39. Paul Arthur, *Special Relationships: Britain, Ireland and the Northern Ireland Problem* (Belfast: Blackstaff, 2000) p. 180.
40. Author Interview, 22 March 2000.
41. McDonald, *op. cit.*, p. 201.
42. O'Connor, *op. cit.*, p. 31.
43. O'Malley, *op. cit.*, p. 288.
44. 'Right Leaders' Solution, *Belfast News Letter*, 23 October 1997.
45. John Paul Lederach, *Building Peace: Sustainable Reconciliation in Divided Societies* (Washington DC: United States Institute of Peace Press, 1997) pp. 45–46.
46. John Paul Lederach, 'Cultivating Peace: a practitioner's view of deadly conflict and negotiation', in John Darby and Roger MacGinty, eds, *Contemporary Peacemaking* (Basingstoke: Palgrave Macmillan, 2003) p. 35.
47. O'Malley, *op. cit.*, p. 286.
48. O'Malley, *op. cit.*, p. 287.
49. See David Makovsky, *Making Peace with the PLO* (Boulder, Colorado, Westview, 1996).
50. Adams, *op. cit.* See Chapter 2 'The Sagart' pp. 13–25 which introduces the reader to Fr Alex Reid, otherwise known as the 'sagart'.
51. Henry Sinnerton, *David Ervine: Uncharted Waters* (Kerry: Brandon, 2002) pp. 136–140.
52. Author Interview, 22 March 2000.
53. Adrian Guelke, 'Negotiations and Peace Processes', in John Darby and Roger MacGinty, eds, *Contemporary Peacemaking* (Basingstoke: Palgrave Macmillan, 2003) p. 53.
54. Godson, *op. cit.*, p. 347 citing Denis Rogan from the UUP.
55. Adams, *op. cit.*, p. 302.
56. Adams, *op. cit.*, p. 302.
57. Author Interview, 22 March 2000.
58. Author Interview, 22 February 2000. This leader said: 'The maintenance of those relationships needs to be built inside the process, and it should be happening here [in Northern Ireland] not in other countries'.
59. Author Interview, 22 March 2000.
60. Walter Ellis, Last Twist of the Orange Card?, *Sunday Times*, 10 September 1995.
61. Robert L. Rothstein, 'In Fear of Peace: Getting Past Maybe', in Robert L. Rothstein, ed., *After the Peace: Resistance and Reconciliation* (London: Lynne Rienner, 1999).
62. Hugh Miall, Oliver Ramsbotham and Tom Woodhouse, *Contemporary Conflict Resolution: The Prevention, Management and Transformation of Deadly Conflicts* (Oxford: Polity, 1999).

63. Dixon 2002, *op. cit.*, p. 739.
64. See Robert J. House and Ram N. Aditya, 'The Social Scientific Study of Leadership': Quo Vadis?', *Journal of Management*, 23, 3 (1997) p. 455.

8   Conclusion: Towards a new understanding of political leadership

1. Robert J. House and Ram N. Aditya, 'The Social Scientific Study of Leadership: Quo Vadis?', *Journal of Management*, 23, 3 (1997) p. 455.
2. Paul Dixon, 'Political Skills or Lying and Manipulation? The Choreography of the Northern Ireland Peace Process', *Political Studies*, 50, 4 (2002) pp. 725–741.
3. John Hume, 'Quote Unquote', *The Independent* (London), 21 December 1996.
4. Paul Routledge, 'Bigger than any bomb; Some say his credibility is lost but the SDLP leader will fight on – John Hume', *The Independent* (London), 18 February 1996.
5. See Owen Bowcott, 'Peace Envoy with a Short Spoon', *The Guardian* (London), 9 October 1993.
6. 'Prize of Peace; Trimble and Hume Receive Nobel Honour' *(Belfast)*, 16 October 1998; also see Suzanne Breen, 'Wisest Move So Far From Hume', *Belfast Telegraph* (Belfast), 5 February 2004.
7. Harold H. Saunders, 'Prenegotiation and Circum-negotiation: Arenas of the multi-level peace process', in Chester A. Crocker, Fen Osler Hampson and Pamela Aall, eds, *Turbulent Peace: The Challenges of Managing International Conflict* (Washington DC: USIP Press, 2001) p. 483. Saunders defines the peace process as 'a mixture of politics, diplomacy, changing relationships, negotiation, mediation, and dialogue in both official and unofficial arenas'.
8. Michael Gove, 'Trimble's long march to a new Unionism', *The Times* (London), 4 July 1998.
9. Margaret Bucholt, 'A Gatherer of Minds', *UMass Boston Alumni Magazine*, Winter/Spring 2002.
10. Padraig O'Malley, 'Northern Ireland and South Africa: Hope and History at a Crossroads', in John McGarry, ed., *Northern Ireland and the Divided World: Post-Agreement Northern Ireland in Comparative Perspective* (Oxford: Oxford University Press, 2001) p. 299.
11. Author Interview, 22 March 2000.
12. Jeremy Smith, *Making the Peace in Ireland* (Harlow: Longman, 2002) p. 241.
13. *Ibid.*
14. Harri Englund, ed., *A Democracy of Chameleons: Politics and Culture in New Malawi* (Uppsala: The Nordic Africa Institute, 2002).

Bibliography

Abse, L., *The Man Behind the Smile: Tony Blair and the Politics of Perversion* (London: Robson Books, 2001).

Adams, G., *Hope and History: Making Peace in Ireland* (Dingle: Brandon, 2004).

Alderman, K., 'Setting the Record Straight', *Parliamentary Affairs*, 54, 1 (2001) pp. 134–138.

Ammeter, A.P., Douglas, C., Gardner, W.L., Hochwarter, W.A. and Ferris, G.R., 'Towards a Political Theory of Leadership', *Leadership Quarterly*, 13, 6 (2002) pp. 751–796.

Arnson, C.J., ed., *Comparative Peace Processes in Latin America* (California: Stanford University Press, 1999).

Arthur, P., 'Some Thoughts on Transition: a Comparative View on the Peace Process in South Africa and Northern Ireland', *Government and Opposition*, 30, 1 (1995) pp. 48–59.

Arthur, P., *Peer-Learning: Northern Ireland as a Case Study* (New York: Carnegie Corporation on Preventing Deadly Conflict, 1999).

Arthur, P., 'Multiparty Mediation in Northern Ireland', in Crocker, C.A., Hampson, F.O. and Aall, P., eds, *Herding Cats: Multiparty Mediation in a Complex World* (Washington DC; Great Britain: United States Institute of Peace Press, 1999) pp. 469–502.

Arthur, P., *Special Relationships: Britain, Ireland and the Northern Ireland Problem* (Belfast: Blackstaff Press, 2000).

Aughey, A., 'Unionism and Self Determination', in Roche, P.J. and Barton, B., eds, *The Northern Ireland Question: Myth and Reality* (Aldershot: Avebury, 1991) pp. 1–16.

Aughey, A., 'Political Parties: Structures and Platforms', in Aughey, A. and Morrow, D., eds, *Northern Ireland Politics* (London: Longman, 1996) pp. 74–82.

Aughey, A., 'The 1998 Agreement: Unionist Responses', in Cox, M., Guelke, A. and Stephen, F., eds, *A Farewell to Arms? From 'Long War' to Long Peace in Northern Ireland* (Manchester: Manchester University Press, 2000) pp. 62–76.

Aughey, A., 'The Art and Effect of Political Lying in Northern Ireland', *Irish Political Studies*, 17, 2 (2002) pp. 1–16.

Barash, D.P., *Introduction to Peace Studies* (Belmont, California: Wadsworth, 1991).

Barash, D.P. and Webel, C.P., *Peace and Conflict Studies* (Thousand Oaks; London: Sage, 2002).

Barker, C., Johnson, A. and Lavalette, M., eds, *Leadership and Social Movements* (Manchester: Manchester University Press, 2001).

Bass, B.M., *Bass & Stogdill's Handbook of Leadership: Theory, Research, and Managerial Applications* (New York: Free Press, 1990).

Bass, B.M. and Steidlmeier, P., 'Ethics, Character, and Authentic Transformational Leadership Behavior', *Leadership Quarterly*, 10, 2 (1999) pp. 181–217.

Bergstrom, A., 'An Interview with Dr Bernard M. Bass', *Leadership Review*, Kravis Leadership Institute (2003).

Bennis, W.G. and Nanus, B., *Leaders: The Strategies of Taking Charge* (New York: Harper & Row, 1985).

Bew, P. and Gillespie G., *The Northern Ireland Peace Process 1993–1996: A Chronology* (London: Serif, 1996).

Bew, P. and Gillespie, G., *Northern Ireland: A Chronology of the Troubles 1968–1999* (Dublin: Gill & Macmillan, 1999).

Blondel, J., *Thinking Politically* (London: Wildwood House, 1976).

Blondel, J., *Political Leadership: Towards a General Analysis* (London: Sage, 1987).

Bloomfield, D., *Political Dialogue in Northern Ireland: The Brooke Initiative 1989–92* (Basingstoke: Macmillan, 1998).

Bloomfield, D., Ghai, Y. and Reilly, B., 'Analysing Deep Rooted Conflict' in Harris, P. and Reilly, B., eds, *Democracy and Deep-Rooted Conflict: Options for Negotiators* (Stockholm: IDEA – International Institute for Democracy and Electoral Assistance, 1998) pp. 29–58.

Boin, A. and Hart, P., 'Public Leadership in Times of Crisis: Mission Impossible?', *Public Administration Review*, 63, 5 (2003) pp. 544–553.

Brocklehurst, H., Stott, N., Hamber, B. and Robinson, G., 'Lesson Drawing: Northern Ireland and South Africa', *Indicator SA*, 18, 1 (2001) pp. 89–94.

Brown, C., *Understanding International Relations* (Basingstoke: Palgrave, 2001).

Brown, M.E., 'Ethnic and Internal Conflicts: Causes and Implications', in Crocker, C.A., Hampson, F.O. and Aall, P., eds, *Turbulent Peace: The Challenges of Managing International Conflict* (Washington DC; Great Britain: United States Institute of Peace Press, 2001) pp. 209–226.

Bruce, S., 'Fundamentalism and Political Violence: The Case of Paisley and Ulster Evangelicals', *Religion*, 31, 4 (2001) pp. 387–405.

Buntman, F. and Huang, T., 'The Role of Political Imprisonment in Developing and Enhancing Political Leadership: A Comparative Study of South Africa's and Taiwan's Democratization', *Journal of Asian and African Studies* 35, 1 (2000) pp. 43–66.

Burns, J.M., *Leadership* (New York; London: Harper & Row, 1978).

Burns, J.M., 'The Difference Between Power-Wielders and Leaders', in Kellerman, B., ed., *Political Leadership: A Source Book* (Pittsburgh, Pa.: University of Pittsburgh Press, 1986) pp. 287–299.

Burton, J., *Deviance, Terrorism and War* (New York: St Martin's Press, 1979).

Burton, J., *Conflict: Human Needs Theory* (Basingstoke: Macmillan, 1990).

Butros-Ghali, B., Bush, G., Carter, J., Gorbachev, M. and Tutu, D., *Essays on Leadership* (New York: Carnegie Corporation of New York, 1998).

Carlyle, T., 'The Leader as Hero', in Kellerman, B., ed., *Political Leadership: A Source Book* (Pittsburgh, Pa.: University of Pittsburgh Press, 1986) pp. 5–9.

Chiozza, G. and Choi, A., 'Guess Who Did What? Political Leaders and the Management of Territorial Disputes, 1950–1990', *Journal of Conflict Resolution*, 47, 3 (2003) pp. 251–278.

Clarke, L. and Johnston, K., *Martin McGuinness: From Guns to Government* (Edinburgh: Mainstream, 2001).

Clinton, B., *My Life* (New York: Knopf, 2004).

Cochrane, F., *Unionist Politics and the Politics of Unionism Since the Anglo-Irish Agreement* (Cork: Cork University Press, 2001).

Colaresi, M., 'When Doves Cry: International Rivalry, Unreciprocated Cooperation and Leadership Turnover', *American Journal of Political Science*, 48, 3 (2004) pp. 557–570.

Conger, J.A., 'Qualitative Research as the Cornerstone Methodology for Understanding Leadership', *Leadership Quarterly*, 9, 1 (1998) pp. 85–105.

Cox, M., Guelke, A. and Stephen, F., eds, *A Farewell to Arms? From 'Long War' to Long Peace in Northern Ireland* (Manchester: Manchester University Press, 2000).

Crocker, C.A., Hampson, F.O. and Aall, P., eds, *Managing Global Chaos: Sources of and Responses to International Conflict* (Washington DC: United States Institute of Peace Press, 1996).

Crocker, C.A., Hampson, F.O. and Aall, P., eds, *Herding Cats: Multiparty Mediation in a Complex World* (Washington DC: United States Institute of Peace Press, 1999).

Crocker, C.A., Hampson, F.O. and Aall, P., eds, *Turbulent Peace: The Challenges of Managing International Conflict* (Washington DC: United States Institute of Peace Press, 2001).

Crocker, C.A., Hampson, F.O. and Aall, P., eds, *Grasping the Nettle: Analyzing Cases of Intractable Conflict* (Washington DC: United States Institute of Peace Press, 2005).

Crozier, M., 'Good Leaders and "Decent" Men: an Ulster Contradiction', in Hill, M. and Barber, S., eds, *Aspects of Irish Studies* (Belfast: Institute for Irish Studies, Queens University, 1990).

Cunningham, M., 'The Political Language of John Hume', *Irish Political Studies*, 12 (1997) pp. 13–22.

Darby, J., *Custom of Fell Deed: The Effects of Violence on Peace Processes* (Washington DC: United States Institute of Peace Press, 2001).

Darby, J. and MacGinty, R., 'Imperfect Peace: The Aftermath of Northern Ireland's Peace Accord', *Ethnic Studies Report*, 17, 2 (1999) pp. 201–225.

Darby, J. and MacGinty, R., eds, *The Management of Peace Processes* (Basingstoke: Macmillan, 2000).

Darby, J. and MacGinty, R., eds, *Contemporary Peacemaking: Conflict, Violence, and Peace Processes* (Basingstoke: Palgrave Macmillan, 2003).

Devine, F., 'Qualitative Methods', in Marsh, D. and Stoker, G., eds, *Theory and Methods in Political Science* (Basingstoke: Palgrave Macmillan, 2002) pp. 137–153.

Dixon, P., *Northern Ireland: The Politics of War and Peace* (Basingstoke: Palgrave, 2001).

Dixon, P., 'Political Skills or Lying and Manipulation? The Choreography of the Northern Ireland Peace Process', *Political Studies*, 50, 4 (2002) pp. 725–741.

Dixon, P., 'Peace Within the Realms of the Possible? David Trimble, Unionist Theology and Theatrical Politics', *Terrorism and Political Violence*, 16, 3 (2004) pp. 462–482.

Doumitt, D.P., *Conflict in Northern Ireland: The History, the Problem, and the Challenge* (New York: P. Lang, 1985).

Edelman, M., *Constructing the Political Spectacle* (Chicago: University of Chicago Press, 1988).

Edinger, L.J., 'Political Science and Political Biography: Reflections on the Study of Leadership (1)', *Journal of Politics*, 26, 2 (1964) pp. 423–439.

Edinger, L.J., 'Approaches to the Comparative Analysis of Political Leadership', *Review of Politics*, 54, 4 (1990) pp. 509–523.

Elcock, H.J., *Political Leadership* (Cheltenham: Edward Elgar, 2001).

Elgie, R., *Political Leadership in Liberal Democracies* (London: Macmillan, 1995).

Elliott, M., *The Long Road to Peace in Northern Ireland* (Liverpool: Liverpool University Press, 2002).

Englund, H., ed., *A Democracy of Chameleons: Politics and Culture in New Malawi* (Uppsala: The Nordic Africa Institute, 2002).

Fearon, K., *Women's Work: The Story of the Northern Ireland Women's Coalition* (Belfast: Blackstaff Press, 1999).

Finlayson, A., 'The Problem of the Political Interview', *Political Quarterly*, 73, 3 (2001) pp. 335–344.

Finlayson, A., 'Elements of the Blairite Image of Leadership', *Parliamentary Affairs*, 55, 3 (2002) pp. 586–599.

Fisher, R.J., 'Prenegotiation Problem-Solving Discussions: Enhancing the Potential for Successful Negotiation', *International Journal*, XLIV (1989) pp. 442–474.

Flackes, W.D. and Elliot, S., *Northern Ireland: A Political Directory 1968–1993* (Belfast: Blackstaff, 1994).

Foley, M., *The British Presidency: Tony Blair and the Politics of Public Leadership* (Manchester: Manchester University Press, 2000).

Foley, M., *John Major, Tony Blair and the Conflict of Leadership: Collision Course* (Manchester: Manchester University Press, 2002).

Gaffney, J., 'Imagined Relationships: Political Leadership in Contemporary Democracies', *Parliamentary Affairs*, 54, 1 (2001) pp. 120–133.

Galtung, J., 'Violence, Peace and Peace Research', *Journal of Peace Research*, 6, 3 (1969) pp. 167–191.

Gidron, B., Katz, S.N. and Hasenfeld, Y., *Mobilizing for Peace: Conflict Resolution in Northern Ireland, Israel/Palestine and South Africa* (Oxford: Oxford University Press, 2002).

Giliomee, H. and Gagiano, J., eds, *The Elusive Search for Peace: South Africa, Israel and Northern Ireland* (Cape Town; Oxford: Oxford University Press in association with IDASA, 1990).

Gilligan, C. and Tonge, J., eds, *Peace or War? Understanding the Peace Process in Northern Ireland* (Aldershot: Ashgate, 1997).

Giuliani, R.W., *Leadership* (London: Little, 2002).

Glad, B., 'Passing the Baton: Transformational Political Leadership from Gorbachev to Yeltsin; from De Klerk to Mandela', *Political Psychology*, 17, 1 (1996) pp. 1–28.

Glaser, B. and Strauss, A., *The Discovery of Grounded Theory: Strategies for qualitative research* (Chicago: Aldine, 1967).

Godson, D., *Himself Alone: David Trimble and the Ordeal of Unionism* (London: HarperCollins, 2004).

Gormley-Heenan, C., *From Protagonist to Pragmatist: Political Leadership in Societies in Transition* (Derry/Londonderry: INCORE, 2001).

Gove, M., 'Preface', in Trimble, D., ed., *To Raise up a New Northern Ireland* (Belfast: Belfast Press, 2001).

Guelke, A., 'Comparatively Peaceful: The Role of Analogy in Northern Ireland's Peace Process', *Cambridge Review of International Affairs*, 11, 1 (1997) pp. 25–41.

Guelke, A., 'Comparatively Peaceful: South Africa, the Middle East and Northern Ireland', in Cox, M., Guelke, A. and Stephen, F., eds, *A Farewell to Arms? From 'Long War' to Long Peace in Northern Ireland* (Manchester: Manchester University Press, 2000) pp. 223–233.

Guelke, A., *The International System and the Northern Ireland Peace Process*, Institute for British-Irish Studies, Working Paper 21 (2002).

Guelke, A., 'Negotiations and Peace Processes', in Darby, J. and MacGinty, R., eds, *Contemporary Peacemaking: Conflict, Violence and Peace Processes* (Basingstoke: Palgrave Macmillan, 2003) pp. 53–64.

Guelke, A., ed., *Democracy and Ethnic Conflict: Advancing Peace in Deeply Divided Societies* (Basingstoke: Palgrave Macmillan, 2004).

Hah, C. and Bartol, F.C., 'Political Leadership as a Causative Phenomenon: Some Recent Analyses', *World Politics*, 36, 1 (1983) pp. 100–120.

Halliday, F., 'Peace Process in the Late Twentieth Century: A Mixed Record', in Cox, M., Guelke, A. and Stephen, F., eds, *A Farewell to Arms? From 'Long War' to Long Peace in Northern Ireland* (Manchester: Manchester University Press, 2000) pp. 275–289.

Hamburg, D., Alexander, G. and Ballentine, K., 'Preventing Deadly Conflict: The Critical Role of Leadership', *Archives of General Psychiatry*, 56 (1999) pp. 971–976.

Harari, O., *The Leadership Secrets of Colin Powell* (New York: McGraw-Hill, 2002).

Harmel, R., 'The Iron Law of Oligarchy Revisited', in Jones, B.D., ed., *Leadership and Politics: New Perspectives in Political Science* (Kansas: University of Kansas Press, 1989) pp. 160–189.

Harrington, J.P. and Mitchell, E.J., eds, *Politics and Performance in Contemporary Northern Ireland* (Amherst: University of Massachusetts Press, 1999).

Hefernan, R., 'Prime-Ministerial Predominance? Core Executive Politics in the UK', *British Journal of Politics and International Relations*, 5, 3 (2003) pp. 347–372.

Hennessey, T., *The Northern Ireland Peace Process: Ending the Troubles?* (Dublin: Gill & Macmillan, 2000).

Hermann, M.G., 'Leaders, Leadership and Flexibility: Influences on Heads of Government as Negotiators and Mediators', *American Academy of Political and Social Science*, 542 (1995) pp. 148–167.

Heskin, K., Cairns, E. and McCourt, D., 'Perceptions of Political Leaders in Northern Ireland: A Factor-Analytic Study', *Irish Journal of Psychology*, 11, 4 (1990) pp. 354–366.

Hite, K., *When the Romance Ended: Leaders of the Chilean Left, 1968-1998* (New York: Columbia University Press, 2000).

Horowitz, D., 'Explaining the Northern Ireland Agreement: The sources of An Unlikely Constitutional Consensus', *British Journal of Political Studies*, 32, 2 (2002) pp. 193–220.

House, R.J. and Aditya, R.N., 'The Social Scientific Study of Leadership: Quo vadis?' *Journal of Management*, 23, 3 (1997) pp. 409–473.

House, R.J., 'A 1976 Theory of Charismatic Leadership', in Hunt, J.G. and Larsen, L.L., eds, *Leadership: The Cutting Edge* (Carbondale, Illinois: Southern Illinois University Press, 1977) pp. 189–207.

Hughes, R.L., Ginnett, R.C. and Curphy, G.J., *Leadership: Enhancing the Lessons of Experience* (London: Irwin/McGraw-Hill, 1999).

Hume, J., *Personal Views: Politics, Peace and Reconciliation in Ireland* (Dublin: Town House, 1996).

Jacobsen, C. and House, R.J., 'The Rise and Decline of Charismatic Leadership', Unpublished Paper (1999).

Janis, I.L., 'Groupthink', in Kellerman, B., ed., *Political Leadership: A Source Book.* (Pittsburgh, Pa.: University of Pittsburgh Press, 1986) pp. 327–346.

Jeong, H., *Peace and Conflict Studies: An Introduction* (Aldershot: Ashgate, 2000).

Jones, B.D., ed., *Leadership and Politics: New Perspectives in Political Science* (Lawrence, Kan.; London: University Press of Kansas, 1989).

Kane, J., *The Politics of Moral Capital* (Cambridge: Cambridge University Press, 2001).

Kaplan, R.D., *Warrior Politics: Why Leadership Demands a Pagan Ethos* (New York: Random House, 2002).

Kellerman, B., ed., *Leadership: Multidisciplinary Perspectives* (Englewood Cliffs, N.J.: Prentice-Hall, 1984).

Kellerman, B., *Political Leadership: A Source Book* (Pittsburgh, Pa.: University of Pittsburgh Press, 1986).

Kellerman, B., 'Hitler's Ghost: A Manifesto', in Kellerman, B. and Matusak, L.R., eds, *Cutting Edge: Leadership 2000* (College Park, Md.: Center for the Advanced Study of Leadership, the James MacGregor Burns Academy of Leadership at the University of Maryland, 2000) pp. 65–68.

Kellerman, B., *Bad Leadership: What it is, How it Happens, Why it Matters* (Harvard: Harvard Business School Press, 2004).

Kellerman, B. and Matusak, L.R., eds, *Cutting Edge: Leadership 2000* (College Park, Md.: Center for the Advanced Study of Leadership, the James MacGregor Burns Academy of Leadership at the University of Maryland, 2000).

King, G., Keokane, R. and Verba, S., *Designing Sound Inquiry* (Princeton: Princeton University Press, 1994).

Knox, C. and Quirk, P., *Peace Building in Northern Ireland, Israel and South Africa: Transition, Transformation and Reconciliation* (Basingstoke: Macmillan, 2000).

Kriesberg, L. and Thorson, S.J., *Timing the De-Escalation of International Conflicts* (New York: Syracuse University Press, 1991).

Kriesberg, L., Northrup, T.A. and Thorson, S.J., *Intractable Conflicts and Their Transformation* (Syracuse, N.Y.: Syracuse University Press, 1989).

Lederach, J.P., *Building Peace: Sustainable Reconciliation in Divided Societies* (Washington DC: United States Institute of Peace Press, 1997).

Lederach, J.P., 'Cultivating Peace', in Darby, J. and MacGinty, R., eds, *Contemporary Peacemaking: Conflict, Violence and Peace Processes* (Basingstoke: Palgrave Macmillan, 2003) pp. 30–37.

Lieberfeld, D., 'Conflict "Ripeness" Revisited: The South African and Israeli/Palestine cases', *Negotiation Journal*, 15, 1 (1999) pp. 63–82.

Lilleker, D.G., 'Interviewing the Political Elite: Navigating a Potential Minefield', *Politics*, 23, 3 (2003) pp. 207–214.

Lloyd, J., 'Only the Naïve Believe that Nelson Mandela's Magnanimity is a Formula for Politicians Seeking to Bring Peace to Other Trouble Spots', *New Statesman and Society*, 19 July 1996.

Lobell, S. and Mauceri, P., *Ethnic Conflict and International Politics: Explaining Diffusion and Escalation* (Basingstoke: Palgrave Macmillan, 2004).

Loughlin, J., *The Ulster Question Since 1945* (Basingstoke: Macmillan, 1998).

Lowe, K.B. and Gardner, W.L., 'Ten Years of the Leadership Quarterly: Contributions and Challenges for the Future', *Leadership Quarterly*, 11, 4 (2000) pp. 459–514.

Ludwig, A.M., *King of the Mountain: The Nature of Political Leadership* (Lexington, Ky.; Great Britain: University Press of Kentucky, 2002).

Lustick, I.S., 'Ending Protracted Conflict: The Oslo Peace Process Between Political Partnership and Legality', *Cornell International Law Journal*, 30, 3 (1997) pp. 741–757.

Machiavelli, N., *The Prince* (Oxford: Oxford World Classics, 1998).

MacGinty, R., 'From Revolution to Reform: Republicans and the Peace Process', in Cox, M., Guelke, A. and Stephen, F., eds, *A Farewell to Arms? From 'Long*

War' to Long Peace in Northern Ireland (Manchester: Manchester University Press. Forthcoming, 2006) pp. 124–138.

MacGinty, R. and Darby, J., *Guns and Government: The Management of the Northern Ireland Peace Process* (Basingstoke: Palgrave Macmillan, 2002).

Major, J., *John Major: The Autobiography* (London: HarperCollins, 1999).

Makovsky, D., *Making Peace with the PLO* (Boulder, Colorado: Westview, 1996).

Mallie, E. and McKittrick, D., *Endgame in Ireland* (London: Hodder & Stoughton, 2001).

Mansergh, M., 'The Background to the Irish Peace Process', in Cox, M., Guelke, A. and Stephen, F., eds, *A Farewell to Arms? From 'Long War' to Long Peace in Northern Ireland* (Manchester: Manchester University Press, 2000) pp. 8–23.

Marsh, D. and Stoker, G., eds, *Theory and Methods in Political Science* (Basingstoke: Palgrave Macmillan, 2002).

Marrinan, P., *Paisley: Man of Wrath* (Tralee, Co. Kerry: Anvil, 1973).

Mastors, E., 'Gerry Adams and the Northern Ireland Peace Process: A Research Note', *Political Psychology*, 21, 4 (2000) pp. 839–846.

McAuley, J., 'Still "No Surrender"? New Loyalism and the Peace Process in Northern Ireland', in Harrington, J.P. and Mitchell, E.J., eds, *Politics and Performance in Contemporary Northern Ireland* (Amherst: University of Massachusettts Press, 1999) pp. 57–81.

McCaffrey, B., *Alex Maskey: Man and Mayor* (Belfast: Brehon Press, 2003).

McDonald, H., *Trimble* (London: Bloomsbury, 2000).

McEvoy, K., *Paramilitary Imprisonment in Northern Ireland: Resistance, Management, and Release* (Oxford: Oxford University Press, 2001).

McGarry, J., 'Political Settlements in Northern Ireland and South Africa', *Political Studies*, 45, 5 (1998) pp. 853–870.

McGarry, J., *Northern Ireland and the Divided World: Post-Agreement Northern Ireland in Comparative Perspective* (Oxford: Oxford University Press, 2001).

McGarry, J. and O'Leary, B., *Explaining Northern Ireland* (Oxford: Blackwell, 1995).

McKittrick, D., *Endgame: The Search for Peace in Northern Ireland* (Belfast: Blackstaff, 1994).

McKittrick, D., *The Nervous Peace* (Belfast: Blackstaff, 1996).

McKittrick, D., *Making Sense of the Troubles* (London: Penguin, 2001).

McKittrick, D. and Mallie, E., *The Fight for Peace: The Secret Story Behind the Irish Peace Process* (London: Heinemann, 1996).

McKittrick, D. and McVea, D., *Making Sense of the Troubles* (Belfast: Blackstaff, 2000).

McMichael, G., *An Ulster Voice: In Search of Common Ground in Northern Ireland* (Boulder, Colorado: Roberts Rinehart, 1999).

Miall, H., Ramsbotham, O. and Woodhouse, T., *Contemporary Conflict Resolution: The Prevention, Management and Transformation of Deadly Conflicts* (Oxford: Polity Press, 1999).

Mitchell, C., 'Conflict Research' in Groom, A.J.R. and Light, M., eds, *Contemporary International Relations: A Guide to Theory* (London: Pinter Press, 1994) pp. 128–141.

Mitchell, G., *Making Peace* (London: Heinemann, 1999).

Mitchell, G., 'Toward Peace in Northern Ireland', *Fordham International Law Journal*, 22, 4 (1999) pp. 1136–1144.

Moloney, E. and Pollak, A., *Paisley* (Dublin: Poolbeg Press, 1986).

Mowlam, M., *Momentum: The Struggle for Peace, Politics and the People* (London: Hodder & Stoughton, 2002).

Murray, G., *John Hume and the SDLP: Impact and Survival in Northern Ireland* (Dublin: Irish Academic Press, 1998).

Nice, D.C., 'The Warrior Model of Leadership: Classic Perspectives and Contemporary Relevance', *Leadership Quarterly*, 9, 3 (1998) pp. 321–322.

Nicholson, M., *International Relations: A Concise Introduction*, 2nd edn (Basingstoke: Macmillan, 2002).

Nordlinger, E., *Conflict Regulation in Divided Societies* (Harvard: Center for International Affairs – Harvard University 1972).

Northouse, P.G., *Leadership: Theory and Practice* (Thousand Oaks, Calif.: Sage 2003).

O'Connor, F., *Breaking the Bonds: Making Peace in Northern Ireland* (Edinburgh: Mainstream, 2002).

O'Doherty, H., 'Leadership and Developing Democracy Where There is None', in Guelke, A., ed., *Democracy and Ethnic Conflict: Advancing Peace in Deeply Divided Societies* (Basingstoke: Palgrave Macmillan, 2004) pp. 118–135.

O'Malley, P., 'Northern Ireland and South Africa: Hope and History at a Crossroads', in McGarry, J., ed., *Northern Ireland and the Divided World: Post-Agreement Northern Ireland in Comparative Perspective* (Oxford: Oxford University Press, 2001) pp. 276–308.

Paige, G.D., *To Nonviolent Political Science: From Seasons of Violence* (Honolulu, Hawai'i: Center for Global Nonviolence Planning Project, Matsunaga Institute for Peace, University of Hawai'I, 1993).

Paris, P.J., *Black Leaders in Conflict: Joseph H. Jackson, Martin Luther King Jr., Malcolm X, Adam Clayton Powell Jr* (New York; Philadelphia: Pilgrim Press, 1978).

Parry, K.W., 'Grounded Theory and Social Process: a new direction for leadership research', *Leadership Quarterly*, 9, 1 (1998) pp. 85–105.

Plato, *The Republic*, translated by Robin Waterfield (Oxford: Oxford World Classics, 2004).

Price, T.L., 'The Ethics of Authentic Transformational Leadership', *Leadership Quarterly*, 14, 1 (2003) pp. 67–81.

Prior, J., *A Balance of Power* (London: Hamish Hamilton, 1986).

Prutt, D.G., 'Flexibility in Conflict Episodes', *The Annals of the American Academy of Political and Social Science*, 542 (1995) pp. 100–115.

Rejai, M. and Philips, K., *Loyalists & Revolutionaries: Political Leaders Compared* (New York; London: Praeger, 1988).

Rejai, M. and Philips, K., *Leaders and Leadership: An Appraisal of Theory and Research* (Westport Connecticut and London: Praegar Press, 1997).

Renshon, S.A., 'Political Leadership as Social Capital: Governing in a Divided National Culture', *Political Psychology*, 21, 1 (2000) pp. 199–226.

Richards, D., 'Elite Interviewing: Approaches and Pitfalls', *Politics*, 16, 3 (1996) pp. 199–204.

Robinson, C.J., *The Terms of Order: Political Science and the Myth of Leadership* (Albany: S.U.N.Y Press, 1980).

Rost, J.C., *Leadership for the Twenty-First Century* (New York: Praeger, 1991).

Rothstein, R.L., *After the Peace: Resistance and Reconciliation* (Boulder, Colo.; London: Lynne Rienner, 1999).

Ryan, S., 'Peace and Conflict Studies Today', *The Global Review of Ethnopolitics*, 2, 2 (2003) pp. 75–82.

Sabia, Jr D.R., 'Weber's Political Ethics and the Problem of Dirty Hands', *Journal of Management History*, 2, 1 (1996) pp. 6–20.

Saunders, H., 'Prenegotiation and Circum-Negotiation: Arenas of the Multilevel Peace Process', in Crocker, C.A., Hampson, F.O. and Aall, P., eds, *Turbulent Peace: The Challenges of Managing International Conflict* (Washington DC: United States Institute of Peace Press, 2001) pp. 483–496.

Sechser, T.S., 'Are Soldiers Less War-Prone Than Statesmen?', *Journal of Conflict Resolution*, 48, 5 (2004) pp. 746–774.

Sharrock, D. and Devenport, M., *Man of War, Man of Peace? The Unauthorized Biography of Gerry Adams* (London: Macmillan, 1997).

Sheffer, G., *Innovative Leaders in International Politics* (Albany: State University of New York Press, 1993).

Sinnerton, H., *David Ervine: Uncharted Waters* (Kerry: Brandon, 2002).

Smith, J., *Making the Peace in Ireland* (Harlow: Longman, 2002).

Sparre, K., 'Megaphone Diplomacy in the Northern Irish Peace Process: Squaring the Circle by Talking to Terrorists Through Journalists', *The Harvard Journal of Press/Politics*, 6, 1 (2001) pp. 88–104.

Spence, H., 'The Great Man Theory Breaks Down', in Kellerman, B., ed., *Political Leadership: A Source Book* (Pittsburgh, Pa.: University of Pittsburgh Press, 1986) pp. 10–15.

Stedman, S.J., *Peacemaking in Civil War: International Mediation in Zimbabwe 1974–1980* (Boulder, Colorado: Lynne Rienner, 1990).

Stein, J.G., 'Getting to the Table: The Triggers, Stages, Functions, and Consequences of Prenegotiation', *International Journal*, XLIV (1989) pp. 231–246.

Stevenson, J., 'Treating Terrorists as Statesmen', *Foreign Policy*, 105 (1996) pp. 125–140.

Todd, J. and Ruane J., *After the Good Friday Agreement: Analysing Political Change in Northern Ireland* (Dublin: University College Dublin Press, 1999).

Trimble, D., 'The Belfast Agreement', *Fordham International Law Journal*, 22, 4 (1999) pp. 1145–1170.

Trimble, D., *To Raise up a New Northern Ireland* (Belfast: Belfast Press, 2001).

Tucker, R.C., *Politics as Leadership* (Columbia: University of Missouri Press, 1981).

Tucker, R.C., 'Nonconstituted Leaders', in Kellerman 1986, *op. cit.*, pp. 265–268.

Waterman, H., 'Political Order and the "Settlement" of Civil Wars', in Licklider, R., ed., *Stopping the Killings: How Civil Wars End* (New York: New York University Press, 1993) pp. 292–302.

Weber, M., 'Politics as a Vocation', in *From Max Weber: Essays in Sociology*. Translated and edited by H.H. Gerth and C. Wright Mills (London: Routledge & Kegan Paul, 1948) pp. 77–128.

Welsh, D. and Spence, J., 'F.W. de Klerk: Enlightened Conservative', in Westlake, M., ed., *Leaders of Transition* (London: Macmillan, 2000) pp. 29–52.

Westlake, M., ed., *Leaders of Transition* (Basingstoke: Macmillan, 2000).

Whyte, J., *Interpreting Northern Ireland* (Oxford: Clarendon, 1990).

Wichert, S., 'The Northern Ireland Conflict: New Wine in Old Bottles', *Contemporary European History*, 9, 2 (2000) pp. 309–322.

Wilford, R., ed., *Aspects of the Belfast Agreement* (Oxford: Oxford University Press, 2001).

Wilson, R., 'Asking the Right Question', in Democratic Dialogue, *Reconstituting Politics* (Belfast: Democratic Dialogue, 1996) pp. 41–59.

Yukl, G.A., Lepsinger, R.P. and Lucia, A.D., 'Preliminary Report on the Development and Validation of the Influence Behavior Questionnaire', in Clark, K.E., Clark, M.B. and Campbell, D.P., eds, *Impact of Leadership* (Greensboro, NC: Centre for Creative Leadership, 1992) pp. 417–427.

Zaccaro, S.J. and Klimoski, R.J., eds, *The Nature of Organizational Leadership: Understanding the Performance Imperatives Confronting Today's Leaders* (San Francisco, CA: Jossey-Bass, 2001).

Index